Ethica IV:
Spinoza on Reason and
the "Free Man"

Spinoza by 2000
The Jerusalem Conferences

Sponsored by

 The Jerusalem Spinoza Institute

The Spinoza Research Program,
The Hebrew University of Jerusalem

Ethica I: God and Nature: Spinoza's Metaphysics

Ethica II: Spinoza on Mind and Human Knowledge

Ethica III: Desire and Affect: Spinoza as Psychologist

Ethica IV: Spinoza on Reason and the "Free Man"

Ethica V: *Amor Dei Intellectualis*:
Spinoza on Intuitive Knowledge and Beatitude

Spinoza as a Social Thinker

Spinoza's Life and Sources

Spinoza by 2000
The Jerusalem Conferences

Ethica IV:
Spinoza on Reason
and
The "Free Man"

Papers Presented
at
The Fourth Jerusalem Conference

Edited by
Yirmiyahu Yovel
and
Gideon Segal

Little Room Press
New York, 2004

Published by Little Room Press
Graduate Faculty Philosophy Journal
New School for Social Research
65 5th Avenue, New York, NY 10003 USA
www.newschool.edu/gf/phil/lrp/
gfpj@newschool.edu

Distributed by Fordham University Press.

ISBN 0-9677102-3-5

Cover design by Jason D. Brown
Cover art is from Light Notations 1986, by Louis Comtois.

The text of this book is set in Palatino

With these few words I have explained the causes of man's lack of power and inconstancy, and why men do not observe the precepts of reason.

The good which everyone who seeks virtue wants for himself, he also desires for others.

A free man thinks of nothing less than of death, and his wisdom is a meditation on life, not on death.

Spinoza

Contents

Preface and Acknowledgments

This is the fourth volume in the series "Spinoza by 2000—The Jerusalem Conferences," organized by the Jerusalem Spinoza Institute. The essays discuss Part IV of Spinoza's *Ethics*, which has a somewhat ambivalent position within the broader work. People tend to think of Part IV (not without good reason) as containing Spinoza's basic ethical theory, which deals with the rational person who has reached a level of experience and action concordant with the teaching of *ratio*, the second kind of knowledge. In this respect it seems Part IV proposes an ethics of freedom. Yet Spinoza reserves the subtitle "On Human Freedom" for Part V, and specifically entitles Part IV "On Human Bondage." This, and the subtitle "or the Powers of the Affects," seems to indicate that Part IV is mostly concerned with non-free experiences and activities, or with "lower" (or weaker) forms of rationality that have not been fully emancipated from the influence of passion, memory, association, fragmented or "perforated" knowledge, and other forms of *imaginatio*.

Then again, freedom is the explicit theme of the climactic final section of Part IV, where Spinoza draws the well-known portrait of the "free man." This admirable text breathes with the genuine spirit of Spinoza's rational ethics, which a mature *ratio* is capable of attaining even prior to *scientia intuitiva* and its attending power of intellectual love, treated in Part V. Incidentally, the several autobiographical allusions hidden here—traits of "the free man" drawn from Spinoza's own life—lead us to see this text also as an idealized self-portrait of the author, depicting, if not how Spinoza actually saw himself in secret, at least what he believed he could be and was about to become.

The ambivalence between freedom and servitude, and between reason and sub-rationality, that characterizes Part IV, came out into the open in the fourth Jerusalem conference, and is also a major theme in the present volume. The largest group of papers deals with the ethics of reason as marked by various forms of limitation and incompleteness, even by inherent finitude. Reason is here not merely "on the way" (both to its own maturity and, beyond it, to *amor intellectualis*); it also needs to rely on auxiliary devices, on time, on "imitation" and self-habituation, on gradual self-acceleration, and on a form of practical reason that is not fully based on clear and distinct ideas.

Another, related theme is how a naturalistic ethics of self-care can produce sociability and benevolence, while drawing its support from the same natural basis—the affects and their driving *conatus*—whose usually aggressive and disruptive outcome it strives to transform. All this makes Part IV, with its impure forms of rationality and the tension of servitude and freedom, egoism and solidarity, most pertinent for a political philosophy—as several authors in this volume make explicit.

Meanwhile, the Fifth Jerusalem Conference—on *Ethics V*—has also taken place, and its proceedings are now being prepared for publication.

* * *

For help in organizing the Fourth Conference and publishing this collection of essays, the Jerusalem Spinoza Institute is grateful to the Yeshaya Horowitz Association and its dedicated legal adviser, attorney Yair Green of Jerusalem; to Mr. Martin Gross of New Jersey, a businessman with a philosophical bent; and to the hospitality of Hebrew Union College in its Jerusalem campus. Ishai Menuchin, director of the Jerusalem Spinoza Institute, was helped by Pini Ifargan and Elena Luria Yoseph in organizing a successful conference, and Steven Barbone translated the papers by Laurent Bove and the late Bernard Rousset from the French. Our sincere and friendly thanks to all.

Yirmiyahu Yovel
Gideon Segal

Abbreviations and Bibliographical Information

The following abbreviations pertaining to the *Ethics* are used throughout this book:

EI (II...V)	*Ethics*, Part, I (II...V)
app	Appendix
ax	Axiom
c	Corollary
def	Definition
def.aff.	Definition of Affect
d	Demonstration
exp	Explanation
gen.def.aff.	General Definition of Affect
lemma	Lemma
p	Proposition
post	Postulate
pref	Preface
s	Scholium

Note: A "," within a citation from the *Ethics* means "and"; e.g., The abbreviation EIIp40d,s2 indicates that both the demonstration *and* the second scholium of Proposition 40 of the *Ethics* Part II, are being cited.

The following abbreviations are used for works other than the *Ethics:*

CM   Metaphysical Thoughts *(Cogitata metaphysica).*

G   Carl Gebhardt, ed., *Spinoza opera, im Auftrag der Heidelberger Akademie der Wissenschaften* (Heidelberg: Carl Winters Universitätsverlag, 1972), vols. 1-4. For instance, GII 8:17-27 = Gebhardt, vol. 2, page 8, lines 17-27.

KV   *Short Treatise on God, Man, and His Well-Being (Korte Verhandeling).* For instance, KVI 2:26 = *Korte Verhandeling,* Book I, Chapter 2, Section 26.

TIE   *Treatise on the Emendation of the Intellect.* For instance, TIE 34 = *Treatise on the Emendation of the Intellect,* Section 34.

TP   *Political Treatise*. For instance, TP 2:8 = *Political Treatise,*
Chapter 2, Section 8.

TTP   *Theologico-Political Treatise*. For instance, TTP 12 =
Theologico-Political Treatise, Chapter 12.

Unless otherwise noted, all of Spinoza's writings, except for his
Letters, *The Theologico-Political Treatise,* and the *Political Treatise,* are
qouted from: Edwin Curley, ed., *The Collected Works of Spinoza*
(Princeton: Princeton University Press, 1985), vol. 1. Citations from
the *Political Treatise* and the *Theologico-Political Treatise* are quoted
from: R.W. Elwes, *The Chief of Benedict Spinoza,* vol. 2 (New York:
Dover, 1951). Citations from Spinoza's Letters, all of which are not
yet included in Curley's edition, are quoted from A. Wolf, *The
Correspondence of Spinoza* (London: George Allen and Unwin,
1928). On occasion, the Gebhardt edition—abbreviated as, e.g., GI
277:10-14 (vol. 1, p. 277, lines 10-14)—is cited in addition to the
reference to the English edition.

Recta Ratio

Bernard Rousset

In the *Ethics*, Spinoza rarely uses the term *Recta Ratio*. When he does, it is never in the demonstrations but only in the prefaces and scholia. Even there the use of this term occurs only at the end of Part IV, in the introduction to the Appendix, and at the beginning of Part V, where he first assays the means by which the mind assures its power over the affections (EVp10s). The term is used again indirectly, in an equivalent but different formula (*recte vivendi ratio*), in the penultimate proposition of Part V (EVp41d), which serves as a general conclusion to the two ethical parts of the *Ethics* (EIV and EV) as discussed in EVpref. This appearance is not accidental, for it was enunciated as early as EIIIpref, dealing with *recta* (not *recte*) *vivendi ratio*, which is the formula Spinoza used at the time to define what will be his response to philosophers' traditional general issue of *vivendi ratio* (without *recte*).[1] Even if it is subtle, the appearance of *recta ratio* thus brings about a formally calculated effect.

Nothing, however, allows this to be foreseen. We do not find any trace of *recta ratio* nor even any clue in the general doctrine of reason unfolding in Part II. The second kind of knowledge—bearing only a theoretical function—proceeds from universal common notions that express nature's laws, and is—like intuition or understanding, although in another way—true and certain knowledge of what is necessary and eternal. None of these characteristics is likewise attributed to *recta ratio*; the penultimate proposition of Part V clearly insists on the distinction. Moreover, we notice that the adverb *recte* is used to modify the verbs *percipere* (EIIp3s), *attendere* (EIp15s), *perpendere* (EIp15s), *intelligere* (EIVapp §32), and *explicare* (EIIp47s), in the same sense that *recto usu* modifies *cogitare* (EVp10s), to indicate the opposition between correct and incorrect or insufficient manners of thinking.[2] This shouldn't come to us as a surprise, for contemporary philosophers often oppose "right reasoning"[3] to that which some of them call "oblique reasoning," and isn't it they who have thus introduced the notion of "right reason"?

1

*

We must insist that the expression *recta ratio* neither only frames nor merely outlines the aim of the *Ethics*, but constitutes the core of a doctrine the importance, specificity, and systematization of which cannot be ignored.[4] This doctrine is constructed through the use—especially in the scholia, prefaces, and appendices—of new key-words of substantives, introduced through verbs that are typically used early in the propositions and their demonstrations. Although seemingly heterogeneous and scattered, these usages together form a coherent whole. What is at stake is an analysis of the activity of reason in the reasoning that carries the mind from principles to consequences in the general theoretical order, and also (and this is what concerns us here) in the practical order.[5]

Reason actually "postulates" (*postulare*), in the logical sense of implication,[6] but with a practical extension (EIVp18s); it "defines" (*definire*; EIVp35d, EIVp36s), it "determines" (*determinare*; EIVp59, EIVapp §25), and naturally, it "teaches" (*docere*; Cf. EIIIp2s and TP 1:5), "persuades" (*suadere*; EIVp73s; see TTP 16 GIII 194), "leads" (*ducere*),[7] and "prescribes" (*praescribere*; EIVp18s, EIVp37s2) the mind, "ordering" (*jubere*; TTP 16 GIII 194) conclusions (in terms of actions), "dictating" them (*dictare*; EVp41d) so that the mind "obeys" (*obtemperare*; EIVp73). All of these terms evidently take on a practical signification since it is a matter of "living and acting and being glad" (*vivere et agere, et laetari*).[8] Given what we know about the use of the adjective 'right,' we understand what Spinoza means by "right acts" (*acti recti*; EIIIdef.aff.27), "right action" (*recta actio*; EIVapp §2), "reason for living" (i.e., reason which makes for living) "rightly" (*recte vivendi ratio*), as well as "right reason of living" (*recta vivendi ratio*).[9]

It is normal to say that a man's life is thus "determined by reason" (*a ratione determinari*; EIVp59), "is born from reason" (*ex ratione oriri*[10]), is led "under the conduct of reason" (*ex ductu rationis* or *ductu rationis*),[11] that it goes "by the prescription of reason" (*ex rationis praescripta*),[12] or by the "commandment of reason" (*ex dictamine rationis* or only *dictamine rationis*),[13] that is, "under the empire of reason" (*imperio*).[14] This is how the mind achieves the power (*potentia*) treated in Part V.

The content of right reason is thus defined, explained, and justified: its "rules" (*regulae*; EIVapp §9), "teachings" (*dogmata*),[15] and "precepts" (*praecepta*; EIVp18s) are "prescriptions" (*praescipta*;

EVp10, EVp41d,s) or "commandments" (*dictamina*).[16] Spinoza himself calls attention to this in EVp41s by highlighting the analogy inherent within this language, constituted by words that are borrowed from a theologico-political vocabulary with an authoritarian nature. This may astound us, once we know Spinoza's philosophy and the sense of his efforts and struggle, and when we meet this vocabulary in the portrait of the free man that follows the description of bondage in Part IV, and in the analysis of the mechanisms of liberation preceding the description of the pleasure of freedom in Part V.[17] This is also why he cares to explicitly specify *ex sanae* or *ex solo rationis ductu*,[18] *ex solo rationis praescripto* (TP 1:5), *ex solo rationis dictamine*,[19] or again *secundum certa nostrae rationis dictamina vivere* or *dictamina propriae rationis agere* (TTP 16 GIII 191, TTP 20 GIII 242) all of which are constituents of *a sui juris omnino esse* that is reminiscent of the Stoics (TP 2:11) and may be contrasted with *ex alterius ratione vivere* (TTP 16 GIII 196). Such an analogy entirely conforms to the whole of Spinoza's method, which consists of repeating traditional questions and analyzing their roots in order to resolve them by substituting his own responses for the traditional ones, the inconsistencies of which are demonstrated by his analysis. Spinoza establishes the truth of his responses in showing, even by using the same words, that his responses fully satisfy all the philosophical, ethical, and even religious demands that had motivated those traditional questions.

The nature and place of right reason is thus well defined, as the second to last proposition and scholium of Part V make clear: it institutes the first ethical level in the *Ethics*, i.e., the rational determination of good that regulates our life without reference to immortality or eternity. This level is distinct from the second level, namely, the knowledge and pleasure of eternity itself in the immanent activity of pure understanding, according to the distinction made in the first line of EVpref. Right reason is realized through what is called 'piety' and 'religion'—terms that have been defined in Part IV—and using the same analogy referred to above.[20]

Still, we must not confound right reason as it manifests itself in the piety and religion deduced, explained, and justified in the *Ethics*, with the morality of the ignorant, who, without using their reason, are capable of a certain salvation as they live correctly in faith and obedience, which is treated in chapter 16 of the TTP.[21] While the conduct of the ignorant throughout their life-works may conform to that which is taught by reason, and give them contentment through their faith, in truth it is not constituted by reasoning reason (*rationcinari*) itself (see EIVapp §§26,27). We see this in Part IV, advancing from "premises" (the model of human nature) to "conclusions" (the affections and good actions) according to a procedure that will be analyzed below. Neither is this conduct that of the "rational life" (*vita rationalis*; EIVapp §§5,8) which "arises" from right reason. Simple conformity to reason, as it is correctly appreciated in the TTP, is not the true rationality established in Part IV—which is still not the pure understanding designated in the second half of Part V.

On the contrary, in the TP (2:20-22) we find an elaborated doctrine concerning how reason constitutes piety and religion, both understood in a strictly Spinozistic sense; its application is exclusively political, with neither ethical extension, nor logical explication, and independent of any question of salvation. This is done with an identical vocabulary (reason, however, is not called right reason),[22] which proves the coherence and the specificity—we might even say sufficiency—of a certain level of rationality.

But once we have discerned the nature of right reason, its place, and the principles that determine its content, it remains to be understood how, beginning from within the general doctrine of reason established in Part II, this specific rationality is constituted, so that, together with Part IV, it defines the first ethical level— first, i.e., in the progressive order in which the good is deduced in philosophy, and in which it is attained in our life.[23]

*

It might be helpful to get our bearings by reviewing succinctly some historical links to this doctrine, the appearance of which was so unforeseen, considering only those doctrines with which Spinoza was familiar.

We cannot avoid considering first Aristotle's *Nicomachean Ethics*, in which the order of books, without speaking of their contents, is incontestably the model that determined the scheme of the last two parts of the *Ethics*, as well as that of most of mediaeval and classical moral works. There is a similar distinction, which is almost a rupture, between a practical good defined by prudence and a contemplative good contained in intelligence. Prudence, situated between opinion and science, is defined with increasing precision as the "power to deliberate properly" (κάλως; 6:5) or, more exactly, "to deliberate rightly" (ὀρθῶς; 6:9, as opposed to κακῶς, "badly"), i.e., "a true practical disposition accompanied by reason" (ἕξις ἀληθὴς μετὰ λόγου πρακτική) or better yet (so as not to confuse it with science, a true theoretical disposition), a practical disposition "accompanied by true reason" (μετὰ λόγου ἀληθοῦς; 6:5), i.e., truth which puts into action the "rectitude of deliberation" (ὀρθότης βουλῆς; 6:9), and finally prudence is defined as "right reason" (ὀρθὸς λόγος; 6:13, repeating what was said as early as 6:1), for "right reason is reason relative to prudence" (6:13), a Greek expression translated directly into Latin as *recta ratio.*[24]

Spinozism has no doctrine of prudence, if only because this Aristotelian notion is tied too much to a philosophy of contingency that excludes a science of particulars. In order to get the equivalent of a doctrine of prudence, it suffices to construct deductively a doctrine of right reason, without mention of a practical disposition, accompanied by reason, which need be true. For with Spinozism, the good is determined, at least in Part IV, without reference to truth, but rather on the sole assurance of the rightness of reasoning.

Ὀρθὸς λόγος or *recta ratio* will occupy a bigger place in Stoicism—well known to Spinoza as well as all his contemporaries—notably in the domain of the moral life, and also in the analysis of our representations. Chrysippus affirms that "all right action is just and legal action," since right action implies *recta ratio*, which implies *lex*, which implies *jus* (δίκαιον).[25] And the whole of our morality, our virtue, is defined by these 'right actions' (κατορθώματα) in general. But the Stoics often distinguish between the perfect morality of the sage who acts 'through reason' (λόγῳ)—his own reason—and accomplishes 'right actions' (κατορθώματα) *stricto sensu*, from the less elevated morality of those who act merely 'conforming to reason' (κατὰ λόγον) remaining with mere 'agreeable actions' (καθήκοντα), which are called *officia* in Latin, '*obligations*' or '*devoirs*' (or even '*fonctions*') in French, and 'duties' in English, as we see in Hobbes. Haven't we seen Spinoza repeat this language when he affirms that the sage is *sui juris*, "autonomous," when he makes clear that our liberty is our *imperium* over ourselves, and when he says that for the utility of our body in particular—thus for the first level of morality which concerns us here—the point is to organize ourselves such that "all its parts can perform their function properly" (*officio suo recte fungi queant*; EIVapp §27; see EIVp60d)?

We must recall that this reason, whose rightness defines right action, is human reason, i.e., calculation—simple inference by implication of propositions comprising sensuous and material impressions from premises that stem empirically from sensuous impressions gathered through common sense: 'common notions,' (ἔννοιαι κοίναι), such as the notion of good in our practical reasonings. Spinoza, no less than Hobbes, is well aware of this, and in the *Treatise on the Emendation of the Intellect* he expressly alludes to this doctrine, if only in order to question it.[26]

On one page of *De cive*, present in Spinoza's library, in the chapter that treats "the law of nature concerning contracts," (I.2.1), Hobbes, in a phrase that contains a note, addresses this "right reason," completing and explicating it:

> Therefore the *law of nature*, that I may define it, is the dictate of right reason [*dictamen rectae rationis*], conversant about those things which are either to be done or omitted for the constant preservation [*conservatio*] of life and members, as much as in us lies.

> [Note:]

> *Right reason*. By right reason in the natural state of men, I understand not, as many do, an infallible faculty, but an act of reasoning [*ratiocinandi actum*], that is, peculiar and true [*propriam et veram*] ratiocination of every man concerning those actions of his, which may either redound to the damage or benefit of his neighbours. I call it peculiar, because although in a civil government that reason of the supreme, that is, the civil law, is to be received by each single [*singulis*] subject for the right; yet being without this civil government, in which state no man can know right reason from false, but comparing it with his own, every man's own reason is to be accounted, not only the rule [*regula*] of his own actions, which are done at his own peril, but also for the measure [*measura*] of another man's reason [*rationis alienae*], in such things as do concern him. I call it true, that is, concluding from true principles rightly framed, because that the whole breach of the laws of nature consists in the false reasoning, or rather the folly of men, who see not those duties [*officia*] they are necessarily to perform towards others in order to their own conservation.[27]

Hobbes thus repeats the Stoic expression and completes it in order to better analyze its practical scope, first across law's then across right's socio-political domain, through the addition of the word *dictamen*, which resonates authority and has a politico-theological connotation, and which thus creates the condensed for-

6

mula that Spinoza will use. To ground this analysis, he has to appeal, as did the Stoics, to 'self-preservation'. Here we have the overarching scheme of Part IV of the *Ethics*, which has its roots in the *conatus* of Part III and ends up as the *potentia seu libertas* of Part V.

We see that Hobbes explains reason through the notion of human reasoning as distinguished from an 'infallible reason' (a simple calculation of consequences), and this in the framework of an empirical, sensuous, materialist, and knowledge-based theory, which, as is evident from numerous passages in the TIE and the *Ethics*, was known by Spinoza. In order to do this, Hobbes relies— not directly or positively, since he forbids himself as well as us from doing so, but rather indirectly and negatively—on a doctrine of 'common notions,' which is written into the framework of a radical nominalist criticism (that moreover needs to be constructive at the same time, because it attempts to make sense, using the analysis of language, of a scientificity distinct from the imaginary—something the Stoics had neither done nor even dreamed of doing). This is a criticism of all universals, abstractions that are only words. Spinoza often repeats his version of this criticism, which he summarizes in EIIp40s1, just before the second scholium to which we ought to return due to its position with regard to adequate common notions. Note that, in the TIE, EIapp and EIVpref, he principally uses this criticism to highlight all the traditional conceptions of the good. But doesn't this seem necessarily to deprive 'right reason' of any basis, to the point of losing its rationality?

*

How, in truth, can such a heritage fit into the general systematization of rationality that is Spinozism? How, in particular, can it be present in the system of modes of perception of the TIE and the kinds of knowledge present within the *Ethics*? Don't these two works privilege understanding and its primacy over reason in all things, especially in the ethical domain, to the point where the TIE relegates reason to a place among the inadequate modes of perception; and if the *Ethics* makes of it a type of adequate knowledge, it is apparently because it sets up, with its doctrine of 'common notions' of EIIp40s2, a rational knowledge the signification of which is theoretical, "scientific," and non-practical, so that the good always remains considered as a relative notion, deprived of objective universality? And isn't this the reason why the appearance of 'right reason' seems both unforeseen and surprising, especially since it is first introduced in an "oblique" manner, by reference to "very distinguished men (to whose work and diligence we confess that we owe much)" at the beginning of the analysis of the affections in EIIIpref?[28]

Let's tarry very carefully over the TIE. The word *ratio* is rarely employed in it (10, 45, 89, 99, and also 95 in the expression 'being of reason') to designate, along with connotations that remind us of Hobbes, the activity by which the mind reasons, an activity opposed to hearsay and to experience on the one hand, and to intuition, the only adequate mode of perception, on the other. It corresponds to the (TIE's) third kind of knowledge, comprising two forms of inference, namely, that which "ascends" inductively toward the universal, and that which "descends" deductively toward the particular.[29]

To which of these two forms can *recta ratio* of the *Ethics* correspond? No doubt the second, the inference from the general, since it constructs its tenets by taking a general 'notion' for a premise, namely, the *exemplar humanae naturae*, which is used to determine the good and the bad—notions produced by our imagination when "we compare things among themselves." This is what EIVpref says (using the word 'notion' three times) in full agreement with EIapp (which uses it four times). These 'notions' are qualified as "extrinsic" (EIVp37s2), in line with, and using the same terms as the analysis performed in the TIE (12-13)— although the TIE does not expound a positive doctrine of a practical *recta ratio*, even in its succinct exposition of the "rules of life," which, as we have seen, can be considered as its prefiguration.

How, then, can the *Ethics* provide such a positive doctrine of practical *recta ratio*, especially after setting up a doctrine of 'common notions' that give the term *ratio* a precise and rigorous signification that the adjective *recta* seems unable to attenuate? Should we say that the *exemplar humanae naturae* is a common notion and that everything deduced from it—good actions and good affections, as well as the laws of the commonwealth, piety and religion—are likewise common notions? Should we say that these are common notions, *at least in a certain sense*? But in what sense? And then, are there second order common notions?

Surely it is not a matter of common notions that define the common essence of all beings in or of themselves, whether one does or does not make the distinction made by Gueroult between "universal common notions"—the laws of nature, these "fixed and eternal things" which are already analyzed in the TIE (99-101)—and "proper common notions" (I would not hesitate to say "specific," as the same passage in the TIE permits us to do), which are the laws proper to a man, e.g., in the association of ideas of his imagination or those of his understanding, or qua *conatus* that produces moral, social or technical actions.[30] For Spinoza makes it clear that it is a matter of "extrinsic" notions.

It can only thus be a matter of relative common notions, notions external in relation to the proper essence of the beings concerned. Here, in the practical domain, men and their human relations are considered not by their definitions and their laws (organic, psychological, social, etc.), but in relation to a notion of the good. Thus, they are considered with regard to evaluation, i.e., in relation to notions common to men who evaluate beings (here again men and human relations) in terms of good and bad, and thus, insofar as they are useful things. We must call these notions common since they are common to all men who have the same general notion of good defined by general usefulness. Insofar as time one can call them subjective, since these notions are relative to men's *conatus*, we should designate them as "needs." This relativized community is just as well founded on the "common properties of things" (*affectus, qui ex Ratione oritur, refertur necessario ad communes rerum proprietates*), as Spinoza insistently claims by expressly referring to the general doctrine of common notions (EVp7d). This is why he allows himself—though only singular individuals exist for him, and though he has gone so far as to criticize the use (by the imagination's being aided by words) of the general, abstract, subjective, and arbitrary notion of *homo* defined as *animal rationale* (EIIp40s1)—to speak in Part IV generically of "men" (*homines*) and even of "man" (*homo*).

Recta ratio *thus manifests itself exactly within the framework of* ratio *that had been declared adequate*, and its appearance represents, therefore, not a logical leap but a thorough deductive examination.

Despite its being a notion produced by the imagination, the *exemplar naturae humanae* is nevertheless a common notion; though it is certainly a general abstraction in the sense of those criticized in EIIp40s1.[31] Still, by its necessity as it is explained by Spinozism, it is universally common—at least inasmuch as it remains an empty formula and is not explicitly cast into a particularly defined image, i.e., in a utopia. Furthermore, we should stress that Spinoza makes no use of this notion, which is explained at EIVpref, to construct the deduction that immediately follows, starting with the first definition that alone serves as a premise.

It is exactly through and in reason, 'right reason,' that this abstract common notion finds its determination—beginning from a definition of good, itself a determination produced by reason—in the construction not of particular images, but of "rules of life"—indeed "laws," not however, the "laws of nature," but what I will call the "laws of conduct," *vivendi regulae*. (This is the most concrete determination, in relation to these practical laws of the common *exemplar humanae naturae*, which is not found and is not to be found in the *Ethics*, but must find its place, in part, in the *Political Treatise*.) The good,along with the laws of its realization, though they are all relative and subjective, are thus truly set up, defined, explained and deduced by reasoning, in a deduction which concedes nothing to the imagination but is the pure fruit of reason. Thus, in this definition and with this determination, we actually deal with a common notion—common since it is universally necessary in and for every man, like the notions defined in the second scholium of the same proposition (EIIp40s2).[32]

We must here take into account the line from EIapp where Spinoza opposes *entia rationis* (which claim to exist) to *entia imaginationis* (which are, in truth, our ideas of good and perfection). We must do this in order to invert the opposition (that allows mathematical entities, evoked a few lines later, to be understood as *entia rationis* and not *entia imaginationis*) and to understand that the good, with its rules (or laws), once rationally determined, ceases to be an *ens imaginationis* (as it used to be together with the *exemplar humanae naturae* in EIVpref), and becomes rather an *ens rationis* once it is defined and deductively explicated in Part IV; although one must not, nor even could one, ever mistake it for an *ens reale*, as one has always wanted to do.

Thus, owing to a deductive determination made from a non-arbitrary definition—both founded on the 'common properties of things'—'right reason' imposes its rationality into the heart of the imaginary, manifesting its specific rationality within the framework of a definition and an explication of Reason in general, which, rather than simply reasoning and calculating from and within the empirical realm, founds itself on and in necessary com-

mon notions. But could it be otherwise? Isn't the function of reason in general to determine experience, and, in the practical order,
to evaluate it, instead of following and ratifying it?

Such *ens rationis,* which is neither an *ens imaginationis* without
any value, nor an *ens reale* constitutive of essential determinations
of things, might be called, in Kantian terms, an *ens ideale,* not *theo-
rico sensu* but *practico sensu* (but, as we have seen, one that is
founded on the reality of the *communes rerum proprietates,* i.e.,
things' relational determinations), as long as our concern is with
what reason "prescribes" to us, rather than with what it makes us
believe.

*

Spinozism thus sets up a *practically rational ideality* that appears
and is expounded, explicated, and even deduced just after
EIVpref with the doctrine of 'right reason.' This rational ideality is
constitutive of that which I will call *notiones communes rationales
atque ideales,* in a manner which can surprise us, for we have not
learned to perceive them here. These are the elements of the portrait that we can make for ourselves of the free man as well as the
instruments of our liberation.

In this ideality 'right reason' enjoys specificity in the heart of
reason, assuring at the same time the specificity of the practical
law, which cannot be reduced to mere knowledge and the simple
application of nature's laws. Morality can and should be neither
observation nor observance.

This is how Spinoza, in a purely rational and fully immanent
manner, establishes in his system of rationality a *practical reason.*

Translated by Steven Barbone

NOTES

1. We see how difficult it is to find a single term in French (or any other language) to translate the word, *Ratio*, which primarily signifies 'calculation,' and thus 'organization.' We cannot forget that it always refers to 'reason', and because of that, to 'motive' (the sense of 'cause', important in Spinozism, does not directly figure here). In a general sense, we must here take into account Spinoza's Latin vocabulary, since this is what explicates the sense of his discourse. We will see that this method makes clear the link between his thought and Hobbes', and explains the role of this doctrine.

2. In the TIE, *recte* is used to modify the verbs *intelligere* (12), *colligere* (25), *concipere* (25), *procedere* (80), and *fieri* (49), and the expression *recta via* (absent from the *Ethics*) is used three times: in a theoretical sense (title and 94) and in a practical sense (17). (See TTP 1 GIII 26, TTP 7 GIII 112.).

3. It is in this sense that the TTP (TTP 5 GIII 73, TTP 16 GIII 190) and the TP (2:20) speak of *sana ratio* and of *ratione recte uti* (TP 2:6, 11).

4. This importance undoubtedly increases in the course of the progressive explication of ideas in the *Ethics*. (See Bernard Rousset, "Eléments et hypotheses pour une analyse des rédactions successives de l'*Ethique* IV," *Cahiers Spinoza* 5 (1985), pp. 129-46; See also "La première *Ethique*. Méthode et perspective," *Archives de Philosophie* 51 (1988), pp. 75-98. I do not wish to analyze this doctrine except in the case where one sees its formation and where one finds it under its more complex form in the *Ethics*. But I will assert that the expression *dictamen rationis* is already found in the TTP, chapters 5, 19, 20 and especially 16, that is, in the same context as that of a sociopolitical analysis found in Hobbes. The whole doctrine is found expressly and systematically summarized, as if it were a matter of it springing from itself, in the framework of a seeming analogy between the practical and theologico-political orders, where the TP deals with piety and religion. There, with a repeated use of the same language, *Rationis dictamen, praescriptum, imperium*, the doctrine of 'Reason' is envisioned with its political significance, yet without Reason being defined in its general philosophical significance as 'Right Reason.'

5. It is not necessary, and perhaps it would be a bit inexact, to analyze the terminological groupings of words which are in the same family in the following list, but we consider it to be a matter of a series of re-editings, corresponding to a deliberate decomposition introduced little by little, starting from Hobbes' condensed formula, *dictamen rectae rationis*.

6. *Ratio postulat* is used in this logical sense in TIE 99.

7. See EIVp37s1, EIVp57d,s, EIVp59d, EIVp62d,s,c, EIVp63,d, EIVp66s, EIVp68d, EIVp70d, EIVp73d, EIVapp §§ 4,9,31, EVp4s; see TP 2:5-6.

8. See EIVp24d, EIVp50s, EIVp59d.

9. This recension is merely indicative and does not pick out the verbs except under their infinitive form (as follows from the substantives under their singular nominative form) without noticing their particular forms in relation to the grammatical construction of phrases. For a complete recension, see Michel Gueret, Andé Robinet, Paul Tombeur, *Spinoza Ethica: Concordances, index, listes de fréquences, tables comparatives* (Louvain la Neuve: Université Catholique de Louvain, 1977). See also Pierre François Moreau, *Spinoza: Traité politique* (Paris: Editions Réplique, 1979); for Spinoza's other works, see Emilia Giancotti-Boscherini's remarkable *Lexicon Spinozanum* (the Hague: Nijhoff, 1970).

10. See EIVp36s, EIVp51, EIVp52,d, EIVp53,d, EIVp54, EIVp61,d, EIVp63cd, EIVp73c,d, EVp7d; cf. EIVp37d; cf. TP 2:5. Cf. *ex ratione ingenerari*, TP 2:5.

11. See EIapp, EIIp49s, EIVp18s, EIVp24,d, EIVp35,d,c1,c2,s, EIVp36d,s, EIVp37d,s1,s2, EIVp40d, EIVp46d, EIVp47s, EIVp50d,s, EIVp51d2, EIVp54s, EIVp63cd, EIVp65,d,c, EIVp66,c, EIVp73c,d; cf. TTP 15 GIII 188, TTP 16 GIII 192-194, 196; cf. TP 6:1; cf. *ratione ducti* TP 1:2.

12. See EIVapp §§13,25; cf. EVp41s; cf. TP 1:5, 2:6, 20, 21, 6:3.

13. See EIIIp59s, EIVp35d, EIVp37d, EIVp39d, EIVp50d,c, EIVp54s, EIVp58s, EIVp62,d, EIVp67d, EIVp72,d, EVp4s, EVp20d; cf. TTP 5 GIII 73, 80; TTP 16 GIII 191, 194; TTP 19 GIII 230.

14. See EVp10s; cf. EIVapp §9, EVpref; cf. TP 2:20.

15. See EVp10s; see also *sua dogmata ratione confirmare*, TTP 9 GIII 152.

16. See EIVp18s; cf. TTP 16 GIII 191, TTP 20 GIII 242. (Cf. *decretum*, TTP 20 GIII 242; TP 2:19).

17. On the linkage between the two last parts of the *Ethics*, and on their complementarity, see Bernard Rousset, *La perspective finale de l'Ethique et le problème de la cohérence du spinozisme* (Paris: Vrin, 1968), vol. 3, p. 1.

18. See TTP 5 GIII 73, TTP 15 GIII 188, TTP 16 GIII 190, 194.

19. See TTP 5 GIII 80, TTP 16 GIII 191, TTP 19 GIII 230.

20. See EIVapp §§15,12, EVp41s. Piety is the practical conviction, without science, but also without superstition, that respects what is good and considers that for which something is good. A good contemporary equivalent would be 'morality'. Religion, on the other hand, is tied to an idea of God, still without an adequate idea born from pure understanding but neither with ideas born in the imagination, and above all without dogmas received from tradition or a teaching magistrate. A classic equivalent would be Rousseauan 'civil religion' or even Kantian moral 'rational religion' (cf. EIVp37s1). Inasmuch as that which is good is defined as such by right reasoning alone, Right Reason manifests itself in such a Piety, and in Religion thus understood, which could accompany it. This is precisely the sense of

the second to last proposition of the *Ethics*. Cf. Bernard Rousset, "Le poids de l'ethique dans l'*Ethique*," *Studia Spinozana* 7 (1991), pp. 39-56.

21. On this doctrine in the TTP, see Bernard Rousset, *La perspective finale de l'*Ethique, III, 3.

22. See the references given in note 3.

23. The first ethical level is found already in the TIE, summarily establishing the *"rules to live by."* These rules, presented in a passage consecrated to the definition of good that would be developed at EIVpref, constitute an *auxiliary morality* that, despite the resemblance, is not a provisional morality like the one proposed by Descartes; it is *definitive* in our enterprise that is to lead the understanding along the *"right path"* (TIE 17) (although it is not a matter of reason). See Bernard Rousset, *Spinoza: Traité de la Réforme de l'Entendement* (Paris: Vrin, 1992).

24. On the Aristotelian doctrine of prudence, see especially Pierre Rodrigo, "Aristote: Prudence, convenance et situation," *Revue de l'enseignement philosophique*, 1992.

25. See E. Brehier, *Chrysippe et l'ancien stoicisme* (Paris: Presses universitaires de France, 1951), p. 267, which refers to Plutarch and Cicero.

26. See TIE 74-76; see 23, 82, 93, 110.

27. *Natural law* (a term that Spinoza does not use in the *Ethics*), the foundation of contracts for Hobbes, is not *civil law*, a product of an authority, that constitutes Right (*Jus*). An allowable Spinozistic equivalent of *mensura* could certainly be *norma*. (The excerpt is taken from a translation of *De cive* attributed to Hobbes himself: Thomas Hobbes, *Man and Citizen*, ed. Bernard Gert (Indianapolis: Hackett Publishing Company, 1991), p. 123.

28. It would be easy to maintain that the condemning of the notion of the good, the critique of universals, and the doctrine of 'right reason,' are all inscribed within the framework of the initial inspiration and of the primary systematization of Spinozistic thought, and that the doctrine of 'common notions,' which allows for a promotion of reason in the realm of adequateness, installs a new systematization in which 'right reason' no longer corresponds to true reason: moreover, it is certain that a stylistic analysis of the texts makes the different editorial layers evident. But such an historical hypothesis would not resolve, but merely deny a problem whose philosophical solution would be relatively easy to reveal.

29. See B. Rousset, *Spinoza: Traité de la Réforme de l'Entendement* (n. 23).

30. M. Gueroult, *Spinoza, II, L'Ame* (Paris: Aubier, 1974), p. 327ff.

31. Turning again to the TIE, we find ourselves here at the level of the first form of the third mode of perception.

32. One can suspect a Kantianism with this use of the word 'determination,' but it is exactly in this sense that the TIE speaks of the "experience that is not [and should have been and is going to be] determined by the intellect" (§ 19).

Incomplete Rationality in Spinoza's *Ethics*: Three Basic Forms

Yirmiyahu Yovel

As is well known, Spinoza makes reason the vehicle of ethical progress, the source of joy, freedom, and affective power. However, a good portion of *Ethics* IV (Propositions 9-17, et. al.) is devoted to proving what seems to be the contrary, namely, that reason is very often impotent, a captive of the passions and a source of grief and suffering. Simultaneously, Spinoza spends much time in the *Theologico-Political Treatise* showing that less-than-genuine rationality can, nevertheless, produce a form of significant liberation for the larger mass of humanity ('the multitude').

So, it turns out that in Spinoza there is a form of *impotent rationality* on the one hand, and a form of *potent and effective semi-rationality* on the other.

This dual fate of reason highlights a significant fact about Spinoza: alongside his far-going rationalism he was deeply aware of the shortcomings of human reason and of the fact that most people can manifest, at their best, only a limited or incomplete rationality. As a naturalist philosopher of reason, Spinoza was more realistic than his classic opponent, the preaching philosophical moralist whose discourse is based on pious, abstract wishes and presupposes a free will to adopt and realize them. Instead, Spinoza grounded human rationality—and its moral precepts—in a strictly natural process that requires the philosopher to pay close and sober attention to the detailed mechanism by which human reason arises, is impeded, and can nevertheless be put to good use even when incomplete.

The natural basis for the rise of rationality is provided by Spinoza's account of common notions. The human body, by being exposed to random causal affection by the rest of nature, accumulates latent information about the world, in the form not only of singular impressions but also of uniform patterns that are the same from every possible point of view, and thus are immune to the distortions of subjective, local perspective. Perceiving these 'common notions' is said to provide the 'foundations of reason' because the mind, when it concentrates on that latent universe in logic, metaphysics, physics, psychology, and eventually ethics, draws the law-like axioms governing these domains.

Elsewhere I have discussed this elaborate doctrine in more detail.[1] It presupposes, against Descartes, that the mind is necessarily *embodied* and that the body primordially exists *in nature*. These are the conditions (necessary and sufficient) for the mind to be there and to think (of itself and of other things), and eventually, to acquire adequate ideas. And since every human being fulfills these ontological conditions, every person can accede to *some* degree of rationality, if prompted by the appropriate causes and if obstacles have been removed form his/her mind.

Furthermore, Spinoza claims in the *Treatise on the Emendation of the Intellect* that once the rational process has been launched, it becomes self-enhancing and even, in a sense, self-engendering, because its exercise amplifies and further accelerates the power of reason.[2] At this stage, so Spinoza seems to hold, the external causes which had triggered the rise of rationality are internalized and transformed into reason's own self-causality operating within the individual and *as* the individual. In other words, reason as a self-engendering, self-enhancing natural power gradually takes over from the external inducements which have initially provoked it to arise in the individual. (If this crucial idea sounds difficult, it is because it basically amounts to explaining human freedom in Spinoza: how a mind-body organism can increasingly be seen as acting from its own resources and power of existence.)[3]

However, Spinoza is far from optimistic concerning the *degree* of rationality people can hope to attain. It cannot be guaranteed *a priori* that all individuals will actually embark on the road toward reason, or that, once started, they will see the process brought to completion. Spinoza views the 'third kind of knowledge' as a matter for the happy few. Even *ratio*, the more ordinary form of rationality which is open to greater numbers of people, will hardly ever become the majority position. Spinoza expects most people to remain at some level of *imaginatio*, either not using their rational capacities effectively, or allowing these capacities to be subordinate to arbitrary authorities, including their own passions and prejudices.

In addition, whatever the degree of knowledge of affective emancipation a person has reached in principle, no one can possibly maintain it invariably on the same level. Even *scientia intuitiva*, the most powerful form of rationality, is not attained *in toto* or once and for all. In every person's life there are dead spots and relapses, moments of oblivion or neglect that fail to express the actual mental level which, nevertheless, has been globally attained. So the effort to preserve that rational level can never cease. Maintaining a mental disposition—that is, an idea—is not the same in Spinoza as acquiring a piece of fixed property. An idea is an activity, a dynamic attitude; having adequate ideas and their affective resonances—that is, maintaining the ethical state of *ratio*—entails a constant effort, an ever active *conatus intelligendi*. We must constantly recreate that idea and renew its tension and alertness in order to be said to "have" or to "maintain" it. And we must also express that idea in terms of whatever new situations arise in our lives. But this is practically impossible for a finite mode to sustain. So *imaginatio* remains a constant possibility, indeed a component of even the most rational person's life.

These are some of the major reasons why, in order to be the natural philosopher of reason he proposes to be, Spinoza must also be the philosopher of *incomplete* reason. He must look into the less-than-rational forms of the mind, explain their role and origin, and try to put them to constructive use. By incomplete reason I do not mean simply error or mere passion. I mean a form of mind that has risen above *imaginatio simpliciter* although it cannot count as fully rational. It is a form of *unfulfilled rationality*, lacking in some essential respect, either (1) because it is still in the process of emerging; or (2) because, although already awakened and even possessing adequate rational ideas, it is powerless to follow their guidance; or (3) because it does not possess adequate ideas but only imitates their effects externally.

We may describe these incomplete forms as:

A. Nascent rationality: Reason as temptation.

B. Ineffective rationality: Reason as bondage.

C. Effective semi-rationality: Reason as external emancipator.

Only the latter two have a direct relationship to ethics; the first is a prerequisite of ratioanlity in general. For completeness' sake, I shall review all three in more detail.

A. NASCENT RATIONALITY: REASON AS TEMPTATION

The first form of incomplete rationality concerns the rise, or becoming, of *ratio* and thus is pre-philosophical. Its main role is to purify the mind of erroneous prejudices and thereby to enable the proper exercise of the mind's *vis nativa*, its innate power to form true ideas. This task has a negative and a positive side. The negative function is to provoke doubt and intellectual unease, so as eventually to evince the main obstacles that blur the mind's view of clear and distinct ideas. This is an enormous task. From childhood on, all humans are burdened with the kind of prejudices described by Descartes: unexamined sense-perception, hearsay, arbitrary association of ideas, and reliance on external authority, especially religious dogma and superstition. How can the mind be purified of its hindering beliefs so as to be ready for a fresh, rational start?

Descartes, a voluntarist and a Christian, assigned this enormous task to the free will. A sweeping act of the will is to suspend judgment about everything that cannot have sufficient rational validation, and thus purify the mind of error and prejudice. The actual false beliefs will not be erased from the mind, but denied affirmation, and error resides in such affirmation.

Spinoza does not see affirmation as a special act, separate from ideation; and he regards the free will as another superstition from which the mind ought to be purified. So Descartes' self-purification by the will is to Spinoza a supernatural miracle, a pure myth. The mind must be purified by other means, natural and causal, and probably in a gradual process. That is the role of pre-philosophical reasoning in Spinoza, consisting in the critique of the senses and in the critique of the Bible.

Because revealed religion has become the main obstacle on the mind's way to clarity, doubt and dissent about revealed religion must be provoked in its believers. God's true word is reason, not the Bible, and God's true 'decrees' are the laws of nature, not the laws of Moses and Jesus. Hence the Bible, which claims to contain God's word and God's decrees, is a major target of criticism—of immanent criticism, using the Bible's own evidence against itself by indicating its contradictions and incongruities. Similarly, the senses, and the sensual values in ethics (pleasure, riches, etc.) are to testify against themselves as a ground for revoking their worth and/or reliability. The aim is to shatter the dogmatic beleiver's confidence, so as to clear the way (and invoke the desire) for better, more adequate knowledge and goals. This is a causal process, using language, experience, rhetoric, and logic to undermine the existing intellectual world of the audience as a way of philosophical purification.

Although this is a phase of nascent rationality, reason is already at work in it. To be moved by rational argument, to recognize its force and feel disarrayed by logical contradictions, one must, to some degree, have already acceded to the use of reason and, at least in part, admitted its normative power. Even those whom Spinoza calls "ignorant" or "superstitious" are often moved by rational argument, be it only momentarily. Later they may censor its consequences or repress the doubt it had caused them, but even so, the seed that was planted may cause them a dissatisfaction that eventually produces further doubt and a greater urge to know. This causal process presupposes that the rudiments of reason (as grounded in 'common notions') are latently at work among the 'ignorant', and certainly in those who are by nature capable of higher reasoning. An educational strategy must be devised for both groups in order to open up their minds to the call of reason, taking into account the psychology of persuasion, illusion, self-deception, etc., and the ways by which different people react to a subtle or overt attack on their entrenched and endeared beliefs. One must equally study and use the mechanisms by which people can redirect their drives from one object to another, shift their allegiance between rival authorities or, more subtly, promote the objectives of a new authority (like reason) while still basically clinging to an old one (like revealed religion).

All this presupposes a perfectly causal process based upon psychology, rhetoric, and logic working together. At first it may seem (and rightly so) that rhetorical persuasion is the main lever: reason must be prompted and awakened by other causes than itself. Yet these causes do not actually create reason, they only entice it to come into operation and they remove obstacles from its way. Fundamentally, reason itself is assisting in its own 'temptation', because, as we have said, one must already accept the validity of some form of reasoning in order to further enhance rationality and turn its latent power into an active principle. At the stage of 'nascent reason', rationality, while incomplete, is therefore its *own* midwife and generator; it is not only the result, but also the substrate and the latent driving force of the process of its own becoming.

Pre-philosophical purification has two goals in Spinoza: (a) to clear the minds of those capable of genuine philosophy, and thus prepare them for a full-fledged life of *ratio*; (b) to subvert the dog-matic beliefs of the majority (the 'multitude'), so as to make it prone to accept a semi-rational system of life, by which social strife and insecurity will be turned into mutual benefit and rela-tive freedom.

On the way to full *ratio* there is another, more dramatic form of incomplete rationality, which I called 'impotent reason' or 'reason as bondage'.

B. INEFFECTIVE RATIONALITY: REASON AS BONDAGE

This, to Spinoza, is perhaps the most troubling part of his rational project. Spinoza analyzes the case of a person fully capable of philsosophical understanding, who has exercised *ratio* and acquired adequate ideas, by which he knows what is truly good and bad, yet is powerless to follow up on his ethical knowledge and remains a slave to his passions. Reason in his case is not merely impotent but harmful, because it causes a special kind of grief which would not have arisen otherwise, a grief which the 'ignorants' are spared.

Those who are ignorant will pursue the bad believing it is good. Later they will probably have to bear the consequences of their ignorance, but meanwhile they are spared the anxiety that afflicts the rational person who watches himself/herself sliding helplessly into a life of danger or empty pursuits.

In addition, because of his failure to follow what he knows to be good, the rational person is torn also by frustration and anger at himself/herself, and these ego-pains, so to speak, can be more agonizing than the simple awareness of sliding into danger. Although Spinoza does not work this second idea out, we can, fol-lowing his logic, easily see such a person suffering from guilt-feel-ings, self-anger, self-pity, self-hatred and depreciation, etc. These are, of course, bad emotions that *ratio* rules out in the true philoso-pher; but here we are dealing with someone who is unable to fol-low the precepts of his/her own reason and might as well violate the rules against guilt and pity too, applying both these emotions reflexively to herself.

Actually, Spinoza's 'geometrical' language deals with some of the most violent and complex human emotions. And there is nothing in his theory to prevent the kind of agony we are dis-cussing from taking on Dostoevskian dimensions at times. Incidentally, Spinoza took an interest in the theater, in which he saw (like some of his friends, notably L. Meyer) a vivid study—

through art rather than science—of the psychology of the emotions.

Of all three forms of incomplete reason, this is the most difficult from Spinoza's standpoint. The other two cases do not involve knowledge of adequate ideas; in one case, *ratio* is immature, and in the other it is present as an external imitation of itself. Here, on the contrary, the person possesses adequate ideas, and yet (indeed, *therefore*) ends up in impotence and suffering.

This kind of anxiety is specific to the knowing ones, who suffer *because* they are rational. Reason in their case is the cause not of joy but of grief; it does not liberate its owner but is itself held in bondage; and rather than invigorating the power of existence it cripples it and creates dramatic evidence of that crippling. This is the sense Spinoza gives to the Biblical verse (which at first may seem to contradict his philosophy): "he who increases knowledge, increases sorrow" (Ecclesiastes 1:18; EIVp17s).

This adds drama to the subtext of the *Ethics*. Underneath the serene geometrical style Spinoza is telling us a story that does not lack in drama and suspense; it is the story of a person struggling to ascend to rationality and freedom yet going through difficult stages of conflict. At the present point in the story the reader, somewhat distressed, may wonder: is there a way out of the agonies of reason? Is the protagonist going to be saved? Spinoza, the narrator of the *Ethics*, assures us in the Scholium to EIVp17 that the bleak outcome we have reached is not the last word. There is a better end to the story—in a separate chapter.

Actually, it is forty-five propositions later that Spinoza starts relaxing (and refining) his stern account of impotent reason. In EIVp62 and its Scholium, and later in EVp6 (and its sequel), he specifies further conditions under which reason becomes subjugated. This will normally occur when we have a general, though abstract, knowledge of the true good and bad—but we fail to know the *concrete apparatus*, or causal chain, by which the good (or the bad) thing might actually happen. The good (or bad) thing appears as a mere vision for the future, without the causal bridge that links the future event to the present.

Thus, the typical case of impotent reason depends on two complementary factors: (1) the true good (or bad) is known as mere *generalization*; (2) it is projected into the *future*. The underlying factor is the absence of a concrete causal chain linking the projected good (or bad) to the agent's present situation. Together, the abstract nature of the good and its location in the future compound its ineffectiveness as an emotion.

As Spinoza makes clear in EIVp62 (which specifically refers to EIVp16 in order to modify it) and again in EVp6, had we possessed knowledge of the complete series of bridging causes, then (a) (by EIVp62) the true good (or bad) would cease to be abstract and would receive detailed concretization; and (b) (by EVp6) we would connect the projected future to the present through a series of *necessary* links, thus transmitting to the distant future the psychological power and the sense of presence that attach to present events.The tighter the causal chain linking the present to the future, the stronger the emotive power transmitted to the predicted event, which enables it to resist and possibly overcome the passions of the present.

The subjugation of reason is therefore not a necesary fate. It can be, if not avoided, at least overcome. But how? Spinoza indicates at least four different ways.

OVERCOMING REASON'S BONDAGE

I. *Knowledge of the future.* Theoretically, reason can be liberated from subjugation to the passions by complete (or nearly complete) knowledge of the future events which are to link the agent's present situation with some true good expected in the future. This eliminates the 'fading out' effect by which the emotive power and vivacity of the expected good diminish in proportion to its cognitive and temporal distance. The tighter our knowledge of the causal chain by which the expected good is to occur, the stronger the emotional attraction of that good and its power to overcome competition from the passions.

Obtaining such detailed knowledge is of course difficult and rare. We depend not only on our individual capabilities but also on the contemporary state of human knowledge. The best we can reasonably expect is to get to know some general outline plus a few fragments of its detailed texture. Yet even that limited knowledge can significantly increase the subjective probability of the future good and thereby transmit to it enough power to tip the balance and to help liberate reason from the passions.

II. *Knowledge of our affects.* The second alternative is also based upon causal knowledge—not of events in the outside world and in the future, but of my own mental processes, past and present. By understanding the reasons for my emotions, conflicts, mental complexes, and vacillations; by knowing their history and causal mechanism and grasping their necessity, I can, in many cases, radically change the quality of my emotions and convert their power from passive to active, from depressing to invigorating. Reason is thereby charged with a strong affective power, capable of overcoming many negative passions and of instilling a sense of joy and power of existence in me. This is the famous theory of mental liberation offered in Part V, which I can only mention here without elaboration.

III. *An overpowering* amor intellectualis. The third way, though different, is related to the second. It consists in cultivating *one* overpowering affect so strong as to dominate the totality of one's mental life and to transform the quality of the other affects—indeed, one's whole personality—to the point of "a new birth." This is the role of the affect known as *amor dei intellectualis*. By dominating the other affects it is supposed to convert the passions into *actiones* (or to dismantle a passion altogether when, like envy, it does not have an active counterpart, diverting its power to other mental formations). At the same time it bolsters the active emotions by linking them to the central experience of the intellectual love of God. Bare reason, although necessary, cannot suffice to produce that experience; one must go beyond *ratio* to 'the third kind of knowledge', in which our metaphysical view of the universe-God is combined with concrete knowledge of particulars—especially, of the particular thing that each of us is—in such a way as to make them mediate one another.

In other words (according to the interpretation of *scientia intuitiva* I have offered elsewhere),[4] the third kind of knowledge entails rational knowledge of my body, my mind, and my environment, as they all proceed from God, exist in God, and—no less important—give God a particularized, finite expression. This is both a form of self-knowledge, mediated by the knowledge of God, and knowledge of God mediated and concretized by self-knowledge. By becoming a form of love, this circular, multi-layered knowledge acquires—by strictly *rational* means—characteristics that are analogous to a mystical unification, and generates an overpowering force, strong enough to change the quality of the emotions (from passive to active) and reorient one's whole life.

Conatus intelligendi

Actually, two stages are involved on the path to that goal.

Before *amor dei intellectualis* can produce its revolutionary effect, *ratio* must also undergo a transformation. At first, working mostly in a cumulative manner, *ratio* increases the number of adequate ideas in the mind and thereby the range of its power and freedom; the more rational I become, the stronger the affective power of reason in me. Increasingly thereby, rationality becomes a drive, capable of competing with other drives, until it takes over the *conatus* itself and becomes *conatus intelligendi*. To better understand this critical shift (textually it is located in the vicinity of EIVp21, the *conatus intelligendi* proposition), I think we should import here a key idea from the TIE concerning the self-accelerating power of rationality. This is important because proposition EIVp21 in itself remains somewhat of an enigma. *Conatus intelligendi* indicates a crucial turn in Spinoza's system, when the power of the original *conatus* is redirected toward knowledge, which has been understood to be the true good, and when the quest for knowledge becomes an effect capable of overpowering the other affects.

With *conatus* becoming *conatus intelligendi* a few crucial things occur in Spinoza's system: nature produces rational culture; self-interest produces an ethics of mutual help; knowledge becomes a driving desire—and Spinoza becomes Spinoza: the philosopher who, characteristically, derives from natural desires the most elevated rational values, indeed a whole religion of reason.

How does this shift occur? Merely recognizing that knowledge is the true good—knowing this as a general truth—is not sufficient. Herein lies our whole problem of 'impotent reason.' Clearly something else is needed in order to produce the transition. Prior to having intellectual love of God we need to have ordinary adequate ideas, in sufficient numbers and in a sufficiently intense context—until at a given point, the 'critical mass' that by then will have accumulated, will trigger in the mind the process of reason's self-acceleration, as described in the TIE. We need the TIE doctrine of reason's self-enhancing character in order to have a mechanism, a natural dynamic, by which to explain the shift from *conatus* to *conatus intelligendi*, upon which so much hinges in Spinoza's system; and we need to have that explanation prior to and independently of *amor dei intellectualis*, which is a different stage.

The plausible answer, then, seems to lie in accumulation plus self-acceleration. The more we have adequate ideas and the denser their systematic context, the more our mental power is strengthened and the closer we come to the turning point where our abstract recognition of the truly good is charged with sufficient emotive power to make it a viable, effective life-project.

Recapitulation: *Ethics* IV and the TIE

At the risk of some repetition, let me recapitulate the problem and the answers we have seen so far. The problem was that a person has acceded to *ratio* and has an idea of the truly good and bad without knowing the causal process leading to the good; he/she recognizes it merely as an abstraction and as something projected into the future. As a result, the affective power attached to the idea of the good fades out in the cognitive and temporal distance and is much too weak to overcome the passions of the present. This situation is described in propositions EIVp26-28 concerning *conatus intelligendi* and the *summum bonum*. Here again, the rational person is said to *recognize* that the truly good is knowledge and that the highest good is knowledge of God; but why can't this be another case of 'impotent reason'? What is to guarantee that my recognition of the true good will be strong enough to re-direct my drives from the pursuit of the passions to the pursuit of reason, thereby converting my *conatus* into *conatus intelligendi*?

Since the text of *Ethics* IV does not seem to supply an explicitly sufficient answer, we supplanted it with ideas from the TIE. The appeal to the TIE is justified because propositions EIVp26-28 echo the beginning of the TIE. In both texts, the true good, as *summum bonum*, is sought and found to reside in knowledge of God; and in both the question then presents itself: what will make us renounce the imaginary goods of the passions like riches, sensual pleasure, and empty fame, and adopt the true good as our new life's project, or (in the language of the *Ethics*) make it the effective goal of our *conatus*? Since the same problem underlies the TIE and the *Ethics*, we may reconstruct Spinoza's answer from both texts, using in particular his theory of the self-enhancement of reason.

First, the answer goes, *ratio* supplies adequate ideas concerning the world at large (not only the true good), including laws of nature and logic and how they apply to various cases in our experience. By forming and accumulating these ideas the mind becomes empowered to form them even more, while further liberating and invigorating itself. The quantitative language describing that process is misleading because it has qualitative aspects as well. Saying that the mind has acquired "more" adequate ideas also implies that it has gained deeper knowledge of the matters at hand and of the nature of knowledge itself—that it has become more intimately familiar with the law-like framework of knowledge, its deductive method and its other essential features. The growth of rationality means more than simply increasing the *particular items* of knowledge in our possession. It entails the deepening of their systematic context and gaining a more profound insight into what knowledge itself is. Also (this is the TIE's version of the same), we become more proficient in the use of *ratio* as we actually go on using it. Again this should not be understood as simple training, as when an artisan or a ball-player improves his skills by exercising them. Rather it is a qualitative deepening of one's reflexive understanding of what one is doing, so as to further contribute to that understanding and its application to further subject matters.

I take this to be the self-enhancing, self-accelerating power that Spinoza attributes to reason in the TIE, and which the cumulative or 'quantitative' work of *ratio* echoes in the *Ethics*. It is also a process that strengthens one's 'power of being', as Spinoza says; that is, it invigorates *one's whole life* rather than promoting reason as some special faculty or 'specialization'. Spinoza takes a clear stand against seeing reason as merely a 'skill' or a special mental department which can, as such, be severed from the rest of one's existence (as in the case of, say, a chess champion or a high-powered logician, who may otherwise be emotionally unbalanced, arrogant, depressed, bigoted, or simply ordinary, lacking in those 'Spinozistic' qualities which reason-as-power-of-being is supposed to promote). To Spinoza, reason affects the whole mind (and the body too); it is an ethical power *from the outset*. Perhaps this view reflects the semi-religious expectations Spinoza placed in rationality.

In Part V Spinoza creates a further layer of the same, when he says that the more the mind knows things, the more it knows (and loves) God, and the greater its own power and capacity. This view restates the self-accelerating nature of rationality on the level of *scientia intuitiva*. Again the process is expressed in a transformed affectivity and is not merely quantitative, but qualitative. However, in this paper I confine myself to the second kind of knowledge and can mention the third only in passing.

The Semi-Rational Maxims

I now turn to the fourth way that Spinoza suggests of escaping "subjugated reason." This way does not consist in acquiring new adequate ideas but in following semi-rational maxims that the rational person shapes with the help of his/her imagination, memory, and habit. These maxims are of two kinds, affective and cognitive.

IV-a. *Focusing on reason's affective parallels.* In one variety of maxim, which is less sophisticated and does not entail a cognitive effort, Spinoza advises his reader to direct his/her attention to the active, joyous side that can be found in most affects, including many passions, and to focus especially on that which, in the passion, could have been produced also by reason and served it. This strategy is based in part on the principle that actions performed from passion can be performed also from reason (EIVp59). To follow the maxim one would have to maintain good spirits and a positive attitude toward other people and things. Instead of finding fault in others, of hating or envying them, I should concentrate on the joyous, enhancing role that the affect can play for me and within me. In addition, the strategy requires that I refer the joy or the passion to my whole organism rather than to some particular part of it. Passions directed to a particular organ, that is, seeking localized pleasure, are usually the source of excess and are ethically bad; whereas the kind of pleasure that affects the organism as a whole (like enjoying good health, a feeling of energy and personal power, a sense of general well-being, or simply good spirits, when not artificially induced) is usually of the positive, enhancing kind and rarely allows of distortions and excess.[5]

IV-b. *Semi-rationality—the imitation of reason by the imagination.* The most important variety of maxim has to do with "right conduct," which Spinoza offers as a major auxiliary to ethics. (It also has far reaching consequences for politics, religion, social policy, and education, which I shall discuss in the next section).

As long as reason is not sufficiently liberated, says Spinoza:

> The best we can do, therefore, so long as we do not possess perfect knowledge of the emotions, is to frame a system of right conduct, or fixed practical precepts, to commit it to memory and to apply it forthwith to the particular circumstances which now and again meet us in life, so that our imagination will become fully imbued therewith, and that it be always ready to our hand. (EVp10s; for technical reasons I have used Elwes' translation.)

These crucially important lines provide the basis for ethical life under incomplete reason, both for the rational individual and for the multitude. In the case of the rational individual they are meant as provisional maxims only, which eventually could be disposed of at least in part; whereas for the multitude they set the *permanent* framework for politics, religion, and other institutions of public education and restraint.[6]

The idea is basically the following. As long as we cannot fully live by reason, we must use the lower powers of imagination and memory to offer a partial remedy. Reason, as we have seen, is impotent because its knowledge of the true good is (a) abstract, and (b) future-oriented. Therefore, we must avoid relying on the future, and provide reason with some concrete cases. This is where memory and the past come into play. Using the mechanism of the association of ideas, I train myself to associate the idea of the true good (and bad) with certain concrete cases that illustrate and realize that good. This concretizes the good, not through causal knowledge of future events (as in alternative I) but through assorted examples which, although they do not form a causal chain, particularize the abstract good by vivid illustration, and thereby endow it with some affective power.

The semi-permanent links that are established between certain ideas are shaped as pragmatic maxims, which the mind trains itself to follow as a matter of habit and routine. (Remember that this is not a rational procedure but one based on association and habit.) These maxims increase in power when the examples they use are drawn from the agent's own past experiences. Recollection of the past, Spinoza argues, is more vivid and impressionable than anything projected into the future. A person who suffered a burn in the past is more strongly affected than one who only fears a burn in the future. In the TIE Spinoza actually used recollection at the critical turning point in his life's project, when saying that past experiences had taught him that most things that are considered good are actually bad. Recollection of the past was linked to the knowledge of the true good and bad as an auxiliary, a psychological support by which to empower the knowledge and sustain the ethical effort. The knowledge of good and bad is no longer abstract, for it is now linked to concrete events and experiences, though the events are in the past, not the future, and the link is maintained through recollection, not causal knowledge.

So, although recollections are a mode of *imaginatio*, not of *ratio*, they can lend affective power to the abstract knowledge of good and bad, and thus help sustain it as a practical force and as a temporary cause of action. This is not an 'adequate' cause of action, of course; it does not entail true freedom, nor can it be relied upon to always produce the desired results. But when effective, it helps to carry on the *transition* between reason as bondage and reason as freedom.

Though it may seem that Spinoza relies here on raw, elementary experience (*experientia vaga*), actually he uses a highly shaped form of experience. Past recollections are shaped to produce a maxim (be it only inductively) which is then impressed upon memory by self-training, so as to pop back to mind whenever a trigger-experience occurs. Memory serves in a dual capacity in this mechanism, first as *recollection* and, secondly, as *association*. The result is a mode of *imaginatio* (memory, association, habituation, etc.) which serves as auxiliary to a mode of *ratio*. In other words, this is a typical case of *semi-rationality*, since the content of our maxim is rational, while the mechanism which leads us to follow that maxim is not. Significantly, this semi-rationality is more effective than pure rationality and may eventually help liberate reason itself.

The idea of semi-rationality has taken us into the third form of incomplete rationality, which has both personal and political implications.

C. EFFECTIVE SEMI-RATIONALITY: REASON AS EXTERNAL EMANCIPATOR

Effective semi-rationality has two applications, for the rational individual and for the multitude, and its function for the rational individual is fulfilled in two versions. The first version concerns the interim stage sketched above, in which reason is still too weak to assert itself. The second version concerns the rational individual in the full sense, in whom reason has become effective as the dominant principle of life. Yet, as finite mode, even this person continues to have passions, relapses, dead moments, areas of ignorance, etc. Therefore, he/she needs a strategy for handling those states, which consists, again, in devising a semi-rational auxiliary to reason. Even those who attain to a form of *scientia intuitiva* need to restructure their imagination and memory so as to turn them into a stable, semi-rational support for the life of reason.

The question facing such a person is, then—how to manage the gaps, reversions, and sheer ordinary periods that lie between the extraordinary rational states that now dominate and color his life in principle, yet cannot be maintatined on the same level of intensity and alertness all the time. Must we, on those occasions, fall back all the way into the depth of sensuality and imagination? If so, how can we expect to rise again when a privileged rational moment recurs? And if not, what will help us maintain a measure of stability even as we revert to ordinary life?

One possible answer is: simply rely on the natural order of things. A person whose life has been transformed by a high intellectual achievement can be expected to enjoy some positive fallout even in the ordinary moments of life. Yet this is simply an incidental assurance and too arbitrary a chance to take. One needs to consciously *shape* this promise, in order to make its outcome, if not actually necessary, at least probable and reliable. The life of reason is *a self-constructed life*; it involves a conscious caring and preparing of means. Thus, a special self-educational mechanism of semi-rationality becomes incumbent even on a person attaning to *scientia intuitiva* and the experience of intellectual love which it generates. No less than those in a sub-rational state, persons in 'supra-rational' states need to rely on a reshaped imagination and recollection to stabilize their mental achievement over time and provide for continuity and constancy—a Spinozistic virtue—by constructing high-level bridges between the relative ups and downs that *any* person's life, at all levels, must undergo.

The same conclusion is reached from another angle. Memory and imagination constitute the mind's empirical individuality. It is through them that, according to Spinoza, an individual mind existing in *duratio* is distinguished from itself as an eternal idea in God's intellect, and is also distinguished from other individual empirical minds. But even as they *constitute the existential individual self*, memory and imagination subordinate the individual mind—whatever its cognitive level—to their other law-determined effects, including the association of ideas and of affects, and the possible recurrence of passion, forgetfulness, decrease in vitality, etc. Therefore, at every stage of knowldge, imagination and memory pose a problem that the rational person will have to handle by attempting to reshape them as semi-rational auxiliaries, and thus transform their effects from negative to positive; i.e., from obstacle to support.

(We may note in passing that this resembles a problem known to mystics, who fall back from the state of elation to ordinary life: how will they return to the higher state? They need to find or shape a new form of ordinary existence which, based on training and investement in self-education, will use elements of *this* world as a launching pad for regaining the transcendent world of Grace.

Most great mystical writers (like Teresa of Avila) grapple with a variety of this problem. Spinoza is no mystic, but his objectives and those of the mystics share certain structural similarities, and therefore also problems of a similar nature.)

The Multitude: Religion and Politics

The element I called "effective semi-rationality" finds its more *specific* role and importance in Spinoza's treatment of the masses— the so-called 'multitude'. Here we are no longer speaking of a method of *self*-education but of educating the general public. Spinoza, a political realist and a student of Machiavelli and Hobbes, shuns a utopian political discourse that only states what is best without pointing to a causal apparatus or mechanism that can bring it about. To him, politics is mostly about the *means* to a desired end—how to pacify a society and ensure general security, which allows for the distribution of labor, proseprity, the growth of learning, and thereby, freedom. By freedom Spinoza means first, political freedom for all, and second—thereby—a chance for the happy few to attain also the mental and metaphysical freedom which he designates as *summum bonum*. This, like everything in nature, is a *causal* process goverend by natural laws, including the laws of human nature that determine our modes of perceptions and emotive reactions and which, in politics as in psychology, must be studied with the natural scientist's objective, self-restrained disposition—"as if they were points, lines, and surfaces." Spinoza sees no use for sheer moral exhortation, because it is doomed to be barren. Exposing the usual attitude of the moral-ist preacher, who prescribes an abstract moral blueprint for the world, he rejects it as an attempt, through mere exhortation, to move an imaginary 'free will' to adopt this ideal and impose it on a resisting world. This attitude is doomed to be barren because it fails to work through the natural causality that alone can promise success—and which, when taken into consideration, will modify or reconfigure one's moral objective in light of what can and can-not be achieved in actual reality.

While freedom and security are the goals of politics, its matter or substrate is the multitude—whose immediate disposition con-tradicts these goals. The causal psychology of the multitude is inclined to produce insecurity, violence, and servitude (servitude to the passions, and servitude to other people, resulting from the drive to vainglory and dominion). Spinoza, a modified Hobbesian, has a grim view of the multitude. In its raw (or pre-political) state[7] the multitude presents a volcanic menace that in essence is preserved also in the civil State. Dominated by ignorance, fear, and superstition, the multitude's reactions are shaped by *imaginatio*, with its distorted, inverse image of what is truly good. This gives rise to other unrestrained passions—greed, lust, ambition, envy, hatred, vainglory—and also to excessive or misplaced love and hope, and to their various offshoots and varieties. This basic disposition of ordinary people defines the problem of politics in Spinoza. Its task is to reshape the multitude's passions and imagination in such a way as to reverse their negative effects: instead of breeding discord and violence, they are to generate behavior that promotes peace, solidarity, social justice, and political cohesion. In other words, through adequate political institutions and laws, a considered use of authority, and effective public education and persuasion, *the imagination is to be re-configured as an external imitation of reason.* This basic disposition defines the problem of politics in Spinoza. Its task is to reshape the passions and imagination in such a way as to reverse their negative effects: instead of breeding discord and violence, they are to generate behavior that promotes peace, solidarity, social justice, and political cohesion. In other words, through adequate political institutions and laws, a considered use of authority, and effective public education and persuasion, the imagination is to be reconfigured as an external imitation of reason.

This will not make the multitude rational, however. Spinoza works on the assumption that, while individual persons could always advance to *ratio*, a large sector, perhaps the majority of the population, will remain motivated by *imaginatio*—and this is what *defines* 'the multitude' for him. The problem is how to use the imagination itself in converting its effects from disastrous to benign. For this purpose Spinoza singles out two elements of *imaginatio* in particular: *fear* (with its constant correlate, hope), and respect for authority (that form of knowledge and action which arises *ex auditio* [from 'hearsay'], namely, from "hearing" the voice of authority and tradition and acting out of respect for them). Fear and respect breed *obedience*, and jointly they promote *social habituation*—the tendency to accept established norms of action, arising from the wish to avoid punishment and/or show respect to an institution, a law, or (above all) a revered text, such as the Bible.

Obedience and habituation thus take the place of first-person rational knowledge as the prime motivation in the reshaped imaginantion, and this cannot work except through *institutions*. The reshaped popular imagination requires, and eventually becomes equal to, a set of institutions—social and political, formal and informal—that structure and regulate the public domain, and toward which the public shows respect and obedience.

The full development of this theory belongs to a discussion of Spinoza's political treatises (TTP and TP). Here I only wish to call attention to their philosophical anchoring in the *same* doctrine of semi-rationality we found in *Ethics* IV. The *Theologico-Political Treatise* and the *Ethics* are not linked only by the overt scholium discussing "the foundations of the state" and natural rights (EIVp37s2), but in a more sepcific and vital way, which states the *method* for answering the problem of politics. This is clearly, though succinctly, offered in the short text of *Ethics* IV we analyzed above, which discusses the use of imagination and memory in creating a mechanism of semi-rationality.

State Law and the Reformed Bible
as Reformed Imagination

The great merit of Spinoza's politics is that it makes the 'multitude'—the many—into a philosophical problem in its own right. Other modern philosophers, from Descrates to Kant and Nietzsche, dismissed the sub-rational domain in various degrees. The philosopher is concerned with the top rational (or mental) achievements; in Kant semi-rationality is not possible—acting from or outside the moral-rational imperative is an either/or dichotomy. In Marx, the multitude itself (as proletariat) is supposed to rise to the height of rational history (as revolution) and redeem all the other human groups too. To Nietzsche the 'many' were an object to spurn and dismiss, which made his philosophy, in principle, politically barren.[8] Spinoza, on the contrary, holds that the problem of the many *as such* (rather than as potential members of a purely rational community) is of the utmost philosophical importance.

The *Theologico-Political Treatise* starts with a forceful short discussion of the psychology of the masses. Spinoza dwells on the dark, volcanic side of the imagination that dominates this psychology, and reaches the conclusion that it must be transformed from the inside into an imitation of reason. The two institutional domains through which this reform is to take place are religion and politics. Religion is based on respect for God's revealed word; by proper interpretation, God's True Word, and therefore commands, are to be shorthanded and identified with the moral-prac-

33

tical principles of justice and *caritas* (meaning solidarity and mutual help) which reason also recommends. No cognitive principle is included in this reduced, purified religion, only practical, semi-rational behavior deriving from motives of the imagination. In parallel fashion, the reformed political state is to pass laws and establish procedures that enact behavior similar to that recommended by reason, which most citizens will follow out of obedience, respect for the law, and social habituation (imagination and memory) rather than pure understanding. Finally, the link between the two institutional domains is to be assured through the subordination of the first to the second—namely, confining the detailed interpretation and concretization of justice and solidarity ('God's True Word') to particular legislation by the civil authorities—since it is the civil, secular state alone which can hold the undivided power of sovereignty. In this way, the institutionally-reshaped imagination has two *non*-symmetrical pillars: the political pillar is higher than the religious, and the religious factor is by and large secularized—into a social creed or civil religion.

This provides a schematic explication of the structure of the *Theologico-Political Treatise,* based on the problem of semi-rationality. Often readers wonder what unites the two parts of this work—what lies behind the hyphen, so to speak. The notion of semi-rationality, and the role of reshaped imagination in constituting it, provide, I suggest, the systematic answer. The TTP is a treatise about the multitude, "the many," and how to transform the effects of their imagination from destructive to benign, from acting as the enemies of security and freedom into serving as their auxiliaries—using memory, habit, respect, fear, dual language, and the reformed institutional powers of politics and religion. Elsewhere I have elaborated on these topics in some detail.[9] In this paper I pointed out how the issue uniting the TTP is anchored in a central problem of *Ethics* IV—namely, that of "effective semi-rationality," and the project of reshaping the *imaginatio* as an imitation of reason.

NOTES

1. See my paper from the Second Jerusalem Spinoza Conference: "The Second Kind of Knowledge and the Removal of Error," in Y. Yovel, ed., *Spinoza on Knowledge and the Human Mind* (Leiden: E.J. Brill, 1994), pp. 93-110.

2. TIE 31. See also TIE 18, 22, 40, 73-5.

3. As in the case of human freedom, what occurs here is an internalization of cosmic forces, which become my own only because I myself am no longer merely particular. Hopefully I shall discuss this in a separate paper.

4. See, e.g., my *Spinoza and Other Heretics*, vol. 1: *The Marrano of Reason* (Princeton: Princeton University Press, 1989), chap. 6.

5. It may seem that this maxim implies free will, but it doesn't. Attention, intention, etc., can be caused by desires, following a calculus or a maxim.

6. These are not the same as the "provisional rules" Spinoza, following Descartes, has set at the beginning of his way (in the TIE), although there are certain similarities. There, the rules were merely pragmatic, unsupported by a theory; here they are part of a whole theory and self-educational strategy.

7. In Spinoza all states are natural, including the civil state; but nature can appear in its raw immediate form or in a worked-out form; the latter is manifest in civilized life, and its basis, the civil State.

8. I elaborated on this claim in *Dark Riddle: Hegel, Nietzsche, and the Jews* (Cambridge: Polity Press, 1998).

9. *Spinoza and Other Heretics*, vol. 1, chap. 5.

Ethics IV: The Ladder, Not the Top: The Provisional Morals of the Philosopher[1]

Herman De Dijn

> We see also that reasoning is not the principal
> thing in us, but only like a stairway, by which
> we can climb up to the desired place.
> —*Short Treatise* II 26:6 [2]

1. The Relationship between Logic, Philosophy (of Nature), and Ethics.

Throughout his life, Spinoza entertained the idea of completing a piece of work that he left unfinished: his logic, the *Treatise on the Emendation of the Intellect*.[3] This *Treatise* was meant to serve as a kind of introduction to his philosophy. His philosophy—as the titles *Short Treatise on God, Man and his Well-Being*, and *Ethics* already indicate—is dominated by ethical considerations. The term 'ethical' is to be taken here in a much broader sense than we conceive of it today: it is basically the pursuit of real well-being, of real happiness.[4] The sum total of Spinoza's philosophizing is ethical in this sense. Paradoxically enough, this ethics is intrinsically linked to what seems a strictly theoretical endeavour: the construction of a genuinely scientific metaphysics; the ultimate ethical end is even said to *consist* in the possession of knowledge (*scientia intuitiva*).

As anyone who has read the first paragraphs of the *Treatise on the Emendation of the Intellect* knows, the origin of Spinoza's philosophizing lies in the profound dissatisfaction with the sort of life dominated by the pursuit of goods like fame, sensual pleasure, and money.[5] In such a life, we are at the mercy of external forces (*fortuna*), particularly because we live under all kinds of illusion concerning these forces and concerning ourselves. Once we realize this, we will look for 'salvation from despair';[6] we will strive for a *real* good, and another sort of life, i.e., another sort of human nature (TIE 13). This pursuit must *at the same time* and in the first place be a pursuit in which we avoid the usual illusions concerning ourselves and our place in reality. Spinoza even tells us that the highest good that we are looking for coincides with truly knowing ourselves and our real place in the cosmos. So what at first looks like a *means* (real philosophical understanding) is somehow *the end*! Philosophy *is* ethics.[7]

Logic, defined as the project of the emendation or purification of the intellect, is the proper introduction to philosophy.[8] It consists basically of two parts: reflexively separating true understanding from untrue understanding, and then, according to the norm of what true understanding is, specifying specific rules, so that, in the *best* and *shortest* way, we can develop the *philosophical* insights about ourselves and our place in nature (TIE 29, 40, 49). Logic thus understood is nothing but the reflexive strengthening of intellectual understanding, leading quickly into philosophy itself. The emendation or purification of the intellect quickly transforms itself into philosophizing itself: there is no absolute distinction between logic and philosophy.[9] The way Spinoza repeatedly describes his logic is such that it can hardly be distinguished from what philosophy as ethics itself is supposed to be. Thus, in EIVapp4 he claims that "perfecting the intellect is nothing but understanding God . . . (and is) to conceive adequately both himself and all things that can fall under his understanding."

But if the new way of life that we must acquire is a life of understanding, then: 1) why does Spinoza say that ethics is *different* from logic (EVpref), and 2) why is there a need to develop a separate ethics *within* the philosophy—why does the *Ethics* not stop at the end of Part II? Do we not there realize our true place within nature? (Compare the end of EIIp49s: "This doctrine . . . in addition to giving us complete peace of mind, also teaches us wherein our greatest happiness, *or* blessedness, consists: viz. in the knowledge of God alone, by which we are led to do only those things which love and morality advise.") Clearly, success in adequately understanding nature, and ourselves within it, is somehow not sufficient to yield the new human nature that we desire.

The problem can also be formulated thus: at the beginning of the *Treatise on the Emendation of the Intellect*, Spinoza, who is here acting as our guide into a new way of life, presents, as our highest and true good, knowledge of our union with God-nature (TIE 13). Why is it then that *after* we have arrived at this knowledge in our philosophy (*Ethics* II), Spinoza reopens the question of what is really good; why does the whole ethical question that stood at the beginning of the logic have to begin all over again? Was, then, the whole endeavour of purification of the intellect and of coming to a real philosophical understanding of ourselves in nature not sufficient? Why is it that *scientia naturalis* has to be complemented by an *ethica*?

The reason clearly has to do with the inevitable persistence (even in the philosopher) of emotions or passions. The fundamental *ethical* problem for the philosopher is that, even though he may come to realize what his real nature is, he still *remains* part of nature, i.e., susceptible to passions that keep him "under the influence" of external things (*fortuna*, EIIp49s), so that he cannot enjoy full happiness. The perfection of our *knowledge* does not immediately and automatically lead to the highest perfection of our *nature*. The real problem is thus the problem of the *power* of our knowledge *vis-à-vis* the emotions, i.e., the relative weakness or strength of our state of knowledge *vis-à-vis* these passions. Ethics arises because of the clash between interiority and exteriority.

This problem of the weakness or strength of our *ratio vis-à-vis* the passions dominates Spinoza's ethics in the proper sense, i.e., *Ethics* IV and V. At the same time, the problem of the relationship between knowledge and real happiness gets a sharper formulation. Indeed, victory over the passions seems to require a *development* in our knowledge that goes beyond the sort of knowledge of the rational man talked about in *Ethics* IV. Real success over the passions and, therefore, real happiness requires a *special* kind of knowledge, namely, intuitive knowledge of our own emotions, linked to intellectual love of God (*Ethics* V).

Spinoza's ethics, properly speaking, turns out to be more related to the issues of self-loss and self-realization—issues intrinsically linked to the search for a meaningful life—than to what today is usually understood by ethics or morals. In the contemporary context, this issue and this search have become closely associated with therapeutic theories and activities, and various methods of self-realization. It is not difficult to find interpretations of Spinoza's ethics (EIV and V) claiming that he advocates a certain kind of therapy against the passions or a strategy (or strategies) of self-liberation.[10] It is well known that Spinoza has been seen as anticipating insights of Sigmund Freud;[11] Georg Groddeck even tried to correct Freud in terms of Spinozist therapy.[12] Wetlesen compares Spinoza to old religious traditions of self-realization and self-liberation (as, e.g., in Mahayana Buddhism[13]), and distinguishes two radically different levels in Spinoza's ethics: one a gradual and one an instantaneous strategy of liberation, to be found in *Ethics* IV and V respectively.[14]

I have mentioned the close connection in Spinoza between salvation and knowledge. So it is not astonishing to see Curley ascribe to Spinoza the idea of a kind of *cognitive* therapy against our passive emotions,[15] in which Spinoza would anticipate therapeutic insights of Nietzsche and Freud. Since the passions contain an element of insight and belief, we can attempt to change them by changing our beliefs. For example, we should be more careful in our interpretations of other people's behavior towards us, be more aware of the inevitability of the natural course of affairs, etc. Such improvements in our knowledge will often mean being less under the influence of the passions. However, we should not have unrealistic hopes about the effects of such cognitive therapy.[16]

In what follows, I shall endorse the general idea of ethics as a kind of cognitive therapy against the passions, but present an interpretation that differs from both Curley and Wetlesen.

2. Why an Ethics in Two Parts?

As we have seen in the first section, ethics is not a matter of knowledge *tout court*, but a matter of our weakness or strength as knowers *with respect to the passions*. It is in this context that we must also try to understand the difference between *Ethics* IV and V.

It has puzzled many a reader why Part IV should bear the title "On Human Bondage, or the Powers of the Affects," while in this very same Part Spinoza paints the picture of 'the free man'. A second problem concerns the relationship between Part IV, which contains this picture, *and* Part V, which bears the title "On the Power of the Intellect, or on Human Freedom." The usual explanation is that the title of Part IV only covers the first part—Propositions 1-18—the rest being concerned with establishing what a life of freedom would be, *if* we could live it.[17] Part V (especially the first part) is then seen as explaining how such a life *can* be lived.

This interpretation can be further developed, taking into account the notion of therapy. Curley, for example, also interprets Parts IV and V as a unity: on the basis of scientific insight into human nature, one can determine what is really useful to man in the realization of the idea of the free man: "the whole of Part IV of the *Ethics* is the construction of the idea of a model human being."[18] *Ethics* IV is then seen as basically an attempt to concretely formulate a *cognitive* therapy, which would lead—at least sometimes—to the implementation of this ideal. In other words, Part V serves to provide ways in which the scientific *knowledge* of our affects can itself—under certain circumstances—become a remedy, so as to moderate or restrain the bad effects.[19] This therapy is based on the following insights:

> If a certain belief is an essential component in a particular affect, and if we can destroy that belief, or weaken it, then we will have destroyed or weakened the affect of which it is a component.[20]

> [O]ne of the services a good therapist can provide is to give you a different perspective on things which, without this aid, you would believe uncritically.[21]

Curley agrees that in his interpretation, we should play down some elements in Part V (and even in Part IV): 1) in Part V Spinoza sometimes seems to suggest that his therapy is easy whereas at other times it is said to be very difficult; 2) the knowledge of God is sometimes presented as an extremely special sort of knowledge; Curley proposes to take this knowledge of God in a very broad sense as meaning any kind of scientific understanding; 3) it would be better to forget completely Spinoza's doctrine of the eternity of the mind (the whole second part of *Ethics* V).

What I call here 'the usual interpretation' (particularly à la Curley) has several disadvantages. First of all, it does not allow us to understand a good deal of *Ethics* V, in particular the theme which, for Spinoza himself and for many of his readers, is clearly something very important: the intuitive knowledge of God, which leads to *amor intellectualis Dei* and to a kind of quasi-religious blessedness (EVp36s). Secondly, and equally important, this interpretation leaves virtually unexplained why Spinoza distinguished *two* parts in his ethics. That these two parts (Parts IV and V) are really different perspectives is indicated in several ways,[22] not only by the two very different titles, but also by strong differences in content: talk of freedom as an ideal versus talk of freedom as a reality;[23] talk of *dictamina* or *praecepta rationis* versus talk of *remedia* through knowledge of the third kind of emotion. What is also left unexplained is the stress in Part IV on a certain weakness of the man of reason, which leads to its own peculiar sorrows (EIVp17s);

this theme is absent from Part V. Finally, although Curley interprets Spinoza's ethics as a form of cognitive therapy, cognition seems in his view only to operate as a means to arrive at a sort of life in which one is less under the influence of harmful affects: the role of cognition is mainly instrumental. This is to miss something important in Spinoza, a line A. Matheron called Spinoza's intellectualism. In Spinoza's view, knowledge is not simply a means to an end. Not only can it help us to overcome the harmful emotions, but it is *somehow* the end itself, happiness itself. Of course, for a contemporary mind, strongly influenced by Hume (and Kant), it is not easy to understand what this could mean, especially since Spinoza interprets this knowledge as identical with (or at least closely linked to) a theoretical endeavour that was establishing itself in his days as a *scientia naturalis*.[24]

Dissatisfaction with this common interpretation, and an attempt to take the differences between Parts IV and V seriously, led me to try and see them as two really *different* ethical perspectives, already expressed in the difference of axioms governing the two Parts. One is the perspective of the rational man who (as EIVpref indicates) cannot help forming the notions of what is really good or bad (useful or obnoxious) and the notion of the exemplar of the free man. The desires of the rational man related to these notions and to this ideal can, however, be easily overruled. This is why the *whole* of *Ethics* IV really deals with human servitude or human weakness. The other perspective is that of another sort of ethical life, *beyond good and bad*, where we intuitively understand our emotions, and thereby and therein are really strong and free.

In this context we can also understand what Spinoza says in the *Preface* to Part V, and why he says it. The question remaining at the end of Part IV is: is freedom, i.e., mastery of the passions, really possible even in a small part of our life? Can we go *beyond* the stage of struggle as described in Part IV? The answer given in Part V, "the remaining Part" of the ethics properly speaking, is positive. The ethical life dominated by the striving towards the ideal of the free man is *only provisional*,[25] and it is not the only sort of life the philosopher is capable of. That there is another possibility is demonstrated on the basis of "the Mind's knowledge alone" (EVpref). Before engaging in these demonstrations Spinoza indicates (again in the same *Preface*) what this alternative does *not* consist in. The solution to the ethical struggle described in Part IV cannot be the work of stoic asceticism;[26] nor can it be the work of an absolutely free will enlightened by reason, a harshly rejected Cartesian solution. Spinoza's own solution, as demonstrated in the first twenty Propositions of *Ethics* V, is (in general terms) this: freedom *is* possible through "the understanding alone" because the understanding can become a real *force* producing effects that constitute real *remedies* against the passions.

An incentive to further develop this unusual view was, for me, the reading of a provocative statement on this topic by the distinguished historian of philosophy, the late Victor Goldschmidt: "It is in this science of the good and the bad that *bondage* consists for Spinoza, and this is why the code of the 'precepts of reason' are necessarily revealed in the Part thus entitled. Freedom neither consists in knowing the precepts of reason, nor in their practical realization. . . ."[27]

If one accepts this interpretation, one reads Part IV as a strange sort of science, a science of *entia rationis*, 'science of good and bad', the possession of which leads to a peculiar form of human weakness: not the weakness of the man steeped in the ordinary anthropocentric illusions, but the *weakness* that still characterizes the desires of the rational man as geared towards the ideal human exemplar.[28]

The knowledge and desires of the rational man of Part IV do not constitute real freedom—as V. Goldschmidt says, real freedom does not consist in knowing the precepts of reason, nor in trying to implement them. As long as one tries to do the good, even to reach the highest good, one is automatically not in that state which constitutes the highest good; indeed one is in a state which is incompatible with the highest good. Thus, for example, the man of reason only really desires with reference to the future (EIVp62s), whereas the really free man simply meditates upon his emotions and is in a state of pure activity and joy (EVp4s).

Expressed in terms of therapy one could say that the best therapy is not the one in which one *tries* to apply, 'externally as it were,'[29] certain truths about what is good and bad to our life. This application may have certain good effects, particularly when we enliven these truths through imagination and memory (EVp10s). But it will not have the effects that Spinoza describes as real *remedies* (EVp20s). The best therapy is the one in which one 'forgets' about good and bad precepts, transcends the attempt to implement them, and simply acts in a certain way *vis-à-vis* one's passions, as determined by our intuitive knowledge of our concrete emotions. What seems decisive is not that certain truths about good and bad, about a certain ideal of freedom, guide us in our concrete daily deliberations, but that we as it were 'lose ourselves' in a meditative activity, in which our passions are not exterminated, but rather are functioning as further occasions for continuing meditative activity and the specific active emotions going with it. So, why are there inevitably *two* parts in Spinoza's ethics properly speaking? For one, the perspective of Part IV is at first and at times inevitable. But also, in order to really reach the goal set in Part IV, one has, as it were, to transcend striving towards this goal in an activity that is different from the desiring of the goal. This activity is the best means to continue to reach the goal, without having to strive towards it.

3. Can We Really Endorse This Provocative Interpretation?

I think we really must. From the *Short Treatise*, through the *Treatise on the Emendation of the Intellect* (§28), up to the *Ethics*, Spinoza's doctrine remains exactly the same: rational knowledge is *not* the proper kind of knowledge to let us enjoy 'salvation from despair'. There is *no continuous path* from one ethical perspective to the other, just as there is no deductive link between rational knowledge and intuitive knowledge: the first are only necessary steps towards the second. It is within this contour that a more detailed analysis has to proceed. To begin such an analysis, I will now discuss a few important themes and problems in *Ethics* IV.

3a.

The first point we have to understand is the *inescapability* of this strange science of good and bad and of the ethical perspective related to it. Why does the *Ethics* not end with Part II, or, better perhaps, why is the ethics in the *Ethics* not simply reduced to what we find in the first part of *Ethics* V? The answer is indicated in the Preface to *Ethics* IV:

> As far as good and evil are concerned, they also (like the terms perfect-imperfect) indicate nothing positive in things, considered in themselves, nor are they anything other than modes of thinking, *or* notions we form because we compare things to one another . . . But though this is so, still we must retain these words. For because we desire to form an idea of man, as a model of human nature which we may look to, it will be useful to us to retain these same words with the meaning I have indicated.

This passage echoes a slightly more elaborate passage we find at the beginning of the *TIE*:

> [I]t must be noted that good and bad are said of things only in a certain respect, so that one and the same thing can be called both good and bad according to different respects. The same applies to perfect and imperfect. For nothing, considered in its own nature, will be called perfect or imperfect, especially after we have recognized that everything that happens happens according to the eternal order, and according to certain laws of Nature. (TIE 12)

> But since human weakness does not grasp that order by its own thought, and meanwhile man conceives a human nature much stronger and more enduring than his own, and at the same time sees that nothing prevents his acquiring such a nature, he is spurred to seek means that will lead him to such a perfection. Whatever can be a means to his attaining it is called a true good; but the highest good is to arrive—together with other individuals if possible—at the enjoyment of such a nature. What [however] that nature is we shall show in its proper place: that it is the knowledge of the union that the mind has with the whole of Nature. (TIE 13)

Although good and bad, perfection and imperfection, and the ideal of human nature, are not objective concepts, *we* cannot help forming and using these notions (EIVpref). 'We' being—so I presume—the rational readers of the *Ethics* who have followed and understood the book thus far, and who are not different from other rational beings engaged in an ethical endeavour. Why is it that even rational people cannot but form the idea of an ideal human nature in function of which all sorts of emotions and activities will be called good or bad? *Not* simply because they are rational: *purely* rational beings would not form any notions of good and bad (EIVp64c, EIVp68). Yet *we* are *not* purely or exclusively rational people, but rational people inevitably forming a part of nature, and constantly assailed by external influences and the passions resulting from these. The ethical predicament is inescapable for the *real* rational man because, on the one hand, he is already more or less rational, yet, on the other hand, he is also living in the real world, which does not exist for the purpose of man. Real life, also for the rational man, is a life of *struggle*, of confrontation, with victories and defeats, a struggle in which both personal strength *and* fortune (EVp10s) play the central roles. Trying to act and live under the guidance of reason is an attempt "to conquer *fortune* as much as possible" (EIVp47s). It rarely happens that men live spontaneously under the guidance of reason.[30] Even the man who is already rational at times, and who experiences the special pleasures involved in rational activity, cannot completely escape dangers and possible defeats. Knowing these pleasures, and confronted with these dangers, the rational man inevitably and self-consciously strives towards more of this life of reason (EIVp26) and forms the notion of an ideal, stronger human nature, in which the possession of rational insight and the concomitant contentment would be more consistent (TIE 13). This conscious desire for the ideal, rational life is informed by the rational information concerning nature, man's place in it, and man's emotions; this leads to ideas of what is good and bad, useful or not for the sake of obtaining this stronger nature. Thus rational man cannot help but to form these notions of the ideal man, of good and bad. It is not absurd to form them either, because through human weakness one cannot grasp the concrete order of causes (to foresee the future) and "at the same time [one] sees that nothing prevents his acquiring such a nature" (TIE 13).

The formation of the ideal by the rational man is therefore linked to the following factors: 1) having gone through certain experiences, he cannot but desire to re-live certain pleasures, and cannot but desire the avoidance of what prevents them; 2) he cannot foresee the course of events, so he forms a certain ideal as a *possibility* for himself (it is thus not an accident that we find definitions of the possible and the contingent at the beginning of Part IV); 3) nothing seems to point to the strict impossibility of obtaining this ideal; on the contrary, the rational man has experienced something of it already (TIE 11). This striving towards the ideal human nature is one mode of the activity of the free man at certain moments and particularly at a certain stage of his development (EIVp67).

3b.

Ideas of what is good and what is bad are really nothing but the consciousness of what gives pleasure or pain (EIVp8d). It is the same with the rational man: his knowledge of what is (really) good or bad is an expression of the awareness of the pleasures of a life of reason since his knowledge of what is bad is indirect (i.e., of what is not good) (EIVp63c). But with the rational person, this pleasure and the desire to have it again are *informed* by *rational* insight in means-end relations (themselves based on cause-effect insights concerning our emotions). These rational insights must 'blend' with the reflexiveness of the pleasure found in rational activity. Insofar as it is linked to the awareness of the pleasures involved in the activity of reason, true knowledge of good and bad is itself an emotion, or part of the affective-dynamic structure, capable of playing a more or less decisive role in the ethical struggle (EIVp63c). In the concrete predicament and struggle of the rational man, these insights into good and bad become his *precepts or dictates of reason* (EIVp19-37), which he tries to keep in mind and to consult, so as to know what to do next and how to react (EVp10s). They are his *precepts*, not of course in the sense that he could freely decide whether to observe them or not, but in the sense that the individual who knows what is conducive to the desired end will necessarily take this knowledge as a guideline in his acting.[31] In light of these precepts, the rational man knows which passions agree with reason and which do not (EIVp38-58). In relation to his desire for a life of reason, the rational man also forms a picture of what sort of life this would be *if* he could act *under the guidance of reason alone* (EIVp59-66): it is the picture of *the free man* (EIVp67-end). This picture in itself does not tell us to what degree it can be realized. It functions as an imperative in the striving of the rational man.[32]

3c.

This knowledge of good and bad is called *true* knowledge, not simply because it just *happens to correspond* to what is really useful to us or not (the notion of truth as correspondence is secondary for Spinoza). It is called true because it is based on reason (as is clear, e.g., from EIVp15d). Therefore, it is inappropriate to call it inadequate[33] or to equate it with knowledge of the first kind.[34] It is *rational* knowledge, even though it has to do with *entia rationis* and even though it is applied under conditions of lack of information and of uncertainty both concerning contingencies and concerning possibilities.[35] While based on rational insights, but applied to concrete circumstances, this knowledge is inevitably 'abstract, *or* universal' (EIVp62s), and is a mixture of reason and imagination, often more imaginary than real (EIVp62s). Thus one can easily understand that even though this knowledge has some affective force, the man of reason often yields to passions. For example, his rational desires informed by knowledge concerning good and bad as regards contingencies and future possibilities do yield to desires for things which are pleasing in the present (EIVp16, EIVp17).

As long as we are in the regime of rational knowledge of good and bad and of the related desires, as long as we do not have intuitive knowledge of our own emotions, the best we can do—Spinoza says in EV10s—is to occupy our mind assiduously with the precepts of reason, "to commit them to memory, and to apply them constantly to the particular cases frequently encountered in life. In this way our imagination will be extensively affected by them, and we shall always have them ready." Even then, there will be vacillation of the mind, but the emotions "will be overcome in far less time than if we had not considered these things beforehand in this way . . . ." And Spinoza concludes: "And he who will observe, these [rules] carefully—for they are not difficult—and practice them, will soon be able to direct most of his actions according to the command of reason."

3d.

The truth is that this true knowledge of what is good and bad not only "often yields to lust of every kind," but that it even "arouses disturbances of the mind" (EIVp17s). In the concrete struggle, our desires, even when informed by knowledge of what is really good, can be overcome and even lead to experiences of sadness. Spinoza repeats here the words of the poet: "video meliora, proboque, deteriora sequor." And he also refers to *Ecclesiastes*: "He who increases knowledge increases sorrow." Which, of course, is *not* to say "that a wise man has no advantage over a fool in the moderating of his emotions." Nevertheless, here we encounter limitations of the life of the rational man in his concrete predicament and struggle.

The question that looms large at the end of Part IV is whether 'we', living the concrete life of the rational man described in EIVp1-18, can ever actually realize the sort of freedom painted in the picture of a truly rational life (EIVp59-66) or in the exemplar of the free man (EIVp67-end). In other words, the question is whether the rational man can ever get beyond this stage of constant struggle and longing; whether he can ever, to some important degree, become a man acting *in a constant manner* under the guidance of reason, and lead a life which, at least in part, is a strong *consistent* flow of active thinking, feeling, and desiring (EIVp63c, EIVp65c, EIV66c). In such a life one is not easily affected by bad emotions (EVp10s), and the passions constitute the smallest part of the mind (EVp20s).

It is perhaps no accident that, at the end of Part IV, Spinoza says that the desire for the ideal (for the possible) should be complemented by a desire for "what is necessary," so that we are contented "with what is true" (EIVapp32), and are able simply "to act well and rejoice *(bene agere et laetari)"* (EIVp73s). These phrases could mean that we should know *no regret* about what happened and what cannot be changed, which would be a repetition of EIVp47s. But maybe Spinoza means more than this here, as seems to be indicated at the end of EIVp73s: the desire for the ideal should be complemented (replaced?) by a desire to conceive things as they are *in themselves*, particularly to conceive oneself and one's own emotions as they are in themselves. How this can ever be realized is not discussed in Part IV: we are referred to Part V.

4. Some Remarks on the Second Part of Spinoza's Ethics: *Ethics* **V, Propositions 1-20.**

The question remaining at the end of Part IV was: is full freedom, i.e., real mastery of our passions, really possible (at least in part of our life)? Can we go *beyond* the stage of struggle as described in Part IV: the stage of knowledge of good and bad; the stage of trying to reach an ideal, with all the attendant fluctuations. The answer given in Part V, "the remaining Part" (EVpref) of the ethics properly speaking, is yes. The ethics of the model (of the free man) is only provisional;[36] the way to solve the ethical struggle is to reach a certain level of pure intellectual understanding.

The answer, says Spinoza (EVpref), is experienced by "everyone," but not accurately noticed, nor distinctly seen to be such (probably because of our being blinded by the ideology of free will, or because of our immersion in the daily struggle). He will demonstrate the answer (EVp1-20) on the basis of "the Mind's knowledge alone" (EVpref).

Freedom is possible through 'the understanding alone' because the understanding is a real force producing effects that constitute real *remedies* against the passions. The vocabulary and notions related to the previous level ('guidance', 'precepts', 'ideals', etc.) are now replaced by a vocabulary and notions indicating real forces and real consequences (the new tone is set immediately by the two Axioms of Part V).

The five remedies recapitulated by Spinoza in EVp20s are none other than the life of active understanding itself. The perspective here is the opposite of that of striving towards a certain ideal; the real remedies against the passions consist in *being* free and active, in reaching another level, a level of free activity, in which all longing is forgotten (likewise, the real remedy against sickness is good health).

Although the solution is said to consist in 'understanding alone', it is not just any understanding, but a particular kind of understanding *oneself* and one's emotions, which is an almost irresistible affective-dynamic force itself. The whole of Spinoza's *Ethics* is geared not towards the acquisition of knowledge in general, but towards "the knowledge of the human Mind and its highest blessedness" (EIIpref): in this sense philosophy is at the same time a real ethics *and* knowledge.

Spinoza's stress on self-knowledge and on knowledge as an affective-dynamic force yielding the result of mastery of one's emotions allows one to effectively compare his ethics with *a cognitive therapy*. Using this concept of cognitive therapy, one could draw attention to different interesting aspects of Spinoza's ethics in its second stage. The best therapy is the one in which one succeeds in forgetting one's problems, in which one finds a way of acting that eliminates the need for therapy. The best remedies consist in the effortless flow of activity itself. Spinoza's remedies consist in *knowledge,* especially of oneself and one's own emotions. Again, as is often stressed with respect to fruitful therapies, it is not sufficient to just know certain truths about human emotionality or even to apply these truths ('externally') to one's own peculiar emotional constitution. Only if held in a kind of *meditative* way can they really change us (EV4s, EVp6s). What seems important is not that these truths guide us in our concrete daily deliberations; it is that we, as it were, 'lose' ourselves in a meditative activity in which our passions are not so much exterminated as functioning as occasions for further meditative thinking, with the active emotions it involves.

The meditative thinking we are talking about is not reducible to an 'external' scientific knowledge of the human mind, but it is also far from being incompatible with it. The assiduous meditation about ourselves and our emotions undoubtedly uses scientific insights like the ones developed in Parts II and III (constituting a sort of 'science of Man'). These scientific insights produce the same kind of detached view of ourselves as the new science of physics produced *vis-à-vis* nature (EIIIpref). Yet in order to be a real remedy against real passions, the scientific outlook has to operate in a special way. It has to become like a predominant attitude, encapsulating everything that concretely happens to *us* and that concretely affects *us* within the objectifying atmosphere of thinking, thereby changing its effect on us radically.

In EVp20s Spinoza enumerates the *five remedies* that together form the solution for our ethical problems concerning mastery of our passions.[37] As has been stressed before, mastery of our passions is reached when we jump beyond the stage of longing for real freedom, when we have succeeded in operating at another level. The remedies work 'automatically', precisely when we are not longing to reach the activity in which they consist.

The first remedy is *knowledge of the emotions.* EVp4s (as well as the whole context) makes it clear that Spinoza means knowledge of our *own* emotions: "We must . . . take special care to know each affect clearly and distinctly (as far as this is possible)." How can this knowledge produce control over the emotions? The answer is given in EVp3d: understanding an emotion stops it from being a passion because, if we form a clear and distinct idea of it, this idea will be distinguished only conceptually from the emotion in so far as it has reference to the mind alone. An emotion is something my mind has (even though it has reference, as a passion, to other things as well; cf. EIIIp3s). If I succeed in adequately understanding *my* emotion, it gets taken up into some other activity, no longer determined from outside; in this way the emotion does not of course disappear, but its previous character (passivity) is lost.

The second remedy consists "in the fact that it separates the affects from the thought of the external cause, which we imagine confusedly." The reference now is to EVp2 and EVp4s. As is clear from EVp4s, this remedy is very closely connected with the first: if we succeed in the first remedy, we can no longer link our emotions with their (supposed) external causes, which brings a halt to the usual train of passions and desires related to the first emotion. Having separated, through our understanding, our emotion "from the thought of an external cause and joined [it] to true thoughts" (EVp4s), a whole new train of activities, emotions, and desires, purely internally determined, will arise.

The first and second remedies do not consist in just any form of adequate understanding. They consist in the way *really occurring* passions *in us* are seen and experienced in the light of our adequate understanding of them. Thus, these passions become encapsulated and defused by being taken up into a different context. They do not hinder, but further the free flow of activity. Whatever happens in us becomes the occasion for adequate thinking and active affects.

The following remedies put great stress on the presence or systematic production of active emotions. These emotions have been described in EIIIp59s as all being subspecies of *fortitude*. They are all basically characterized by profound joy and deep quietude.[38] The remaining remedies all show how active emotions hang together with adequate knowledge (in general) and how they can 'spontaneously' override many passive emotions due to the very laws governing both kinds of emotions (laws having to do with the sorts of cause of the emotions, with their relation to time, modalities, etc.). Active emotions are real causes, related to real objects and operating in time. The very way detached understanding sees things (according to their common properties, as necessary, as not unique, as modifications of God, etc.) brings it about that the active emotions accompanying such understanding will be stronger than many passive emotions. As soon as active emotions are present in the mind, especially if they are produced there in a systematic way, they constitute formidable remedies against the passions. This systematic production is particularly stressed in the fifth remedy. It consists "in the order by which the Mind can order its affects and connect them to one another (see Proposition 10 and, in addition, P12, P13, and P14)." In the propositions referred to here, Spinoza invokes the role of the *bodily* counterparts of our (active) ideas and emotions, i.e., bodily images and bodily power-fluctuations.[39] The ease with which many images of things can be linked with images corresponding to adequate ideas and vice versa, as well as the ease with which bodily emotions corresponding to (mental) active emotions can be evoked by any image of any thing, creates a real flow of activity. Each thing we encounter can become a further occasion for adequate thinking and active emotions.

When we look at the remedies taken all together, we notice, as has already been stressed, their ethical rather than logical character. What gives mastery and freedom is of course adequate understanding, but especially adequate understanding of *our own emotions*, as well as adequate understanding in general insofar as it is productive of active emotions in a more or less systematic way (creating a special kind of emotional atmosphere). Even though the remedies cannot remove the passions entirely,[40] they can bring it about that the flow of active thought and feelings grows into an almost unassailable stronghold, and that the passions constitute only the smallest part of the mind (EVp20s). This is particularly so, says Spinoza (in the same Scholium), when adequate thinking gives rise to the intellectual love of God.

It is strange that this *love* of God is not mentioned as a *special* remedy; on the other hand, it is extensively discussed in the second part of Part V (from EVp21 onward), which no longer deals with the ethical remedies for an actual life of freedom in time, but 'with the eternity of the mind'. It looks as if the love of God, though not unimportant from the ethical point of view, nevertheless is not so much a remedy against the passions, as an experience having a significance that goes beyond the ethical perspective altogether.[41]

NOTES

1. This paper is an extensively reworked version of my earlier (1990) paper: "Spinoza's *Ethics*: From the Sorrows of Reason to Freedom and Beyond," in *La Ética de Spinoza. Fundamentos y Significado*, ed. Atilano Dominguez (Acts of the International Congress, Almagro, 24-26 October, 1990; Castilla-La Mancha: Ediciones de la Universidad de Castilla-La Mancha, 1992), pp. 493-503.

2. "zo zien wij ook, hoe dat de redenering in ons niet en is het voornaamste, maar alleen gelijk als een trap, langs de welke wij na de gewenste plaats opklimmen," *Korte Verhandeling*, II 26:6, in: Spinoza, *Korte Geschriften*, eds. F. Akkerman, H.G. Hubbeling, F. Mignini, M.J. Petry, and N. & G. van Suchtelen (Amsterdam: Wereldbibliotheek, 1982), p. 378.

3. Arguments for this view are to be found in my paper, "The significance of Spinoza's *Treatise on the Improvement of the Understanding*," *Algemeen Nederlands Tijdschrift voor Wijsbegeerte* 66 (1974), pp. 9-11.

4. This point is developed in the first part of my "Spinoza's Ethics: From the Sorrows of Reason," pp. 493-4.

5. Harry Frankfurt interprets Spinoza's philosophizing in this respect as originating in "an Oedipal syndrome" expressing itself in an exaggerated anxiety concerning certain competitive and sexual urges (H. Frankfurt, "Two Motivations for Rationalism: Descartes and Spinoza," in: A. Donagan, A.N. Perovich, Jr. and M.V. Wedin, eds., *Human Nature and Natural Knowledge* [Amsterdam: Reidel, 1986], pp. 47-61). This simplistic interpretation does not have to be adhered to, if only because of the anti-ascetic views of Spinoza, e.g., in his *Ethics*.

6. This expression is used by E.E. Harris as a general characterization of Spinoza's philosophy. See E.E. Harris, *Salvation from Despair–A Reappraisal of Spinoza's Philosophy* (Den Haag: M. Nijhoff, 1973).

7. See my paper, "Metaphysics as Ethics," in *God and Nature: Spinoza's Metaphysics*, ed. Y. Yovel (Papers presented at the First Jerusalem Conference, *Ethica* I; Leiden: E.J. Brill, 1991), pp. 119-31.

8. This point is developed in my paper, "Conceptions of Philosophical Method in Spinoza: *logica* and *mos geometricus*," *The Review of Metaphysics* XL (1986), pp. 55-7.

9. See my paper, "Conceptions of Philosophical Method in Spinoza," pp. 61-4, and Bernard Rousset, "Introduction," in Spinoza, *Traité de la Réforme de l'Entendement*, Introduction, texte, traduction et commentaires par Bernard Rousset (Paris: Vrin, 1992).

10. Concerning Spinoza and therapy, see: S. Hampshire, *Spinoza* (Harmondsworth: Penguin, 1967), but also, E. Curley, *Behind the Geometrical Method–A Reading of Spinoza's* Ethics (Princeton: Princeton University Press, 1988). Concerning Spinoza and strate-

gies of self-liberation, see: J. Wetlesen, *The Sage and the Way: Spinoza's Ethics of Freedom* (Assen: Van Gorcum, 1979).

11. See among many others, S. Hampshire, *Spinoza*, p. 141; E. Curley, *Behind the Geometrical Method*, p. 125; and C. De Deugd, "Spinoza and Freud, an Old Myth Revisited," in this volume.

12. See R. Lewinter, "Georg Groddeck, ou la psychanalyse selon Spinoza," *Les Temps Modernes* 24 (1968-9), pp. 47-70.

13. J. Wetlesen, *The Sage and the Way*, p. 308.

14. Ibid., p. 217, 319.

15. E. Curley, *Behind the Geometrical Method*, p. 128ff.

16. Ibid., pp. 134f.

17. See Spinoza, *Ethics*, ed. G.H.R. Parkinson (London: Dent-Everyman's Library, 1989), pp. 244-5, translator's note 132.

18. E. Curley, *Behind the Geometrical Method*, p. 123.

19. Ibid., pp. 128-9.

20. Ibid., p. 130.

21. Ibid., p. 131.

22. See also B. Rousset, *"Recta Ratio,"* in this volume.

23. "The model of a free person . . . should not be confused with the free person himself" (J. Wetlesen, *The Sage and the Way*, p. 277).

24. See further my paper, "Wisdom and Theoretical Knowledge in Spinoza," in *Spinoza: Issues and Directions. The Proceedings of the Chicago Conference*, eds. E. Curley & P.-F. Moreau (Leiden: E.J. Brill, 1990), pp. 147-56.

25. See J. Wetlesen, *The Sage and the Way*, p. 30.

26. Spinoza is strongly anti-ascetic; See EIVp45.

27. "C'est en cette science du bien et du mal que réside, pour Spinoza, la *servitude*, et c'est pourquoi le code des 'préceptes de la raison' se trouve nécessairement exposé dans le livre qui porte ce titre. La liberté, elle, ne consiste, ni a connaître les préceptes de la raison, ni a les mettre en pratique. . ." (V. Goldschmidt, "La place de la théorie politique dans la philosophie de Spinoza," *Manuscrito. Revista de Filosofia* II [1978], p. 114). In the meantime, a similar view has been worked out by W. Bartuschat, "Die Theorie des Guten im 4. Teil der Ethik," in *La Ética de Spinoza. Fundamentos y Significado*, pp. 331-9; and by B. Rousset, *"Recta Ratio,"* in this volume.

28. "[R]eason, then, has no power to bring us our well-being . . ."; KVII 22:1.

29. See KVII 4:3, note in margin: "De 2 [= tweede] uijtwerkinge (van de reeden), dat ze ons verstandelijke doet genieten de zake die zij *buijten ons* aanwijst en vertoond; dat is klaar en onderscheide kennen,

niet de zake zelve, maar wat ze moet zijn (The second effect [of true beliefs] is that it makes us enjoy in a rational way the thing it points to and shows us *outside us*; i.e., [it brings us] to clear and distinct knowledge not of the thing itself, but of what it should be"; Dutch text from the critical edition: Spinoza, *Korte Geschriften*, p. 305; my translation and italics.

30. EIVp35s; EIVp37s2; EIVp54s; EIVp58s; EIVapp13.

31. See Wernham's introduction to *Spinoza: The Political Works*, ed. and trans. A.G. Wernham (Oxford: Clarendon Press, 1958), pp. 19-20.

32. In KVII 22n. 1 Spinoza compares *ratio* to the religious notion of the law, and intuitive knowledge to the religious notion of grace.

33. As Parkinson does in his translation of the *Ethics*, p. 247 n. 158.

34. As Wetlesen does in *The Sage and the Way*, p. 303 (and passim).

35. All these points are beautifully discussed in Rousset's paper in this volume.

36. J. Wetlesen, *The Sage and the Way*, p. 130.

37. J. Wetlesen also distinguishes two fundamentally different levels in Spinoza's ethics, roughly coinciding with the division between Parts IV and V, and which he opposes as gradual versus instantaneous strategies of liberation (*The Sage and the Way*, pp. 278, 319). Yet, he does not adequately understand the cohesion of the five remedies discussed in EVp1-20, due to his unclear grasp of the relationship between time and eternity in Spinoza (p. 304-5). Still, he rightly interprets EVp10s as a reminder, within Part V, of the perspective of Part IV (p. 298).

38. For an enumeration of these active emotions, see J. Wetlesen, *The Sage and the Way*, p. 209.

39. This may mean that Wetlesen's talk of a certain kind of (meditative) body-awareness, as a major element in Spinoza's instantaneous strategy of liberation (J. Wetlesen, *The Sage and the Way*, p. 313), is not so farfetched after all.

40. On this point, see also the interesting observations made by Menachem Brinker in the last section of his "Spinoza on Desire and the Impossibility of Utopia," in this volume.

41. See my paper, "Spinoza's Ethics: From the Sorrows of Reason to Freedom and Beyond," pp. 501-2.

"Strange Science of Paradoxical Desires . . .": De Dijn on *Ethics* IV

J. Thomas Cook

In recent years, Herman De Dijn has produced a series of papers that, taken together, seek to make sense of Spinoza's *Ethics* as a whole. Of course, it is notoriously difficult to articulate a single interpretive approach that reconciles the diverse threads of Spinoza's system without having to dismiss or explain away important doctrines. But De Dijn is trying to articulate such a unified vision of the system, and I find that I have learned something from each of his recent papers, just as I have learned from the paper presented in this volume.

Two things especially strike me about De Dijn's work in this area, and I mention them here, for they are both very much in evidence in "*Ethics* IV: The Ladder, Not the Top." First, there is a certain tone in his writing that suggests that he does not think of his efforts as a purely 'academic exercise'. His writings read like those of a man interested not only in articulating and defending a particular interpretation of the text, but in undertaking the kind of meditative reflection that promises to convert *ratio* into intuitive self-knowledge. This attitude I find engaging, and as a reader I find myself drawn along by the flow of ideas, almost mesmerized by the earnestness of tone.

The other striking aspect of this series of De Dijn's papers is that, while seeking a consistent overall interpretation, he does not shy away from the apparent paradoxes and threatening incongruities in Spinoza's text. In this paper he points out how strange it is that Spinoza offers an extended and elaborate ethical analysis whose basic concepts—good and evil—are ideas destined to be overcome, mere "notions we form because we compare things with one another." De Dijn highlights, too, the paradoxical character of certain desires—for example (as he puts it in an earlier version of the paper), "the desire for a state which is such that when one is in it, one cannot have such desires." Of course, many commentators focus on the apparent tensions in the system, often in an effort to convict Spinoza of self-contradiction or to highlight ways in which his reliance on disparate traditions has led him into inconsistency. De Dijn, on the other hand, seems to hold that the apparently paradoxical doctrines are important because they lead us more deeply into the system, preventing us from settling for a superficial understanding. I think that De Dijn is right in this, for I think that we do well not to downplay but rather to emphasize the seemingly paradoxical elements in the *Ethics*. These tensions in the doctrine mark interpretive hotspots in the text—subterranean pressure-points in the system that deserve attention precisely because they lie deep under the surface, near the foundations of the structure.

Usually the two striking features of De Dijn's writing are mutually complementary. Sometimes, though, these two aspects are at cross-purposes. We, the readers, follow De Dijn through Spinoza's text, borne along by the engaged and engaging tone of the writing. But, preoccupied by the beauty of the view and the sincerity of the exposition, we may fail to notice some of the incongruities in the text that announce important pressure-points in the system. As I noted above, I think it is important that we take notice of these, and so I want to focus my comments on a few places where Spinoza's path is less smooth than De Dijn's sympathetic exposition would lead one to believe.

1. Why The Life of Reason is Good

De Dijn refers to that part of Spinoza's ethical program laid out in Part IV as the "first part of the ethics." This is the stage of ethical development at which we experience both pleasure and pain—the stage at which we enjoy our increased power and suffer from our decreased power to persevere in our being. Wanting to maximize this power, and hence wanting those things and actions that are effective means to this end, we judge some things good and other things bad. Ultimately, these concepts of 'good' and 'bad' will be left behind, but at this stage they are indispensable for us concrete, finite individuals who experience ourselves as struggling for survival in a hostile environment.

In presenting this stage of the ethical program, De Dijn emphasizes, from the beginning, the role and importance of reason. According to his exposition, the doctrines that make up the first part of the ethical program are designed and intended for those who are "already more or less rational," and who know "the special pleasures involved in rational activity." Thus, "knowing these pleasures . . . the rational man inevitably . . . strives toward more of this life of reason (EIVp26), and forms the notion of an ideal, stronger human nature, in which the possession of rational insight and the concomitant contentment would be more consistent (TIE 13)."[1]

This is an interesting approach, and it has a certain important strength as an interpretive strategy. Let it be noted, though, that the order of exposition in De Dijn's account of the formation on the ideal of human nature is different from Spinoza's own. According to De Dijn, the process goes as follows: We, the readers of the *Ethics*, being rational sorts, have experienced the joys of reason, and so, naturally, when we set out to judge good and bad, we appeal to our experiences of joy and sadness, and judge those things as good which are conducive to reason and those as bad that impede rational activity. According to this account, we the readers enter midway into the process that Spinoza is describing and explaining in the *Ethics*. Our joys are those of reason, and since our judgments of good and bad are nothing but affects of joy and sadness, our conception of the good is a conception of rational activity.

There is a minor problem here, I think, in that De Dijn describes so vividly not only the pleasures of reason, but also what he elsewhere calls the "sorrows of reason"[2] that inevitably attend the pleasures. In the long run, of course, the pleasures will presumably predominate over the sorrows of reason. But De Dijn's interpretation of the first part of the ethical program depends upon it being the case that the pleasures outweigh the sorrows from the very beginning—from the very first experiences of reasoning activity. I'm not sure that we can be so confident of that.

To return to the main point, De Dijn's account suggests that we embrace the "dictates of reason" and adopt the reason-oriented model of human nature because we begin from first-hand experience of the special pleasures of reason. This account is consistent with Spinoza's view, but, I think, it does not follow his own order of exposition. According to Spinoza, the desire that leads us to form a conception of the model of human nature is a desire to persevere in being. It is this desire that is foundational in the account, and Spinoza emphasizes repeatedly that this is the very basis of virtue. Where De Dijn would have us directly experience the joy and hence the goodness of reason, Spinoza undertakes to derive the goodness of reason and understanding from the more basic desire for preserving one's being. Now, these two approaches are not necessarily inconsistent with each other, but by focusing on the one, De Dijn has bypassed the opportunity to explore another of those incongruities that he rightly finds so interesting.[3]

I say that there is an incongruity here, for I find Spinoza's attempt to connect understanding with perseverance in being singularly unconvincing.[4] His approach to this issue commits him to the task of demonstrating that the desire to persevere in one's being, seen aright, is identical with the desire to understand. On the face of it, this is not a very plausible claim. The crux of the argument comes in Propositions 26 and 27 of Part IV, where Spinoza tries to prove that understanding and those things that are conducive to understanding are the only things that we can certainly know to be good. The proofs of these propositions make formal sense, given the abstract definitions of adequate cause and adequate idea. But they make no sense in terms of mental acts of inference-drawing, and the relationship between the mind's endeavor to act, in this sense, and the body's endeavor to persevere as an organism is quite unclear.

The human individual is an organism whose bodily identity consists of a constancy of ratio of motion and rest among the parts that make it up. The body tends to maintain its physical integrity, and that homeostatic tendency—the body's endeavor to persevere in being—is the very essence of the individual, and the source of all virtue.

The same individual, when viewed not as a body under the attribute of extension, but as a mind under the attribute of thought, is a complex idea, made up of the ideas of those many extended things that constitute the body as well as ideas of the ways in which the body is affected from without. The mind's power of understanding consists of its power to form what Spinoza calls adequate ideas, also known as "common notions," which are ideas of those things that all things have in common, and which are equally in the whole and in the part of all extended things. The mind's endeavor to understand is an endeavor to form, and thereby become, such "adequate ideas."

Now it is not immediately obvious how the body's endeavor to maintain its homeostatic integrity as a complex physical organism is identical with the mind's endeavor to become ideas of that which all extended things have in common. And yet Spinoza tells us that these endeavors are indeed identical. If Spinoza were only claiming that understanding is needed for distinguishing those things which are truly conducive to our perseverance in being from those that are not, there would be no problem. But he is

claiming much more than that. Not only is understanding a necessary means for distinguishing the true good from the apparent
good; understanding *is* the true good—and Spinoza uses this
identification extensively in the development of his model of
human nature and in that "strange science of good and bad."

Perhaps later, after demonstrating the direct power of reason
over the passions, early in Part V, Spinoza could plausibly make
the case that reason and understanding constitute the good for
human beings. But at this point in the *Ethics* it seems to me not
only unconvincing but incongruous—one of those interesting
incongruities that deserve our attention. De Dijn simply sidesteps
the issue, ignoring the weakness of Spinoza's derivation and offering, instead, an appeal to the reader's first-hand experience of the
"special pleasures of reason."

I wish that De Dijn had done more with this issue, for I think
that it dovetails nicely with his focus on the two discontinuous
ethical stages found in the *Ethics*. De Dijn's way of dealing with
those two stages provides a hint about how we might approach
the incongruity outlined above. According to De Dijn, one adopts
notions of good and bad which serve as guideposts in attaining
one's desired state of being. Paradoxically, though, to the extent to
which one truly attains the desired state, one knows nothing of
desire and nothing of good and bad.[5] Also, Spinoza tells us that
understanding is most conducive to—indeed is identical with—
success in one's effort to persevere in being amidst the conflicts
and hostilities of the natural and social environment. Perhaps the
extent to which we understand—the extent to which our minds
come to be dominated by the 'common notions'—is the extent to
which we have no ideas of conflict, of effort, or of perseverance. In
this way our minds are constituted primarily by ideas of effortless
activity, and the ethical problem simply goes away.

This might work as an unusual interpretation of Spinoza's
identification of rational understanding and the good, but it will
only work for an individual to the extent that his or her mind is
constituted by common notions—by the ideas of that which all
things have in common and is equally in the whole and in the
part. It would be important to minimize ideas of those states of
one's own body that indicate passivity, pain, or confusion. But, as
De Dijn rightly points out, that is precisely *not* what Spinoza
urges. On the contrary, he urges that we focus our cognitive attention on just those passive states, arguing that understanding can

provide not only effective distraction from the passions, but a direct remedy for them.

2. Impossible Remedies

When De Dijn passes to what he calls the second part of Spinoza's ethical program, he rightly focuses on the five "remedies" enumerated by Spinoza in Proposition 20 of Part V. But in depicting, sympathetically, these concrete remedies, it seems to me that De Dijn misses, again, an interesting and important paradox in Spinoza's views.[6] As De Dijn rightly points out, the concrete remedies are, first of all, based on the knowledge of our own emotions. The emotions for which we most need remedy are certain passions, of course, and so the chief concern is to gain knowledge of these passions. In EVp3 and EVp4 Spinoza speaks of "forming a clear and distinct idea of the affects." It sounds as if it is the 'second kind of knowledge' that is at issue here—but that would be problematic, for the second kind of knowledge, based on the common notions, is universal and general, whereas it sounds as if Spinoza is talking about knowledge of a specific occurrence of an emotion in an individual, at a specific time.[7] Perhaps Spinoza is trading here on a type-token ambiguity, but that should not detain us, for there is a much deeper problem involved in the suggestion that we achieve knowledge of the passions.

Among the most troublesome passions—certainly among those from which I most want liberation—are painful passions. According to concrete remedy number one, as De Dijn designates it, Spinoza is recommending that I achieve an adequate understanding of my own painful emotion. But in recommending this, Spinoza is recommending something that is, by his own view, strictly impossible. Pain is, by definition, a transition to a state of lesser perfection or power. If I could have an adequate knowledge of my pain, an idea of a transition to a state of lesser power and perfection would have to follow from ideas adequate in my mind. Were this the case, my mind alone would be the adequate cause of this idea of transition to a state of lesser perfection. But this consequence is absurd, for nothing can follow from my mind alone except that which is conducive to my perseverance in being—and ideas of transitions to states of lesser perfection are *not* conducive to my perseverance in being. So, in recommending that we gain an adequate idea of painful passions, Spinoza is, paradoxically, recommending the impossible.

The natural response to this line of reasoning is to take it not as a damaging objection, but as a confirmation of the efficacy of understanding in overcoming painful affects. The same principles that entail that painful passions cannot be adequately understood also entail that that which is adequately understood cannot be pain. This sounds like the path that Spinoza is pursuing, for he says that a passion "ceases to be a passion as soon as we form a clear and distinct idea of it."[8]

This would be a welcome conclusion indeed, and it would resolve what seemed just now to be a paradox. But it will only be satisfactory if the way it achieves this ethically salutary end makes sense.[9]

Spinoza's explanation is found in EVp3d. It reads:

> An affect which is a passion is a confused idea (by Gen.Def.Aff.). Therefore, if we should form a clear and distinct idea of the affect itself, this idea will only be distinguished by reason from the affect itself, insofar as it is related only to the Mind (by EIIp21 and EIIp21S). Therefore (by EIIIp3), the affect will cease to be a passion, q.e.d.

Here we have a confused idea (a passion) and a clear and distinct idea of that passion—and these two are distinguished from one another only "by reason." Now it must be the case that two things that are distinguished only "by reason" can nonetheless be quite different since, by hypothesis, one of these ideas is confused while the other is clear and distinct. On the other hand, the doctrine of the *idea ideae*, to which Spinoza adverts here, emphasizes that an idea and the idea of that idea are "one and the same thing conceived through one and the same attribute" (EIIp21s). Indeed, Spinoza's proof relies on there *not* being a great difference between these two. If I understand Spinoza correctly, the crux of the argument is the suggestion that two things as different as a confused idea and a clear and distinct idea could not possibly be distinguished only "by reason"—so the confused idea must have ceased being confused.

I hope that I have said enough to remind the reader that a straightforward effort to understand the demonstration of EVp3 can itself feel like an effort to form a clear and distinct idea of a confused idea. Let us look at what De Dijn does with this. His account follows Spinoza's exposition closely, and his version of the proof of EVp3 is as follows:

> understanding an emotion stops it being a passion because, if
> we form a clear and distinct idea of it, this idea will be distin-
> guished only conceptually from the emotion in so far as it
> has reference to the mind alone. . . . If I succeed in adequately
> understanding *my* emotion, it gets taken up into some other
> activity, no longer determined from outside; in this way the
> emotion does not of course disappear, but its previous char-
> acter (passivity) is lost. (p. 51)

I find this a helpful gloss on the proof, and in some ways I
understand De Dijn's words better than Spinoza's own. The central suggestion is that my passive emotion, when understood, gets
"taken up into some other activity no longer determined from
outside." I take it that the "other activity" in question here is the
activity of understanding itself—but I'm not entirely sure what it
means to say that the confused idea which is the passion is "taken
up into" that activity. De Dijn also says that they are "encapsulated" and "defused" by being "taken up" into this different context. If I understand him correctly, De Dijn is claiming that we
come to see these emotional states as following from the general
principles of the science of man that Spinoza has been developing.
To view one's passions in this way is to focus on the way in which
they are manifestations of the regularities of the workings of
nature, rather than singular instances caused by a specific individual external object. More technically, the emotion is seen to follow
from ideas that are adequate in my mind, and since indeed adequate (i.e., active) ideas can follow from adequate ideas alone, the
passive character of the emotion is lost.

So I understand De Dijn. I have an experiential sense for what
it is like to reflect on some painful passion and, in the process,
become somewhat detached from it and less susceptible to its
painfulness. This is an attractive view, beautifully expressed, and I
find myself leaning toward it.

But the fact remains that the paradox with which we began has
not been resolved. If my emotional state is indeed a passion, then
a knowledge of that state which does not know the state *as* a passion is not a knowledge of *that state*. This is a plausible reading,
and the upshot would be that in fact we cannot achieve knowledge of our passive states as such. At best, with this reading, we
could get an abstract, universal sort of knowledge of emotions of
that type, though no adequate knowledge of my own specific
emotional state.

Alternatively, we might say that if an adequate knowledge of a
state reveals that state to be without passive character, then that

state is not a passive state. In this view, its *apparent* passivity is a function of our nescience or confusion. The passive character of the emotion is lost in an adequate understanding of it because the emotion is not, in fact, a passion (and by extension never really was). This seems to me the more plausible and the more Spinozistic of the proposed alternatives, but De Dijn seems reluctant to go in this direction on this issue.

3. Conclusion

The two cases that I have discussed here are cases in which Spinoza makes a very strong and somewhat strange claim in favor of the importance of reason and understanding in dealing with an ethical problem. In each case, De Dijn has provided a plausible, attractive, experientially-based interpretation of the doctrine that sidesteps the system-related difficulties or paradoxes of the claim. I have tried only to bring these difficulties back into focus.

I take it as significant that in each case the tendency of the problem is to push us toward an extreme solution—a solution according to which understanding provides the answer to the ethical difficulty, because such understanding reveals that there is no difficulty. I take this as significant because I think that the logic of the system will drive us inexorably in this direction. There is an inherent instability in any position short of full intuitive self-knowledge—the *amor intellectualis Dei* of the final propositions of the *Ethics*. Any such position is, as De Dijn says, merely the ladder, not the top.

NOTES

1. H. De Dijn, "*Ethics* IV: The Ladder, Not the Top—The Provisional Morals of the Philosopher," in this volume, p. 44.

2. H. De Dijn, "Spinoza's *Ethics*: From the Sorrows of Reason to Freedom and Beyond," in *La Ética de Spinoza. Fundamentos y Significado*, ed. A. Dominguez (Acts of the International Congress, Almagro, 24-26 October, 1990; Castilla-La Mancha: Ediciones de la Universidad de Castilla-La Mancha, 1992), p. 497.

3. The textual sources on the issue of the motive in establishing the model of human nature are meager, but clear. In the TIE Spinoza says that "man conceives a human nature much stronger and more enduring than his own," and judges as good whatever can lead to the acquisition of such a nature. In the Preface to Part IV of the *Ethics*, he speaks of a "model of human nature which we may look to," and suggests that the model is one of maximal "power of acting, insofar as it is understood through his nature." The latter might be thought to be a direct reference to reason or rationality, but, as I read it, the order of exposition in Part IV itself does not support that view.

4. Much of the material in the next three paragraphs comes from my "Self-Knowledge as Self-Preservation?" in *Spinoza and the Sciences*, eds. M. Grene and D. Nails (Dordrecht: Reidel, 1986; Boston Studies in the Philosophy of Science, vol. 91), pp. 191-210.

5. As De Dijn states the point in an earlier version of the paper, a person desiring a state of rational, free activity has a paradoxical desire "in the sense that it is a desire for a state which is such that when one is in it, one cannot have such desires" ("Spinoza's *Ethics*: From the Sorrows of Reason to Freedom and Beyond," p. 497).

6. The issues raised in the following paragraphs served as the focus of my contribution to the fifth Jerusalem Conference (on Part V of the *Ethics*) in June, 1999. My thanks to the organizers of that conference for providing the opportunity and occasion to think through this issue in greater detail. The paper (forthcoming in the Proceedings of the fifth Jerusalem Conference) is entitled "Adequate Ideas of Inadequate Ideas: Power and Paradox in Spinoza's Cognitive Therapy."

7. I take it to be the case that Spinoza is talking about a specific occurrence of an emotion in an individual at a time because he speaks of the emotion's "ceasing to be a passion." The term "ceasing" suggests a specific temporal event. This seems to be De Dijn's view as well.

8. Earlier discussions of these issues in the *Ethics* do not entirely prepare us for this claim. EIVp7, for example, states that an affect can be "restrained or taken away" only by an opposite and stronger affect. Also, the discussion of the image of the sun (EIIp35s) is at best ambiguous in its implications for this issue. Does the imagining of

the sun "cease to be an imagining" if we achieve an adequate understanding of it? These questions are considered more fully in the above-mentioned paper for the fifth Jerusalem Conference (see note 6 above).

9. Two recent critical discussions of the passage in question (EIVp3d) are quite helpful—Jonathan Bennett, *A Study of Spinoza's* Ethics (Cambridge: Cambridge University Press, 1984), pp. 335-7, and a recent exchange between J.-M. Beyssade and Margaret Wilson in *Spinoza: Issues and Directions*, eds. E. Curley and P.-F. Moreau (Leiden: E.J. Brill, 1990).

Is the Rational Man Free?

Elhanan Yakira

> Je suis spinoziste, il faut résister, combattre, affronter la mort. Ainsi l'exige la verité, la raison.
> —Jean Cavailles, London, 1940, explaining to Raymond Aron the reasons for his decision to join the *Résistance*[1]

> It was—I don't know how to say it—a feast of fools, a magnificent carnival . . . On the mountains with Dolcino, before we were reduced to eating the flesh of our companions killed in battle, before so many died of hardship that we couldn't eat them all, and they were thrown to the birds and the wild animals on the slopes of Rebello . . . or maybe in those moments, too . . . there was an atmosphere . . . can I say of freedom? I didn't know, before, what freedom was; the preachers said to us 'The truth will make you free.' We felt free, we thought that was the truth. We thought everything we were doing was right.
> —The cellarer's explanation of the Dolcino rebellion; Umberto Eco, *The Name of the Rose*

To the question posed in the title of this paper, many would answer in the negative. In our postmodern age, many would even say that reason, or rationality, is tyrannical by nature and injurious to human freedom. Spinoza, of course, thought differently: for him reason is not only the condition of freedom, but practically identical with it. So much so that some critics, liberals and so-called postmodernists alike, think that his ideas, like those of some of his contemporaries, are the source of modern ideologies which, in the name of reason and freedom, institutionalized some of the worst forms of servitude. This is the general background to the present study in which I shall try to better understand Spinoza's way of conciliating reason and freedom. I want to suggest that whatever might have been its historical role in the subsequent emergence of modernity, one may still find in Spinoza a pertinent philosophical attempt to reconcile reason and freedom.

Usually, the question concerning this reconciliation is framed around the theme of determinism. How is it possible, we are endlessly asked, to reconcile human freedom with causal determinism and logical necessitarism, both of which are doctrines that Spinoza adopts. The problem of determinism is closely related to the theory of reason, whose most cogent and full articulation in the seventeenth century is given by Leibniz's *Principle of Sufficient Reason*. As is well known, the formulation of this principle is said sometimes to have lead Leibniz to a Spinozistic kind of determinism. If, it is claimed, for every fact it should be possible, at least in principle, to give a reason why it is so and not otherwise, and if, moreover, *causa* is *ratio*, then nothing, including man's will and action, can be said to be free.

This, however, is not the angle from which I want to approach the problem; there is much more to the opposition between reason and human freedom than the alleged incompatibility between freedom and determinism. The line I am going to follow in the present study is not based on one more reconstruction of Spinoza' reconciliation of causal determinism and logical necessitarism with freedom; instead, I shall investigate the relationship between Spinoza's theory of reason and his conception of the free man as elaborated in Part IV of the *Ethics*.

Why is it that reason is seen as injurious to human freedom? One property that has been always considered as essential to reason and which is of great importance in Spinoza's theory is that the rational is *universal* and *general*. I think—and I schematize a lot concerning this very complex issue—that the crux of the problem is that the particular thing is thought to be ontologically determined and epistemologically known through what, by its very universality and generality, is transcendent to its individuality. Even when no suspicion is cast on the rationality of reason, and even when its claim to universality is accepted, it is sometimes felt that the individual must revolt against this claim if freedom is to be achieved. I believe that much of the criticism of rationality is based on the feeling that reason and rationality menace human freedom largely because it is difficult to see how rational generality is an adequate expression of one's real self. Abstract theoretical constructions as well as alienating social and political institutions are felt to threaten and dehumanize our real selves.

70

Who is more of a rationalist than Spinoza? It is often claimed that in his metaphysics of substance, individuality is hopelessly lost in the generality of the laws of nature and in the universality of infinite essences. If this is so, then even if he succeeds in formulating a coherent semantics of freedom based on its reduction to the necessity of essences or natures,[2] and a coherent theory of the freedom of God, this is of no much avail when the question of human freedom is posed. Yet, it is my suggestion that Spinoza's attempt to overcome the alleged opposition between reason and freedom is largely based on a highly original theory of reason, whose main thesis is that generality and universality should not be considered as essential properties of rationality, but rather as secondary and derivative ones.

*

Spinoza's definition of reason (in the strict sense of *ratio*, i.e., of knowledge of the second kind) is based on his doctrine of the *notiones communes*, developed in Propositions 37-44 of *Ethics* II.[3] In the important first Scholium of EIIp40, these common notions are explicitly contrasted with universals and with general notions which are said to be confused and obscure. 'Commonality', rather than 'generality' or 'universality', is thus supposed to be the real foundation of our science of the world. It is on the basis of it that we predict, for instance, how a particle of matter will behave in certain circumstances. Science, as knowledge of the second kind, is not knowledge of singular things but of their common properties. In what way do common notions, which are the ideas of common properties, differ from knowledge of general notions? We shall restrict our discussion to the properties of bodies, as Spinoza does. He says in the second Lemma after EIIp13 (which he refers to explicitly in the text of Proposition 37 itself—an unusual procedure), that "All bodies agree in certain things." This allusion is supposed to explain the term 'common notions'. The Demonstration of this Lemma sheds more light on what is meant by this 'agreement':

> [A]ll bodies agree in that they involve the concept of one and the same attribute (by D1), and in that they can move now more slowly, now more quickly, and absolutely, that now they move, now they are at rest.

71

They agree primarily because the concepts of these bodies are related to the concept extension—they *involve* it. The concept of the attribute is not a general concept, and all bodies (or their concepts) are not subsumed under it as its extension. This holds also for *common notions*: the objects they refer to are not their extensions. The fact that these notions commonly refer to them does not group them in classes, and common notions are not names of classes. Classes do not exist, except in the imagination of human beings; and our talk of things as members of classes is epistemologically deficient or, more precisely, inadequate.

General notions refer to objects semiotically; since we cannot properly know many things at once, we designate them by certain linguistic signs which are cognitively poor. Since Spinoza saw no role for syntax and form in the constitution of knowledge and meaning, he had very little taste for semiotics and did not assign much epistemological value to knowledge through signs. Whatever value they have is due to their conceptual or representational content; but, as they are the outcome of processes of abstraction, their content is diluted in proportion to the advancement of the abstracting process. The further away we are from singular concrete things, the greater the number of things we refer to, and the poorer is the content of our discourse.

Moreover, abstraction is necessarily subjective. It is the work of a finite mind, and its inadequacy means that its character is imaginative. This is why general notions and universals are only general in one sense, that is, in the sense of referring to a large number of objects. They are not general in the sense of being shared by a large number of knowers. Every abstraction is different, and the representation Peter has of a dog is different from the one Mary has. Common notions, on the contrary, are the same for all minds.[4] But this is only an outcome of their fundamental nature, and not what defines them as such. And although it may seem paradoxical, I suggest that their 'objectivity' (in this latter sense, which is their 'intersubjectivity') is based on their 'subjectivity' (except that this word has a very special sense in the Spinozistic system).

What I mean can be better understood if we briefly consider Spinoza's analysis of our knowledge of external bodies. The discussion, contained mainly in EIIp16-17, is best summarized by EIIp16c2: "the ideas that we have of external bodies indicate the condition of our own body more than the nature of external bodies." In other words, what we know, what we feel, what we per-

72

ceive is always only our body. Knowing external bodies is knowing our own body insofar as it is affected by something outside it (the idea of this modification of our body involves that of its external cause). Is Spinoza a solipsist? Of course not: the idea each one of us has of his own body (which is the only idea he has—it is his Soul or Mind) involves the ideas of the properties our body has in common with other bodies.

Now these ideas are necessarily adequate ideas;[5] we know they are adequate not because we compare them with their objects, which is impossible (since we cannot jump out of our bodies). Moreover, this is a conception of truth based on a completely erroneous understanding of the nature of ideas. Adequate ideas are not defined either by their relation to the objects they refer to (Spinoza does not have a correspondence theory of truth), or by their representative character, or by their resemblance to ideas in God's understanding, taken to be archetype of all true ideas. Truth or adequacy is its own sign. We can determine the adequacy of our ideas by their compliance with the rigorous criteria of adequacy, which are intrinsic.[6] Objectivity (i.e. the correspondence with 'external objects') is only a consequence of adequacy, and thus it is what can be described as intersubjectivity and can account for the accord between different objects.

The significance of this doctrine is far-reaching, since it is based on a conception of ideas as non-representative and non-intentional entities. Strictly speaking, (adequate) ideas do not *refer* to their objects. The soul is the idea of the body; but this does not mean, of course, that someone thinks the body through this idea which is the soul. The soul is the idea of the body because it is the *objective reality* of which the body is the *formal reality*. Basically, then, ideas are defined without reference to a subject; but ideas are constituents of *knowledge* and not only of *truth*. In other words, Spinoza tries to formulate an epistemology, and not a formal logic (which he abhors), where the concept of a subject does not have a constitutive role. We do not have to presuppose someone who performs the act of thinking (as Descartes and most of us do), in order to understand what thinking is. Bizarre as it may sound, I still think that to the extent that to refer presupposes a subject who performs an act of referring (and is not just understood as signifying a purely formal distinction between 'idea' and 'object'), it can be maintained that adequate ideas *do not* refer to their objects.

The idea of the body *involves* the conditions of its being (the idea of substance and the idea of extension), which are also the semantical conditions of its intelligibility or of the very possibility of thinking it. 'The idea of the body', however, is the particular idea (or soul) of the particular body of which it is the idea. And it is this idea—a concrete, particular, private, and unrepeatable one—that involves the adequate common notions, as well as the other adequate ideas. These ideas are such that knowing them, that is, bringing them explicitly to our awareness, is our rational science and, eventually, our intuitive science. What is important for us is that rational knowledge does not consist in the knowledge of general truths, but that it is fundamentally a form of self-knowledge. We know the world through our body and not vice versa.

Even in the second kind of knowledge, in what is usually—and I think rightly—said to be scientific knowledge in the sense in which, say, Galileo's *New Science* of motion is scientific knowledge, what is adequate never comes to us by abstraction or by idealization, but is always knowledge of the concrete and is a form of self-knowledge. Even scientific knowledge is based on knowledge of the particular; not, though, in the empiricist way, which leads us back to abstraction, but through the knowledge of the body. Generally speaking, Spinoza's epistemology is not one of going beyond the subjective (as, for instance, in our perception of 'secondary qualities') towards knowledge of the 'objective' (pure 'primary qualities'), but a sort of hermeneutics based on self-knowledge or on knowledge of the body (of one's own body).

Rational Man

We shall now describe Spinoza's phenomenology of the rational man. The theme of the rational man appears here and there in the course of the discussion of *Ethics* IV, but most explicitly and systematically (though still in sketchy and condensed form) in EIVp61-66. EIVp65 and EIVp66 (each of which has one Corollary) describe very clearly the things we follow under the guidance (or rather under the command—*ex rationis ductu*) of reason. The basic thing we do under this guidance is to simply "follow [*sequemur*] the greater of two goods or the lesser of two evils" (EIVp65). The Demonstration of this most obvious Proposition is not really a demonstration, but rather a clarification of its significance: good and evil are relative and, as such, are always a matter of comparison. Reason gives us the principles according to which we can calculate a correct account of goods and evils, of utility and loss. Reason dictates that we suspend our desire for various goods for the sake of greater ones, or accept some evils in order to save us from greater ones.

Is the rational man, then, something like Adam Smith's profit-maker or consumer? Or is he a Hobbesian subject (in the political sense), who, like those famous prisoners of the dilemma, calculates the best way to survive? In this context it is interesting to note that the description of the rational man's ends, and the discussion of human freedom, begins with the assertion that the free man "thinks of nothing less than of death, and his wisdom is a meditation on life, not on death" (EIVp67). This could perhaps be interpreted as an expression of a sort of Hobbesian rationality, if it were not for the Demonstration, which sends us to EIVp63, where it is said that "he who is guided by Fear, and does good to avoid evil, is not guided by Reason."

In complete opposition to the Hobbesian rationalist, the Spinozistic one is not guided by fear. The fear that does not guide the rational man is a very specific fear—the fear of death. I suggest that what Spinoza is really talking about here is the fear of human finitude, and in this he is closer to Pascal than to Hobbes. Usually, as the famous opening paragraphs of the *Treatise on the Emendation of the Intellect* show, this 'anxiety' is overcome by some sorts of 'distractions' (money, pleasure, honor). Where Spinoza differs from Pascal is in the remedy he prescribes for this distress. The best way to serve self-interest is not to bet on God, but to know him: "Knowledge of God is the Mind's grestest good; its greatest virtue is to know God" (EIVp28).

Reason is the condition of self-transcendence. If earlier in the text we were given the principles of the immediacy of the passions (e.g., "an affect whose cause we imagine to be with us in the present is stronger than if we did not imagine it to be with us," EIVp9), we now have the principles of overcoming it. It was also established (EIVp63-64) that reason's guidance is positive, the rational man does not do things out of fear or out of other negative motives. This raises the difficulty with which we began our discussion: in the name of what is self-transcendence preferred to immediacy? What is the source of the normative character reason now appears to possess? More generally, the language employed here is reminiscent of the usual language based on the image of competing forces or faculties, the 'upper' (reason) against the 'lower' (will and desire), of an inner struggle for control and supremacy—in short, of precisely what seems to be contrary to true freedom.

It is, then, quite significant that the next group of porpositions, 67-72, which concludes *Ethics* IV, discusses the *free man* (except for EIVp73, the very last one, in which the notion of rational man reappears). The transition from Propositions 65-66 to Propositions 67-72 occurs in a Scholium in which Spinoza points out what he considers to be the difference between a 'slave' and a free man. The former,

> does those things he is most ignorant of, whereas the latter complies with no one's wishes but his own, and does only those things he knows to be the most important in life, and therefore desires very greatly. (EIVp66s)

It is interesting to note that what Spinoza opposes to the ignorance of the man of passions is not the intelligence and knowledge of the rational man, but his refusal to comply with other men's wishes and his insistence on satisfying his own desires. Though very brief, this is a powerful portrait of a man of character who has personal autonomy. The same impression is made, and with even more power, by what I take to be the real *naturae humanae exemplar*, namely, the notion of *animositas* (translated by Curley as Tenacity).

EIVp69 says that:

> the virtue of a free man is seen to be as great in avoiding dangers as in overcoming them.

The Corollary adds that:

> in a free man, a timely flight is considered to show as much Tenacity as fighting; or a free man chooses flight with the same Tenacity, *or* presence of mind, as he chooses a fight.[7]

One should reflect on the reasons that lead men to fight—such as the will to glory or the pressure of a peer group, or those which lead them to run away, such as fear—to understand what Spinoza has in mind here. What is no less significant is the choice of example: the man who goes to war. The warrior is certainly at odds with the usual images we have of the Spinozistic sage, on whose emblem the word *Caute* is engraved.

Animositas is defined in EIIIp59s:

> All actions that follow from affects related to the mind insofar as it understands I relate to *strength of character* [*fortitudinem*], which I divide into Tenacity and Nobility [*generositatem*]. For by

76

> *Tenacity* I understand *the Desire by which each one strives, solely from the dictate of Reason, to preserve his being.* By *Nobility* I understand *the Desire by which each one strives, solely from the dictate of Reason, to aid other men and join them to him in friendship.*

It is true, as we learn from EIVp73s, that 'strength of character' is also the basis of political virtue, law-abiding conduct, and civility. Spinoza then adds, in this concluding Scholium of *Ethics IV*, that "these and similar things which we have shown concerning the true freedom of man are related to Strength of Character," and goes on to say what there is actually no need to say, namely, that the man of the *fortitudinem* hates no one, is angry with no one, envies no one; in short, that he has all the virtues that religion and traditional morality cherish. There is no doubt that Spinoza, here and in other places, both in the *Ethics* and in other writings, reintroduces or defends many of the 'traditional' values; but there is much more to his conception of human morality than offering, as some of his recent students think, a non-theological or naturalist foundation for the same old values. It is not only in the light of Part V of the *Ethics* that the radical and, so to speak, non-vegetarian character of Spinoza's thinking becomes apparent. For as the recurring theme of Strength of Character shows, and as is made even clearer by the insistence on this Strength of Character as meaning the ability to overcome any pressure and to follow one's own desires without paying real attention to anything but one's own judgement, there is little left of the traditional well-meaning morality of kindness and compassion, of altruism, or of religious charity.

Rational Freedom

In light of what has just been said, Proposition 72 (the last but one of *Ethics IV*) looks curious and, as Curley remarks, 'difficult to reconcile' with the spirit of Spinozism. It says that "a free man always acts honestly, not deceptively." Its Demonstration is basically intuitive, and is based on the logical impossibility that a free man, insofar as he is rational, would do something that cannot be expected of all rational men:

> If a free man, insofar as he is free, did anything by deception, he would do it from the dictate of Reason (for so far only do we call him free). And so it would be a virtue to act deceptively (by P24), and hence (by the same Proposition) every-

one would be better advised to act deceptively to preserve his being. I.e. (as is known through itself) men would be better advised to agree only in words, and be contrary to one another in fact. But this is absurd (by P31C).

Then follows a Scholium which looks like a piece of Kantian practical reasoning:[8]

Suppose someone now asks: what if a man could save his life from the present danger of death by treachery? Would not the principle of preserving his own being recommend, without qualification, that he be treacherous?

The reply to this is same. If Reason should recommend that, it would recommend it to all men. And so Reason would recommend, without qualification, that men make agreements, join forces, and have common rights only by deception—i.e., that really they have no common rights. This is absurd.

This seems not only difficult to reconcile with 'the spirit' of Spinozism, but is also explicitly in contradiction with other affirmations of Spinoza, such as the one that states that a promise given under threat may be broken once the danger is over. This is permitted by the most 'general law of human nature', which says that a man should not give up a good, except for the sake of a future greater good (TTP 16 GIII 192). But Spinoza's reasoning here is based neither on the formal impossibility of conceiving the idea of reaching an agreement and, at the same time, breaking it, nor on utilitarian considerations. In order to see what he does have in mind, I suggest we start by reminding ourselves of the exmple of the *Animositas* man as warrior, and also of the words of Jean Cavailles, which serve as a motto for this study. This exceptional man understood Spinoza very well, and his description of the resolution to risk his life as 'Spinozistic' is perhaps less paradoxical than it looks at first sight. But we can claim that the paradox is merely apparent only if we can say that risking one's life is not necessarily contradictory to the principle of life, action, and virtue. This principle is, of course, the *conatus*, and it is the basis on which it is possible to assert that "no virtue can be conceived prior to this (viz. the striving to preserve oneself)."

One should also recall what Spinoza says about suicide: this cannot be a rational, and hence free, act. The act of suicide is always determined by external causes, and it is done in a state of bondage. But engaging in a fight is sometimes what reason dictates. Whether it is a worthwhile battle, and what its value and importance are, should be determined, as we already know, in the most personal manner through a decision (no choice involved!) free of outside instigation and irrelevant motivations.

This can happen only if life is sometimes worse than death, if there are some forms of life that are not worth living, at least not for the rational man. Furthermore, since it is always a matter of necessity, risking one's life must sometimes be the correct way to self-preservation. A careful reading of EIVp72 and its Scholium would show, I suggest, that this is not as paradoxical as it seems. What is really important in this Proposition and its Scholium is not a Kantian-style reasoning about the universality of norms as the foundation of the duty to obey them; it is rather the fact that, although one can indeed do certain things, one loses both one's rationality and one's freedom by doing them. And by losing one's freedom and rationality one loses one's essence, which is not a specific form but an actual effort, concretely deployed, to persevere in existence.

The impossibility of deception is not the impossibility to will a universal maxim of generalized deception; it is the impossibility that the rational man, qua rational, would will certain things, precisely as it is impossible for him to will a triangle of 170 degrees. It is true that, as in Kant, the universality of a rule's application is a condition of its rationality; but in this case the universality is not in itself the motive for willing it. First of all, there is no such thing as free will; and secondly, the point is that by repudiating the rule or declining to act according to it, one ceases to be rational. It's simply impossible to want certain things and still be rational, because there is always one truth, and this truth is reason.

For reason, like will, understanding etc., is not a faculty. The soul is a mode and not a substance; the subject and its individuality are not absolute but derivative. They are, as shown in the groups of lemmas after EIIp13, a product. One of the consequences of this is that the soul, or mind, is defined as an idea (of the body) and should not be seen as the *locus*, so to speak, of ideas. Reason, then, is not a thing in the world, some obscure power, or agent within the agent, a 'ghost in the machine' or what have you. It is either truth, or even better, true ideas; or an adjective qualifying what we say and how we act. If we act according to what is true, i.e., to what can be deduced from true propositions, we are rational and free; otherwise, we are neither. For Spinoza this is an affirmation of fact, and not, as it was for Kant, a motivation of the will. It becomes what we experience as an act of will through the fact that knowledge of necessary things has a high affective value, not by an illusory overcoming of desire by reason. There is no struggle here between two different, mutually exclusive and alien entities, but an inner passage from partial to fuller knowledge.

Now all this becomes intelligible only when we discover the metaphysical signification of the phenomenological analysis. Without rigorously establishing the connection of all this with the ontological foundation of things, it risks remaining purely verbal. And one of the main ways in which this ultimate justification—and clarification—of the theory of rational freedom is achieved, is through the theory of reason. I shall have to ask you, then, once more to recall soemthing that was said above, namely, that Spinoza, in contradistinction to most other rationalists, defines reason and truth not by generality and universality, but by commonality. We also saw that adequate knowledge of physical reality is knowledge of the common properties of all bodies (by way of common notions), and that this knowledge is gained through self-knowledge or through knowledge of one's own body. Actually, all adequate knowledge is *knowledge of one's own body*, or *knowledge of this knowledge*.

And precisely as it is in scientific knowledge, so it is in moral action. The necessary rational truth of one's practical knowledge is self-knowledge in the strict sense, and it is not universal, transcendent, and necessarily alien norms that one complies with when one acts rationally. this is why rational man is free, and this is why Spinozistic 'positive freedom' does not amount to a tyrannical oppression of one's real self by universal reason. On the contrary, it is a theory that should be seen as a serious attempt to relate, or even to identify, personal freedom and authentic self-affirmation on the one hand, and rationality on the other.

Recall what was said before: if we consider, as I think we should, the two citations at the opening of this article as expressions of two 'legitimate' concepts of freedom, maybe there is not such a great opposition between them after all; at least not from the point of view of Spinoza's theory of human freedom. Of course, there is a dramatic contrast between the orgiastic licence of the terrible Dolcino, and the serene and tragic valor of the *resistance* philosopher. And the wild hilarity of destructive frenzy that one senses in the cellarer's story is surely very different from

Spinoza's *laetitia*; but still the two share a very basic common property, perhaps the most basic of all when it comes to freedom: in both cases freedom is an expression of the innermost self and its affirmation.

NOTES

1. "I am a Spinozist, one must resist, fight, affront death. Truth, reason require this" (R. Aron, preface to J. Cavailles, *Philosophie mathémathique* [Paris: Herman, 1962], p. 14, my translation).

2. "That thing is called free which exists from the necessity of its nature alone, and is determined to act by itself alone" (EIdef7).

3. For the historical sources of this doctrine, and for an analysis of some of the points on which Spinoza differs from them, see M. Gueroult, *Spinoza: l'Ame; Ethique II* (Paris: Aubier-Montaigne, 1969), pp. 358-62 and appendix 12, pp. 581-2. Gueroult talks mainly about the non-formal nature of Spinoza's *common notions*, in contradistinction to both Aristotle and Descartes; I shall not repeat here what Gueroult says, but add to it what he seems to have omitted. His commentary on this doctrine is on pp. 324-73.

4. There is a certain difference here between what is referred to (by Gueroult for instance) as "universal" common notions and "proper" ones; this difference does not bear on our discussion.

5. "Those things which are common to all, and which are equally in the part and in the whole, can only be conceived adequately" (EIIp38).

6. This whole conception is based on mathematical truth as a model.

7. Curley translates the last word as 'contest'.

8. Or is it Socratic? See H.F. Hallett, *Creation, Emanation, and Salvation* (The Hague: Nijhof, 1962), p. 191, n. 3.

Time, Rationality, and Intuitive Knowledge

Gideon Segal

Time and Rational Action

Extensive literature is devoted to Spinoza's concept of time, but almost none of it adresses the relation of time to rational action. Whereas the eternity of the human mind is considered a major subject, the temporality of human beings as agents has become only a secondary, derivative issue. Given the importance ascribed to rationality by Spinoza, and the corresponding expanse of its treatment in the *Ethics*, this inequality of attention is unjustified. In contrast to the overtones of the opening sentences of the *Treatise on the Emendation of the Intellect*, where Spinoza defines his goal to be the *superceding* of emotional afflictions of daily life by the "love towards the eternal and infinite thing" (TIE 10), the fourth, longest part of the *Ethics* is dominated by an orientation toward day-to-day emotional and practical hardships. To meet the latter, Spinoza puts forth a set of rules that are aimed to free human beings of their servitude to passions as well as base their daily activity, including their relations with all other human beings, on rational principles. To be sure, temporality is an indelible and, in fact, indispensable feature of rational life led according to these principles, and, inasmuch as an agent is rational, his agency involves a distinctive realization of the temporal nature of his own activity. What, then, is a practically rational attitude toward time? In an attempt to answer this question, I shall inquire into the role that temporal images and concepts play in shaping human behavior. Eventually it will turn out that:

(a) An agent can become thoroughly rational only through intuitive knowledge of himself as an agent, for only then can he apply rational rules to actual life.

However, it will also be clear that

(b) rather than being devoid of temporality, as some interpretations of Spinoza would suggest, an agent's rationality depends upon his adequate knowledge of the temporal nature of his own activity.

Affection and Temporal Perspective

Temporal images partake in the shaping of our affective lives. As long as an image of an object is isolated from the temporal terms of past, present, and future, it affects us equally whether or not the object itself is present, for then the object is *indistinctly* cognitively present (EIIp18d). If, on the other hand, the image of an object involves a temporal aspect, i.e., the object is conceived as existing in the past (a memory) or in the future (an expectation), then, other things being equal, the strength of the image is correlatively diminished: the more remote either in the past or the future an object or event is conceived to be, the weaker is its impact on our minds (EIVp9c). Thus, other things being equal, a future or a past quarrel is less agonizing than a present one, and the moment of receiving a coveted prize is happier than all other moments in which we might expect or recall that prize.

It should be remembered that having an idea of a present object[1] is simply having this idea without a temporal qualifier,[2] whereas an idea of a past or future object is a complex of two ideas, namely, that of the object as well as that of its past or future position. In Spinozistic terms, this latter idea excludes the presence of the object, positioning it within our imagination as nonpresent, i.e., in the past or in the future (EIIp44s). A temporal qualifier is an image that, associated with the image of the object or event, temporally relates it to other things or objects that necessarily exclude its present reality. Thus, e.g., my waking up this morning is associated with a certain position of the sun in the sky; the latter is linearly related to the sun's position experienced now; and since the sun's position now excludes the image of it as seen while I was awakening, my awakening, associated with that position, is excluded from the present. Again, an imagined object or event is always present unless associated with another image that excludes its presence.

By excluding the present reality of an object, a temporal qualifier diminishes the affective power of the idea of that object, and does so in correlation with the temporal distance it sets between the present and that object (EIVp10,d). Hence, if a map of objects emotionally affecting our minds is to be drawn, in which the degree of effect of each object is to be inversely correlated with a spatial distance representing it on the map, then the remoteness of objects from the present should form one of the factors that determine the distances on the map. Generally, the more remote from the present an object is known or imagined to be, the weaker is its affective power.

This Spinozistic principle of a negative correlation holding between, on the one hand, the imagined temporal distance from the present of an object or event, and, on the other hand, its cognitive and emotional affective impact, does not come as a surprise. Rather, from our daily experience we know that the closer a future inconvenience (e.g. a surgery) is, the more alert we are, and, likewise, that the joyous memory of a past event (e.g., a birthday party) usually diminishes as time passes. Thus, there seems to prevail a *temporal perspective* governing the strength and conspicuousness of objects[3] in our cognitive and emotional field that is somewhat analogous to the spatial perspective governing our visual field: the more an object is distanced from us spatially, the smaller part of our visual field it covers, and, other things being equal, the weaker is its sensual impact; similarly, the more an object is distanced from us temporally, the smaller the part of our cognitive field it occupies, and the less powerful is its impact on our thoughts and emotions.

Temporal Images and Rational Action

a. The Negative Role of Temporal Images

Temporal images partake in the determination of the strength of our affective states. Therefore, they also influence our motivation, and, *ipso facto*, play a role in determining our actions. For, according to EIIp56d, each specific desire on the part of a person is his *conatus*, i.e., his striving to persevere in existence, which is specifically shaped by his actual affective state. We desire to create or perpetuate joyful situations, and to stop or shun those that are saddening, e.g., to stay with those whom we love and to avoid hated enemies. Now, it is a person's desires, i.e., his more or less conscious drives or appetites for this or that object (situation, event, etc.), that motivate him toward specific actions (EIIp9s). Therefore, inasmuch as temporal images determine our emotional constitution, and hence also our desires, they also shape our actions. Thus, e.g., a danger in the near future is more frightening than one that is similar yet more remote; accordingly, we are less motivated to take precautions in the second case than in the first. In this way, temporal images are practically relevant, for the temporal perspective they involve plays a powerful role in determining our desires.

Now, one might suggest that a rational agent's motivation toward action should be free from the influence of the temporal perspective. If not, he may find himself unprepared for a danger that he ignored when precautions could still be taken, or sacrificing a long-run profitable project for a meager benefit expected shortly. For in Spinozistic terms, a purely rational agent would plan his activity on the basis of pure conative calculation, i.e., he would coordinate his actions so as to achieve the highest possible perfection or power at any future point. And since the temporal perspective may shape our desires against our conative interests, i.e., our interests of power or perfection, it may seem that an agent's rationality depends upon his eliminating temporality from his conception of the reality within which he is active. In order for the true conative value of alternative actions to be practically operative, one's images of those actions should be free of temporal qualifiers involving both temporal perspectives as well as the affective biases they entail. An agent should consider an action in accordance with its net contribution to his perfection, and for this to be the case, the remoteness of the result from the present should not form an evaluative factor, lest it improperly affect the agent's practical reasoning and distort his motivation for action. Such a description seems to be confirmed by Spinoza's statement that "insofar as the Mind conceives things from the dictates of reason, it is affected equally, whether the idea is of a future or past thing, or of a present one" (EIVp62). A rational agent will always opt for the better, i.e., "the greater of two goods or the lesser of two evils" (EIVp65), deliberately ignoring the relative positions of the various options along the time-axis. Proceeding from this we find the following major practical proposition:

> From the guidance of reason we want a greater future good in preference to a lesser present one, and a lesser present evil in preference to a greater future one. (EIVp66)[4]

b. The Positive Role of Temporal Images

However, inasmuch as it ignores the positive role that temporal concepts must play in planning one's action, this conception of rational action is fallacious. A person's ability to face daily challenges depends on his appreciating their temporal relations. In particular, a rational agent must incorporate the time factor of events in his behavior, and for an agent to be virtuous, i.e., (by EIVp24), to rationally persevere in his being and seek his own advantage, his motivation toward action should reflect the respective weights that he should ascribe to his ends, in accordance with their relative temporal distances. This means that what has been described above as a distorting influence of temporal images upon an agent's behavior is, from the point of view of a rational agent, a necessary link between planning rationally and acting in accordance with one's plan. Thus, e.g., a farmer *wisely* takes action to forestall this year's floods *before* heeding to next year's drought, notwithstanding that in both cases an equal loss of crop is expected. For that to happen, his motivation to action must reflect the spread of future climates over the time-axis. Innumerable similar preferential considerations are made daily by everyone. Their efficacy requires that the temporal relations holding between events be part of the agent's mental constitution. For no activity takes place unless the agent's *conatus* is shaped by his affective states, and these affective states must be differentially aligned in accordance with the temporal ordering of practical needs. Spinoza's recognition of the indispensability of temporal concepts for rational action is explicit in EIVp66 and its corollary:

> From the guidance of reason, we shall want a lesser present evil which is a cause of greater future good, and pass over a lesser present good which is the cause of a greater future evil. (EIVp66c)

Thus, while temporality obstructs rational behavior inasmuch as it appears as a temporal perspective, distorting our evaluation of the relative conative value of objects and events and influencing our motivation to action so that our perfection and power are diminished rather than augmented, no remedy is provided by ignoring temporal relations. Rather, knowledge of the latter is indispensable to rationality, a point which Spinoza quite explicitly makes in EIVp62s, where he relates our irrationality to the inadequacy of our knowledge of the duration of things. Note also the role of temporal perspective in this regard:

> [W]e can have only a quite inadequate knowledge of the
> duration of things . . . , and we determine their times of exist-
> ing only by the imagination . . . , which is not equally affected
> by the image of a present thing and the image of a future
> one. That is why the true knowledge we have of good and
> evil is only abstract . . . and the judgement we make concern-
> ing the order of things and the connection of causes, so that
> we may be able to determine what in the present is good or
> evil for us, is imaginary, rather than real.

But then how are we to understand the recommended disre-
gard of time, presented to us as a dictate of reason in EIVp62? In
what way should we become emotionally indifferent to whether a
possibly dangerous occurrence, or a happy one, is past, present, or
future, and to whether it is close to the present or more remote?
Spinoza's answer to this must have been that a rational agent's
practical considerations, while incorporating the temporal factor,
should do so in a way that would eliminate its distortional effect
upon our motivation toward action. The differential affection we
undergo, in correlation with the temporal distance from the present of the affecting object, should be rationally controlled so as to
avoid its effect when it turns against our real conative interests.
This happens whenever an object (situation, event) is emotionally
charged in accordance with its temporal distance *without regard to
the causal relevance of this distance*. Therefore, a rational agent
should not ignore time. Rather, he must rationalize his conception
of time, so as to avoid the emotional and practical *bias* of temporal
perspective.

The Rationalization of Temporal Images

Reason is the knowledge of things that is attained through 'common notions,' and through adequate ideas of the properties of
things (EIIp40s2). Thus, for instance, the essence of an entity can
be studied through inferring from its effects (which, according to
Spinoza, are its properties; cf. EIp16d,c1). Then we can derive
other properties of that entity from the known essence (TIE 19; GII
10:16-18). One example Spinoza gives of such a process is particularly relevant to the perception of time:

> [W]e infer [one thing] from another in this way: . . . after we
> have come to know the nature of vision, and that it has the
> property that we see one and the same thing as smaller when
> we look at it from a great distance than when we look at it

from close up, we infer that the sun is larger than it appears to be. (TIE 21)

In other words, we learn how to estimate the size of seen objects when we become aware that, the closer the object, the greater the part of our visual field it covers. And, once we have learned this rule (in early childhood), we can also use it the other way around: by means of the part of our visual field being covered by an object we know the size of, we can estimate its distance from where we stand.

As explained above, an analogy can be drawn between the phenomenon of spatial perspective and what I call 'temporal perspective.' Just as with space, the closer in time a thing or an event is to the present, the greater is the part of our cognitive field it occupies, or the greater is the attention, emotional arousal, and alertness it affects in us. This similarity between spatial perspective and temporal perspective, both accompanied by perceptual distortion, is matched by a similarity in the cognitive remedy for the distortion. For how do we "come to know . . . that [vision] has the property that we see one and the same thing as smaller when we look at it from a great distance than when we look at it from close up" (TIE 21)? Spinoza's answer would no doubt be: by comparing the distances between objects that are estimated under unchecked perspectival bias with measured distances between them.[5] Similarly, real temporal distances are known by way of measuring, and therefrom also stems our awareness of the phenomenon of temporal perspective.

One may here recall that the middle of the seventeenth century witnessed a rapid development of techniques and tools for the measurement of time. These innovations, also prompted by the growing need for accurate navigation, were well within Spinoza's field of scientific interest. In his library he had a book by Christian Huygens, in which the famous Dutch scientist described with much detail a pendulum clock that he had invented in 1656,[6] and, in Letter 41, reporting some experiments he had done in hydraulics, he remarks that he could have measured time using a pendulum clock if he had one in his possession; he also describes an ingenious substitute that he had prepared for himself.[7]

But what specific cognitive distortion is rectified through measurement? As we noted earlier, the increase of our attention and alertness as expected significant events approach, is, far from being irrational, sometimes vital for our survival. What does require amendment is miscalculated behavior, and this owing to our inability to adequately grasp the things in their causally-relevant temporal relations. For example, amendment is needed when we are overwhelmed by the image of a present thing and fail to take the steps needed in order to forestall a future event the possible results of which are far more significant to us. Contrariwise, amendment is needed when a memorized event, or one expected in the remote future, overpowers us to the point that we ignore present urging needs. By taking a disproportionate hold on our cognitive and emotional 'field,' it comes to dominate our motivations against our true (correctly calculated) conative interests. In such a case, awareness to actual temporal distances of events from the present may restore balance in our array of motivations. This is analogous to the rectification of bias born out of uncontrolled spatial perspective: measuring spatial distances enables us to assign true sizes to objects, thus rectifying mistakes in our visual field. Similarly, measuring time makes it possible to assign importance, e.g., true causal efficacy, to temporally distanced objects, and rectifies the improper emotional charge due to bias in our cognitive and emotional field.

Thus, rational cognition of time does not mean indifference to the temporal ordering of things. It rather means adequate cognition of the things in their causal relation to each other and to us, and these relations include temporal terms. In this respect, our cognition of temporal perspective is necessitated by daily life no less than our cognition of spatial perspective.[8] Yet some kind of indifference *is* required—an indifference to the affective bias in favor of the present, and against past and future. One needs to overcome the natural tendency to pay more attention to things the closer in time (and space) they are, or imagined to be to oneself, irrespective of whether their temporal remoteness is relevant to one's rational goals.

Thus we find that the time perspective is in one way part of rationality, and in another way it should be dispensed with in order for rational behavior to take place. For, on the one hand, past and future things that have a causal bearing on us should be considered *as past and future things (correspondingly)*; as such they should motivate behavior in accordance with their temporal relation to the present. For example, a more closely imminent danger or opportunity should make us more alert and ready to act than do more remote dangers; and a past case of grave sickness should not affect us or draw our attention if not for present (or future) practical purposes. On the other hand, for this time-oriented balancing of motivation to take place, we should first overcome time-perspective bias, i.e., the natural tendency to be more affected by things the closer they are, or imagined to be, to the present (see EIVp10); for unless we annul this cognitive bias, we cannot avoid the corresponding motivational bias. Such is our natural bias for acting upon images of the present rather, that is, than dispassionately considering the causal bearing on us of all things and events of the past, present, and future; our natural bias for acting as if from outside the time continuum.

* * *

Given these requirements for a rational treatment of time, it would seem that the way seventeenth century scientists utilize the concept of time may serve as a paradigm for moral theory. For within this conception events are put together along a (theoretical) time-axis, and their temporal relations are described in time-units. This procedure enables one to record regularities, leaving no room for the affective bias that otherwise accompanies the perception of time. Put together along a line, the time points make a homogeneous continuum, excluding the possibility of an affective preference or bias for any of them over the others. In scientific thought the present moment has no privilege over other moments, and all the time points are indiscriminately taken as empty denominators of actual occurrences—ones that have no intrinsic content or value.

In view of the testimonies to a newly gained control over the phenomenon of time, Spinoza would be expected to conceive of a practically rational attitude toward time as consisting of its accurate measurement and the building of scientific theories that incorporate measured time;[9] from such theories, together with principles like EIVp66c—"From the guidance of reason, we shall want a lesser present evil which is a cause of a greater future good."—one can derive practical maxims and specific decisions in daily life. Moreover, by rationalizing the perception of time, one can overcome the bias involved in temporal perspective dealt with above.

Adequately acknowledging temporal relations as part of causal scientific comprehension of things can counter-balance our tendency toward untimely actions. With the powerful means of scientific theory at hand, such as one that incorporates measured time, one is freed from the differential impact of images stretched along time's continuum back into the past or forth into the future. Thus, one can rationalize one's behavior by acting upon a long-term plan, devised for the attainment of one's goals, which, for Spinoza, should all derive from one's *conatus*—the striving for self-preservation and hence for self-strengthening.

Yet, to serve as a practically rational conception of the temporal dimension of reality, the scientific concept of time would have to retain one aspect of the time-perspective—that of referring all memorized events, or things of the past, and all anticipated events, or things of the future, to the present moment lived by the agent. For what use would one have of a practical rule that utilizes a scientific concept of homogeneous time-continuum, and of one's knowledge of natural, physical, psychological, and social laws that incorporate such a concept, unless, when applying these laws, one knows and takes into one's practical consideration which of the moments along that continuum is the one lived at the present?

* * *

Is this the rational attitude toward time that we were looking for? If it is, one should expect it to be feasible and practical. Before we can answer this question, we must do some more work toward clarifying the nature of the concept of time in question. We may start with Letter 12, where Spinoza treats the concept of Time together with those of Duration, Quantity, Measure, etc. Spinoza distinguishes between two ways of conceiving Duration: it can be conceived by the intellect, as it is in itself, i.e., as one indivisible flow "from eternal things," and it can be imagined as finite, composed of parts and divisible. From the latter mode of conceiving Duration there arises the notion of Time by which we 'determine' Duration. The notion of time is the quantifiable, scientific mode of conceiving Duration. In a similar way Measure is the imagination's way of perceiving Quantity. Thus, Spinoza contrasts two levels, that of Quantity and Duration, and that of Measure and Time. Quantity and Duration are real modes of substance, of which Measure and Time are, respectively, imaginary 'determinations', themselves determined further by Number.

That in Letter 12 the concept of measured quantity, both spatial and temporal, is relegated by Spinoza to the realm of imagination: "Measure, Time [determined 'Duration,' i.e. temporal quantity], and Number are nothing but Modes of thinking, or rather, of imagining" is rather puzzling. For, given Spinoza's recognition of the newly born scientific concept of time, and generally his whole–hearted participation in seventeenth century embryonic modern science, so amply demonstrated in his correspondence,[10] one wonders why he regarded conceptual cornerstones of that science as unreal *entia imaginationis*.

A natural answer is that measured duration, based as it is on the divisions of Substance, is incompatible with its unity. This is the main thrust of Spinoza's argumentation in EIp15s, as well as in Letter 12, where it is also supported by Zeno's famous paradoxes. But Spinoza may have had an additional reservation. To see this we need to probe further into the way the scientific notion of time is attained. The view taken by the scientist Isaac Barrow, Spinoza's contemporary, can provide a clear initial illustration. According to Barrow:

> it accords with reason to consider [time] as a quantity endowed with a single dimension; for we conceive it constituted either by the simple addition of successive moments, or by the (so to speak) continued flow of a single moment, whence we are accustomed to attribute to it length alone. . . . And just as the quantity of a line depends on length alone . . . so the quantity of time follows from a single succession spread out, as it were, in length; which the length of the traversed space proves and determines. So we shall always represent time by a straight line.[11]

It turns out that perceiving time as a quantifiable magnitude requires its comparison with a spatial continuum. This is also clear from an early treatment of time by Spinoza himself in *Metaphysical Thoughts*, where he defines time as follows:

> [T]o determine . . . duration, we compare it with the duration of other things which have a certain and determinate motion. *This comparison* is called *time*. (*Metaphysical Thoughts* I,4)[12]

Note that the notion of time requires that of motion, which in turn involves the notion of space. If we ask how much time it took a certain event to occur, the answer is given by the number of units of *spatial* magnitude that were traversed by some "certain and determinate motion," such as the sun, a clock's hands, etc., during that occurrence. Similarly Barrow says that,

> [S]ince time ... is a quantity uniformly extended ... proportionately to the parts of space traversed by an equable motion, it can be represented to our mind or phantasy ... by any homogeneous magnitude; especially by the simplest, such as a straight or a circular line; between which and time there are also not a few similarities and analogies. (ibid., p. 152)

However, the simulation of time by spatial analogues has its limitations. Considered by itself, the duration of an entity seems to make up a continuous flow of that entity the being of which as a whole constitutes one indivisible existence, stretching—or progressing—in temporal dimension. This aspect of duration is also expressed by Barrow when he describes time as "the path of [a single] instant continually flowing, possessing a certain indivisibility . . . ."[13] However, in order to be rationally 'determined,' and thus conceived as Time, that is, divided and measured, this durational unity must be recast by imagination into space, in which it is reified, and where all of its 'points' are laid out simultaneously. Thus, time is an imaginary spatial representation of duration.

That the mediation of space is a necessary condition for the conception of time is further confirmed by Spinoza's explanation of the way we perceive temporal phenomena, grounded in his theory of the physiological basis of perception. According to the latter theory, our body, as an organ of sense-perception, is a dynamic physical system that preserves the imprints of external bodies that affect it. These imprints are not adequate copies of the affecting bodies, but are, rather, confused representations of the nature of one's own perceiving body as well as those of the affecting bodies (EIIp17cd,s). Nevertheless, temporal relations are consistently translated by this perceptual mechanism into correlative body-configurations. For example, upon seeing the morning light, a person "will immediately imagine the sun taking the same course through the sky as he saw on the preceding day, or [sive] he will imagine the whole day" (EIIp44). This is explained by the fact that dawn is associated in one's mind with the full temporally-stretched picture of a day (or of the sun's diurnal course), on the basis of the physiological mechanism of perception (see EIIp18,d). Spinoza even sketches the structure and operation of this perceptual mechanism, and although he ascribes to this scheme a merely heuristic role within his theory of mind

(EIIp17cd,s), he holds on to the general view that it supports with regard to the perception of time, namely, that our ability to quantify duration depends upon the formation of some corporeal analogue to the phenomenon of passage. Such a corporeal analogue records temporal relations in spatial images (*imagines*) wherein time points are simultaneously displayed. We should here recall that techniques of time measurement, whether old or new, are all based on this or that physical device—an hourglass, a sundial, a pendulum clock, etc.—in which successive time points are represented in spatial dimension. Thus, any means for recording, comparing and measuring time-intervals requires a spatial (material) substrate.[14]

This should not be considered a deficiency of our temporal concepts, so long as time is merely taken to be, as in Letter 12, an aid of the imagination, which we can use for the purpose of scientific theorizing and for technical purposes—i.e., as long as we do not confuse imaginary temporal constructs with the real notion of a thing's duration. But let us recall our original motivation for the present inquiry into the concept of time. We opened our discussion asking: what is a *practically* rational attitude to time? In view of this, the inadequacy of the imagination's spatial simulation of duration seriously endangers Spinoza's moral program. I shall now try to explain why this is so.

Human action is a durational entity. When Spinoza recommends a technique for correcting one's own behavior on the basis of previously internalized practical rules (EVp10s),[15] he assumes the applicability of these rules to real actions. But the implementation of a practical rule necessarily takes time, i.e., it stretches in a temporal dimension. For, unlike such things as geometrical propositions, scientific theories, or even bodies, an action simply cannot be understood without a temporal dimension. Inasmuch as a rule is dealt with in connection with theorizing and planning, it can incorporate the scientific, imaginary concept of time without risk of error; but when practically implemented, a rule is to be realized regarding action stretched in time.

An action is a change that evolves with the progressing duration of the agent as well as that part of his environment that receives the action. Each stage of an action stems out of and depends upon the preceding stage, and the whole series of stages together form a unified durational being. Grasping this character of action is absolutely necessary for the application of rules for rational action. And since this 'evolving' nature of an action is a genuinely temporal (durational) property, it seems that the reification in space of the duration component of a rule or a plan amounts to a nullification of its very nature.

Earlier we asked whether the scientific concept of time was a feasible remedy to human beings' tendency to be affected by an object more intensely the closer to the present it is imagined to be, and to act accordingly. Now, our latter clarifications, regarding the spatial and imaginary reification of time involved in this modern concept raise a problem in connection with the applicability of rules. Can there be any common ground between an a-temporal rule—a-temporal since its originally temporal parameter is clothed in a spatial image—and the essentially temporal action through which the rule is to be realized? Is there any common cognitive ground between a straight line that represents the duration of an envisioned action, and the action itself, progressing in time—a ground that would make the rule's quasi-temporal element applicable to the action as a genuine durational event? If not, an agent who entertains such a reified cognition of time cannot bring forth a projected action, because his abstract cognition of what he is about to do is incongruous with his awareness of himself as acting within the temporal dimension of his own reality, i.e., with himself as an enduring being.

Thus the problem we are dealing with is at once epistemological and practical. It frustrates whoever tries to apply practical rules to his own life, insofar as he conceives himself, the supposed subject of these rules, in abstraction—cutting his existence into slices, each a state along a time-continuum—without re-uniting these slices (commonly considered as forming a causal sequence) into a flowing unity continuously manifesting his essence or *conatus*.

However, rational rules are formulated and implemented, and the question that should concern us here is: How is a rule implemented on the basis of a rational conception of its temporal parameter? My answer to this question is that the role of activating practical rules, and specifically that of overcoming their incommensurability with real action, due to the inadequacy of their spatialized temporal component, is assigned by Spinoza to the third kind of knowledge.[16]

* * *

My discussion of these matters centers on EVp29, its demonstration and scholium. Here Spinoza claims that one's knowledge of things in relation to duration and time depends upon conceiving the "present actual existence" of the body. Spinoza bases the demonstration on EVp21, and through it on EIIp17s and EIIp18s, which affirm the necessity of one's body for imagining and memorizing. Spinoza thinks that, since imagining and memorizing are ideas of non-present things, they necessarily require bodily impressions as their substrate.[17] This fits well with my former claim that knowing an object in relation to time stems from positioning it by the imagination on a line together with other objects the temporal relation among which is simulated through a bodily analogue. One cannot ascribe the content of ideas to the past or to the future, and, generally, one cannot conceive of temporal relations between things, unless one can presently visualize these relations; this requires an imaginary reification of duration in some spatial analogue, onto which one imaginarily projects successive temporal positions, and for which our body is needed as a (spatial) substrate.[18]

Thus far, the bodily perceptual mechanisms are required in order for abstract temporal cognitions to take place. But what is extremely significant here is that this very same body, the perceptual mechanisms of which provide a physiological basis for our abstract conception of things as enduring and as existing in time (EVp21, EIIp18s), is the object of our conception of the eternal being of things as well:[19]

> Whatever the Mind understands under a species of eternity, it understands not from the fact that it conceives the Body's present existence, but *from the fact that it conceives the Body's essence under a species of eternity.* (EVp29, my emphasis)

To probe into the meaning of this distinction, between 'the body's present existence' and 'the body's essence conceived under a species of eternity' (*sub specie aeternitatis*), we should turn to EVp29s, which recapitulates EIIp45s.[20] Put together these scholia complement the distinction as follows: the body's "present existence" is simply its "duration, i.e., [its] existence insofar as it is conceived abstractly, and as a certain species of quantity" (EIIp45s, my emphasis); the body's essence conceived under a species of eternity is its conatus ("the force by which each one perseveres in existing"; EIIp45s), when conceived as 'following from the eternal necessity of God's nature'. Now, according to EVp31d, conceiving a thing 'under a species of eternity' is knowing it by the third kind of knowledge, i.e., knowing it 'intuitively', whereas, in contrast, a thing's duration is its existence "insofar as it is conceived abstractly, and as a certain species of quantity" (EIIp45s, my emphasis).

This distinction thrown into relief provides a conceptual scheme that can be applied to the issue of rational action. So long as an agent conceives of himself abstractly, as a temporal entity, he cannot but remain on the theoretical level. For then, inasmuch as he abstractly conceives of himself as a series of successive states projected onto an imaginary, reified temporal dimension, a cognitive barrier necessarily separates his true agency from his knowledge. In contrast, in order to rationalize his activity, an agent should, while acting, be conceiving himself-qua-agent as continuously realizing the rules of reason.

As long as we think of our endurance under the abstraction involved in the concept of time, our rationality necessarily remains precarious and sporadic. Substituting rational rules for casual experience cannot free us from the distortion effected by temporal perspective.[21] For, inasmuch as those rules comprise a projection of our activity onto an imaginarily spatialized temporal dimension, they cannot actually supplant the affective efficacy of this perspective, with its resulting distortion of our motivations. Our ability to ground our behavior in reason is necessarily obstructed due to our perception of things and of ourselves as spread over a temporal continuum; for then our abstract envisioning of our activity, in accordance with the dictates of reason, remains detached from our concrete grasping of ourselves as agents.

Thus our implementation of practical rules is sporadic, if not totally impossible, inasmuch as these rules are entertained on the level of the second kind of knowledge. So long as we grasp ourselves-qua-agents through this kind of abstract cognition, which depends on spatialized temporal images (which function as auxiliary imaginative aids to Reason; see Letter 12), we cannot realize our rationality in actual life. To overcome this obstacle, we must free ourselves from this imaginative abstraction, and this is just the practical import of Spinoza's conceptual scheme developed in the scholium to EIIp45, and their derivatives in *Ethics* V.

We have seen that Spinoza contrasts the conceiving of a thing's *conatus* as it necessarily follows from God's nature, 'under a species of eternity,' to conceiving its duration, i.e., its 'present existence' flowing in time. Now, if we substitute an agent, *qua agent*, for the "singular things" of which Spinoza speaks in EIIp45s and its derivatives in Part V, we find that, conceiving intuitively of himself as the subject of a rational rule, the agent knows himself to be flowing from God's eternal nature. Instead of projecting his imaginary self onto a causal sequence of consecutive states spread over time, he grasps the actual flowing of his life as a specific, unified realization of the laws of nature, manifested in and through his activity as a rational agent.

Thus, one's intuitive cognition of his *conatus* as evolving from God's eternal nature is nothing but his directing his behavior in agreement with the dictates of reason. This is so because, when one conceives of oneself intuitively, one is free of the temporal abstraction of his perseverance in existence. In and while acting, one's actions evolve adequately as effectuation of a rule of reason flowing from oneself as agent, instead of imagining oneself—as is the case in abstract rational thought—as being theoretically projected into a causal sequence over spatialized time. A free agent's activity is an expression of *conatus*, in accordance with rational rules, known intuitively as the ongoing manifestation of God's eternal nature.

Finally, a person's intuitive knowledge of himself, his body, and of external things, is at once both detached from and attached to the present: it is *detached from* the present inasmuch as the present is an idea of a temporal locus in which the person imagines himself to be situated. Such imagining of one's enduring existence constitutes a context within which the person perceives himself in a self-alienated way, since his supposedly real present life turns out to be, for him, a mere moment in a line of things that he imagines to be spatially related to each other.

But in another way, a person's intuitive knowledge is *attached to* the present. For the object of intuitive knowledge is the existence of things following from God's nature, conceived by an agent as an evolving reality that includes himself as actual dynamism, rather than as a concatenation of causes and effects abstracted from their actual being. Thus, Spinoza claims in EVp30d that "to conceive things under a species of eternity [hence intuitively; cf. EVp31d] . . . is to conceive things insofar as they are conceived through God's essence, as real beings, or [*sive*] insofar as through God's essence they *involve existence*" (emphasis mine). The existing things of which he speaks, rather than being abstract eternal essences, are things actually persevering in existence. This is expressly stated in EIIp45s, to which he here refers, and the content of which permeates Spinoza's discussion of these matters in *Ethics* V. "I am speaking," he says, "of the very existence of singular things," each persevering in existence by a force that "follows from the eternal necessity of God's nature."

* * *

A Concluding Note on Action and Intuitive Knowledge

In Spinoza's discussion of the kinds of knowledge provided in EIIp40s2 three numbers are given, "and the problem is to find a fourth which is to the third as the second is to the first." In the third kind of knowledge "we *infer* the fourth number from the ratio which, *in one glance*, we see the first number to have to the second" (my emphases). An otherwise discursive process of *inference* is here reduced to a single act of comprehension. I suggest that we apply this description to the comprehension of ourselves as agents. When someone actually applies rational rules, he abides by the dictates of reason, i.e., knowledge of the second kind, but he does so by intuitively comprehending himself as acting according to these dictates. This means that the agent activates these rules as immanent effects of his own nature, rather than conceiving his rule-governed actions as transitive effects of his agency, separated from him in time. The latter way would not be through and through rational behavior, since: a) it involves imaginary reified time concepts; and therefore b) it also involves one's alienation from himself as a real temporal agent; hence c) it cannot efficiently realize rational rules. Only through intuitive knowledge, free of self-alienating projections of our agency, can we fully realize the dictates of reason in real, temporal activity. Thus, practical rules, the knowledge of which is achieved by the second kind of knowledge, cannot be fully realized but through knowledge of the third kind.[22] Due to the inadequacy of our temporal concepts—and we cannot overcome this inadequacy within the domain of discursive theoretical knowledge—reasoned activity can take place only if we incorporate the rules we implement into our intuitive knowledge of our acting selves. Thus, all the cases of proper implementation of a plan or a rule are instances of intuitive knowledge, in and while acting, of ourselves and of other things causally related to us. Sometimes these are mere glimpses of absolute self-control; but we can train ourselves by "ordering and connecting the affections of the Body according to the order of the intellect" (EVp10,s). Our activity can then constitute rationality in a prolific, blessed way of life.[23]

NOTES

1. The word 'object' here refers to material things as well as non-material ones, events, and any other entity, in the broadest sense of this term.

2. The term 'qualifier,' denotes here an idea that, forming a part of a complex idea, qualifies in some way another idea in the same complex. Thus, recalling yesterday's lecture (thinking of it as a lecture that was given *yesterday*) is (to simplify the matter for clarity's sake) a complex idea formed by the idea of the lecture and the qualifying idea of yesterday, which assigns the idea of the lecture to the past.

3. See note 1 above.

4. Note that, as a practical prescription, this proposition (as well as its corollary) is no more than a commonplace. Its importance for Spinoza's theory of rationality turns on its presentation not merely as a prescription, but as a description of what a rational person as such would necessarily do. Always considering practical matters *sub specie aeternitatis*, a rational agent is motivated to action equally, whatever the relative positions of the relevant entities (objects, events) are over the time-axis.

5. Thus, it can be assumed that babies learn to estimate distances through accumulating experiences of correlations between, on the one hand, distances directly experienced, e.g., by stretching out their hands, and, on the other hand, the parts of their visual field covered by the distanced objects.

6. Christian Huygens, *Horologium Oscillatorium. Sive de Motu Pendulorum ad Horologia aptato Demonstrationes Geometricae* (Paris: F. Muguet, 1673). See J. Freudenthal, *Die Lebensgeschichte Spinozas* (Leipzig: Veit & Comp, 1899), p. 160.

7. In the apparatus he built, Spinoza used uniform flow of water for time-measurement. He probably did not invent this technique (which in any case is but a sophisticated improvement of the old clepsydra), since we know that Galileo also used it at his youth for the same purpose. See E.A. Burtt, *The Metaphysical Foundations of Modern Physical Science* (London: Routledge & Kegan Paul, 1932), p. 63.

8. Compared to geometrical abstraction, spatial perspective is sometimes taken to be a perceptual distortion. Imagine, though, what would have been the fate of someone who suddenly lost his ability to grasp bodies in spatial perspective.

9. See in this regard Letters 26, 29, 32, and 70.

10. See note 9 above.

11. Isaac Barrow, "Lectiones geometricae," in: *The Mathematical Works of Isaac Barrow* (Cambridge: W. Whewell, 1860), quoted in: Burtt, *The Metaphysical Foundations of Modern Physical Science*, p. 152, n. 76.

12. Curley's translation, p. 310.

13. Burtt, ibid., n. 76. This notion of time mixes properties that in Spinoza's terminology belong to two different levels of our temporal concepts. Whereas the continuous flow of a (temporally) indivisible entity is termed Duration, only the notion of Time, i.e., duration divided and measured, requires the spatial image of a path, or a line.

14. Time is measured by recording any kind of uniform change, such as the accumulation of sand in the lower part of an hourglass, or the behavioral pattern of elementary particles in an atomic clock. In these and all other cases the measurement consists of the manifestation, in some patterned corporeal occurrence *in* time, of the uniform flow *of* time itself.

15. Especially GII 287:24-288:5.

16. Since a mind that entertains *scientia intuitiva* is said to that extent to be eternal, my final answer to the question, what is a practically rational attitude to time, should also constitute an outline for an interpretation to a central aspect of Spinoza's concept of eternity, namely: what does it mean to act *sub specie aeternitatis*.

17. See especially EIIp18c,d which, together with EIIp18s, provides an explanation, on the basis of bodily mechanisms, of how we can imagine things that are not present.

18. Thus Spinoza's argument in EVp29d, with its reference to EVp21 and through it to EIIp17s and EIIp18s, constitutes a confirmation to my contention as to the indispensability of a spatial substrate for the formation of the notion of time. In the scholia of EIIp17 and EIIp18 Spinoza describes the body-correlate of our ideas of things imagined or memorized. The fact that this description serves as a justification to his claim, in EVp29d, that only insofar as the mind perceives the present existence of its body does it conceive things in time, inescapably proves that he regards our temporal concepts as dependent on the bodily substrate.

19. Generally speaking, things' eternal being, which Spinoza contrasts with the reified temporal existence we ascribe them, is not devoid of physical reality, despite some expressions in *Ethics* V that hint at that possibility. More specifically, an interpretation of Spinoza's concept of the eternity of the soul as maintaining mental existence without a body would directly contradict Spinoza's theory of the mind-body unity. See EIIp12 and EIIp13, especially as they are interpreted at the beginning of EIIp21d.

20. In EVp29s Spinoza cites EIIp45, where this distinction is implied for the first time, but he probably has in mind EIIp45s, which explicitly focuses on the distinction.

21. Note that, according to EIVp62s quoted above, p. 88, it is "the *true* knowledge we have of good and evil" that remains inoperative as a practical basis for rational behavior, due to our inadequate conception of duration.

22. There is much to support the view that in the *Ethics*, Spinoza is basing the third kind of knowledge on the second kind, i.e., to his intending *scientia intuitiva* to ensue from *ratio* (see EIIp47s; GII 128:14-18). Accordingly, he means morality at the level of *scientia intuitiva*, with its eternal blessing, to be consequent upon rational behavior. However, I will not elaborate on this here.

23. [This paper, which was presented at the fifth "Spinoza by 2000" conference, is added to this volume for thematic reasons—Eds.]

Spinoza and the Motives of Right Action: Some Remarks on Spinoza's *Ethics* IV

Timothy L.S. Sprigge

1.

Though this volume centers on Part IV of Spinoza's *Ethics*, this is so closely bound up with what precedes it, in particular Part III, that perhaps a few remarks situating my attitude to Spinoza's thought in general may be allowed.

I shall start with a brief comment on Spinoza's definition of love (EIIIp13s) as "pleasure accompanied by the idea of an external cause."[1] I have always found this definition very helpful when I ask myself whether I really love someone or something. Taken just as it stands it is perhaps open to some criticism on the basis of more recent theorizings about intentionality. Surely the pleasure has to be pleasure taken in something rather than just known or believed to be caused by it. Moreover, the loved object is experienced as suffused with a charm which we may follow George Santayana in calling objectified pleasure. But still, the real gist of Spinoza's point, that to love someone is to take pleasure in the thought or awareness of them, seems to me extraordinarily suggestive in its pithy way.

An associated claim is the assertion that "there are as many kinds of each emotion as there are kinds of objects by which we are affected" (EIVp33d drawing on EIIIp56). This might mean either: 1) pleasures and pains are in themselves qualitatively unvarying sensations but we give them different names according to their causes; or 2) the felt quality of a pleasure or pain varies according to the object that produced it. I certainly prefer to take it the second way, supported by EIIIp56d. In that case Spinoza has a phenomenologically richer conception of the mind than might at first appear. For if our pleasures and pains differ in their inherent nature according to the essence of what evokes them, and differ also from person to person in virtue of the difference between their essences (so that the emotions based on them likewise differ) we avoid the impoverishing reduction of our emotional life to three unvarying factors distinguished only by the propositional contents which accompany them. And there is a good deal to suggest that this was indeed Spinoza's view. (Besides EIIIp56, see EIIIp57 and EIIIp58 with proofs and scholia.)

The most striking thing, of course, about Spinoza's treatment of human emotion and behaviour is his uncompromising determinism and claim that its truth is ethically helpful rather than the reverse. When philosophers discuss determinism and free will today they usually dwell on the 'compatibilism' of such thinkers as Hume, Schlick, and Ayer. But Spinoza's 'compatibilism', if it be so called, is much subtler. Freedom is not merely being able to do what you want; it is a matter, rather, of the type of mental causation occurring within one. In the free man this is rational causation via rational insight rather than irrational causation by ill understood emotions. I believe this to be the true and profound solution to the problem.[2] Just as striking is his insistence on the calming effect in human relations of recognition of the truth of determinism:

> This doctrine assists us in our social relations, in that it teaches us to hate no one, to despise no one, ridicule no one, be angry with no one, envy no one. (EIIapp)

These pervasive ideas are those which, along with the identification of God and Nature, have most inspired me in Spinoza, and they underlie the whole treatment of the emotions in Part IV.

There is much in Part IV with which no one could plausibly disagree. Who, for example, could reject the following claim?

> It is impossible for a man not to be part of Nature and not to undergo changes other than those which can be understood solely through his own nature and of which he is the adequate cause. (EIVp4)

Similarly persuausive are the various remarks about the way in which distance in time affects the power of emotions. So too with most of what Spinoza says about the emotional effect of viewing things as necessary, contingent, or possible. Rather more involved are such short essays on human nature as the discussion of pride in EIVp57s.

2.

Part IV of the *Ethics* is mainly important for its account of how a free man will partake of the good life. Basic to this account is the claim that the free man lives this type of life because it is the one that serves him best in his quest to preserve his own being. This is, in fact, the motivation of all human conduct, but it can only be pursued clearly by the man who is aware of what he is doing in his action. The man in bondage, in contrast, acts thoughtlessly in response to passing passions which reflect the action upon him of external things, rather than his own creative response to them. Moreover, the *conatus* which drives the conduct of the man in bondage is in many cases not the *conatus* of the man as a whole but that of some part of him, some bodily need or psychological obsession which is seeking its own good in opposition to the good of the whole.[3] See EIVp22c: "The *conatus* to preserve oneself is the primary and sole basis of virtue"; and EIVp43d: "Thus every man, insofar as he really understands what he is up to, seeks to preserve his own being, and this is the basis of virtue."

Several questions arise. Does Spinoza then think that there is nothing that we should value more than the preservation of our own lives? This is an ethical claim which few would find altogether admirable. Does Spinoza think that no one ever values anything more than the preservation of his own life? Surely if he does think this, he is wrong. The company of martyrs, and of many brave soldiers, and other such heroes, clearly belies any such claim.

However, it seems out of the question that Spinoza did mean quite this. What he meant was that all our active behaviour—indeed anything which can properly be called *our* behaviour at all—is the expression of the urge to self-preservation of a certain personal essence. But this personal essence is not simply the physical organism whose identity is a matter, as we now tend to put it, of spatio-temporal continuity. For my organism can survive me, as did the organism of the Spanish poet discussed in EIVp39s. Moreover, although Spinoza takes a dim view of suicide, he does not (how could he?) think it impossible. He himself gives the example of Seneca, and there were examples nearer home, such as Uriel da Costa. Nor is it clear that he condemns suicide in all cases. Seneca seems to be respected for choosing 'a lesser evil to avoid a greater'. And apart from suicide, I doubt whether he really wanted to condemn the soldier who risks his death in battle, to preserve a nation to whose welfare he is committed, on the grounds that he could not so act if he were intelligently bent on preserving his own being.

As for the ethical side of the matter, one must presume that Spinoza would reply that a voluntary death is sometimes the only way to preserve one's spiritual integrity. In short, to live under some circumstances would be for one's personal essence to be overcome by the *conatus* of lower aspects of one's person.

The question still stands whether it is the mere persistence of one's essence at which the *conatus* is directed, or whether it is not equally its persistence in an enhanced, more fulfilling form. Nietzsche, we may recall, regarded his main doctrines as having been anticipated by Spinoza, and he thought our fundamental motivation was will to power, rather than will to survive. It was precisely on this point that he thought he was making an advance on Schopenhauer, who is supposed to have seen mere will to survive as the basis of everything.

Was not Spinoza likewise also meaning something rather more than the urge merely to survive when he spoke of the *conatus*? Was it not rather *will*—not perhaps so much to power—as *will* to an enhanced, more full and complete type of existence? There are some indications that this was Spinoza's real thought. (For example, the idea of pleasure as transition from a lesser to a greater perfection.) Of course, the mere wish to survive is basic, but surely we must postulate this as being continuous with a will to a more complete form of existence, not just because this makes existence of some kind more likely, but for its own sake.

If we can ascribe this view to Spinoza, we can say that for him the proper and rational way to justify a moral code is that we will all find ourselves best fulfilled by living according to it. More specifically, this is the ground of our duty to work for, or if it exists, support, a stable society, in which rules are laid down which allow for the resolution of conflict and co-operative pursuit of human fulfillment for all. It is not simply a matter of avoiding disruption of one's own pursuits by others. For one cannot reach the highest human good except with the help and encouragement of others and through the kinds of relationships one can establish with them.

Many have denied that such considerations are sufficient to ground an adequate morality. They fear that someone who rationally pursued simply his own interests, in however enlightened a way, would not always behave in a way of which they would approve.

Spinoza is, of course, aware of this objection. A large part of his answer to it is given in EIVp36, its Demonstration and Scholium. "The highest good of those who pursue virtue is common to all, and all can equally enjoy it." "Somebody may ask: 'What if the highest good of those who pursue virtue were not common to all?' . . . Let him take this reply, that it arises not by accident but from the very nature of reason that men's highest good is common to all." I shall come back to this later. (Compare EIVp72s.).

But the uneasiness lingers. Perhaps it is more pressing on us today, when there are more possibilities of our becoming involved in the welfare of those remote from us. For example, people in Britain, a relatively peaceful and prosperous society still, watch scenes of mass starvation in Somalia on their television sets and of terrible warfare in former Yugoslavia [this paper was written in 1993—Eds.]. Should the individual contribute to alleviating the starvation by giving to appropriate charities? Should he urge his government to raise taxes so that more aid can be given? Should he be ready to have his own countrymen die, intervening in a fairly remote civil war? These are, indeed, difficult questions. Some wonder how much good the charities really do, and there is a more serious debate as to what good military intervention in various trouble spots by outside powers, under the UN or otherwise, might do. But suppose it granted that the charity can do real good from the point of view of the starving, or military intervention from the point of view of the victims of war. Should we not accept that this imposes a duty on us, even if it has no bearing on our personal survival or self fulfillment as rational beings? Most of us will answer 'yes'. In that case we are rejecting the adequacy of the foundation of morality apparently proposed to us by Spinoza.

But what better foundation can we supply? What really is forceful in Spinoza's approach to these matters, I suggest, is his determination that ethical recommendations should not be mere emotional exhortations, but should draw attention to what we will really want to do, the better we understand ourselves and our situation. He wants, that is, to link ethical recommendations to real human motivations. Without this they are largely pointless, or at any rate can only influence us by a misunderstanding.

Where Spinoza seems lacking is in denying empathy any positive role in ethics. Clearly he very much acknowledges the fact of empathy; indeed, it plays an important part in his psychology (see EIIIp27 and EIIIp31). But he thinks that it is something destructive to the good life rather than helpful to it. Or at best it is a substitute for moving the masses to do what the free man does because he realizes that to do so is in his own enlightened best interest (see EIVp50s).

I fully support Spinoza's wish that ethical recommendations should point to genuine and stable motives for conforming to them; they are largely pointless otherwise and lead to a contempt for ethical discourse. But why should not the desires we have as a result of empathy, the desire for a happier world, or at least a happier community around one, not be a main motivator? In fact, I believe that giving empathy a substantial role in the foundation of morality grafts very appropriately onto Spinoza's metaphysics and psychology. He attributes to each of us an urge to understand the world around us, an urge to grasp the truth of things. Thus:

> [T]he mind is active only to the extent that it understands. . . . So the absolute virtue of the mind is to understand. But the highest thing the mind can understand is God. . . . Therefore the highest virtue of the mind is to understand or know God. (EIVp28d)

> The highest *conatus* of the mind and its highest virtue is to understand things by the third kind of knowledge. (EVp25)

But, as we understand God, and therefore the world around us, more fully, we come to grasp more of what the victims of such evils as famine and war are enduring. This sets up an imitation of their emotions and felt needs within one. An urge to do something to satisfy these needs, if we can, necessarily follows, for their needs have become ours. (Of course, they will be motivationally weaker needs than those which arise from our own more personal situation.) Certainly, it may often be more pleasant at one level to close our eyes to the sufferings of others. But that is also to close ourselves off to the truth of their situation, and here I am taking it that Spinoza is right in treating the urge to truth as a basic human motivation.[4]

There are traces of thoughts of this sort in Spinoza. His insistence that a belief in determinism, and an understanding of the causes of people's feelings, will quell our inclination to mock them points in this direction somewhat. Yet it should surely be taken further.

But how much further? Should we become so dominated by concern for suffering humanity at large that we cease to be able to make the best of our own situation? Nietzsche for one thought not. And he thought it a deplorable feature of Christianity that it had led to a decline in human excellence precisely through promoting such concern. For those who might otherwise have lived really worthwhile lives were being drained of their energies by the emotional tug of people less fortunate in abilities or circumstances. Spinoza, to some extent, thought likewise. It lies behind his striking remark, to which we shall turn our attention shortly, that pity considered in itself is an evil. And I would agree with Spinoza if he meant that too great a demand upon us to concern ourselves with the welfare of remote others can be psychologically so unrealistic that the belief that morality requires it may lead to a slackening of the influence of other less extreme moral demands upon us. But I still think that the proper Spinozistic message would have been: Gain the clearest and most distinct ideas which you can both of yourself and of the world around you, and act in the light of these. Thereby you will increase your own pleasure in life. Nevertheless, you will find that those of your clear and distinct ideas whose *ideata* are the mental states of others may sometimes force you, if you want to be at ease with yourself, to activity which when less enlightened you thought were against your own best interests, and which, indeed, do sometimes run counter to what you will continue to want in your less enlightened moments.

Part of the problem in thinking about this whole matter is that the distinction between self-regarding and altruistic activity is not clear-cut, not through any fault in our concepts, but because there is no sharp distinction between the things. Insofar as one is concerned about others, their happiness or unhappiness, even their survival or otherwise, has become (to echo J.S. Mill) a 'part' of one's own happiness or unhappiness, one's own survival or otherwise.

3.

Is Spinoza in fact moving to such a view when he claims that rational people pursue the same good because it is genuinely a common good? For propositions EIVp29-40 contend that the interests of free men are common interests in a sense in which those of unfree men cannot be. Thus:

> No thing can be evil for us through what it possesses in common with our nature, but in so far as it is evil for us, it is contrary to us. (EIVp30)

> The highest good of those who pursue virtue is common to all, and all can equally enjoy it. (EIVp36)

> The good which every man who pursues virtue aims at for himself he will also desire for the rest of mankind, and all the more as he acquires a greater knowledge of God. (EIVp37)

The argument here is not always easy to follow, and some of the inferences seem a little dubious. However, the general case, that the overriding goal of free men (rational understanding of themselves and the world) is intrinsically non-competitive, since another man's rational understanding cannot threaten, but can only assist the increase of it in myself, seems right. In contrast, the goals of unfree men, though at times they may provide a basis for cooperative activity, cannot be guaranteed to do so for long. This is fairly obvious if the goal is material wealth and its advantages, or political power. Similarly in academic life, if the goal is a particular chair of philosophy, or a prize, then those who are aiming at it are bound to enter into more or less gentle competition. Likewise in the pursuit of knowledge, wherever the really motivating goal is the desire for reputation or position, the goal is necessarily a competitive one leading to friction. But to the extent that all are really aiming at, say, philosophical or scientific understanding, then the increase of it in one must assist rather than threaten the increase of it in others.

What of political conflicts? Surely it is true that any increase in people's delight in simply understanding the human world (how different cultures and societies have developed, how conflicts have arisen) must contribute to the reduction of conflict. Although this may seem an unlikely ideal to be actualized in the modern world, it is true, nonetheless, that the more real understanding of the world people share, the more they will be ready to come to some sort of *modus vivendi*. Spinoza, of course, does not expect too wide a spread of such rationality, but he is asking those who have to some extent attained it to participate in whatever looks likely to promote the tranquillity and peace most favourable to its development.

Is the kind of rationality which should culminate in the intellectual love of God the only good which necessarily unites rather than divides people? What of artistic activity, for example? On the face of it the same seems to apply. An artist may be devoted to artistic beauty (or some alternative aesthetic ideal) as something he wishes to prosper in the world, or he may be devoted more to his own personal success as an artist with the consequent worldly rewards. In the latter case he may enter into conflict with rival artists with whom he is competing; in the former the aesthetic creations of others will please him for themselves, and encourage him in his own work.

Perhaps the distinction which Spinoza should mean is that between the pursuit of great transpersonal ideals[5] for their own sake on the one hand, and the pursuit of personal success in a worldly sense (whether by way of contribution to such ideals or otherwise) on the other hand. But perhaps he is also right that there is something peculiarly uniting about rational understanding, not only because it is a good which, when genuinely desired, cannot be competitive, but also because, insofar as it is directed at the sources of strife, it tends to lessen them, by showing how the behaviour of other groups was the necessary result of their circumstances, a result however which may be modified to the extent that both sides can share in a rational understanding of what is happening.

Though, upon the whole, Spinoza's case for the necessarily unifying character of rationality as an aim seems well taken, it is doubtful if it can quite bear the weight put upon it. Sometimes, so it would seem, my rational understanding might be impeded by that of another, if we both, say, need the same books which are in short supply or indeed both need medical treatment where resources can only save one of us. For, as Spinoza himself effectively affirms, if you want rational understanding you must also want the physical survival which, on the face of it,[6] is its requisite. Spinoza's answer seems to include an appeal to a more mystical sense of the solidarity of free men than we have so far been considering. For there are puzzles as to just how strongly Spinoza posits that something one and the same is present in all free men. Is the free man aiming at rationality for himself, or is he aiming at the increase of rationality in the world? If the latter, EIVp72s, where it is said that the free man would not liberate himself from danger by deception, because if so reason would advise all to do the same, becomes more intelligible than it has sometimes seemed. But that does suggest a rather mystical rational essence shared by us all, in our rational aspect, which has its own goals quite apart from its persistence in the individual who is sustaining it. It becomes rather like a gene, as socio-biologists now describe it, which does not mind, so to speak, whether it survives in its present home or in that of one of its kin. But it is by no means certain that this is Spinoza's meaning. If not, then although in general my rational understanding is promoted by that of others, the question remains whether, since, if I am to understand, I must survive, I should not break faith if necessary to ensure this.

4.

Both in his psychological and in his ethical thought Spinoza is quite close to hedonism. It is true that theoretically pleasure is valued because it is our experience of our mind's and body's 'transition from a lesser to a greater perfection', and pain disvalued as the converse (EIII def.aff.2,3), rather than as mere indefinable feelings, but the practical upshot is close to a hedonistic system in which pleasure is the only real positive value. (EIVp41-3 do not say that pleasure and pain are the only things which are respectively good and bad, but the general line of argument which follows from them implies this.) Not that I think the worse of it for that. It would be interesting to examine in detail how Spinoza's ethics compares with such great hedonistic systems as that of Epicurus, Bentham, and Mill. The most striking contrast is the way in which Spinoza's hedonism, if we can call it that, treats rational thought as the highest human pleasure.

5.

A special feature of Spinoza's approach to pleasure and pain, and the emotions defined in terms of them, is his insistence that it is better to be motivated by the prospect of pleasure than in the hope of avoiding pain. This is because motivation by pleasurable emotions is more powerful as a form of control of oneself or others than control by painful emotions. Thus EIVp18: "Desire arising from pleasure is, other things being equal, stronger than desire arising from pain"; and EVp63 (based on EIIIp58d): "He who is guided by fear, and does good so as to avoid evil, is not guided by reason." The logic of Spinoza's position is clear enough. Pleasure marks a strengthening of our vital powers (at least when it exhibits the flourishing of the organism as a whole rather than merely of some wayward part of it), pain a weakening of our vital powers (See EIIIp11,d). Therefore when we act on the basis of painful emotions we are acting with weakened powers. Now, if one treats this as an empirical claim (and even if Spinoza's method is not empirical, it is supposed to yield empirically correct results), there seems to be a good deal going for it, but it requires qualifications that may not have been available to Spinoza.

Suppose I am in desperate need of a job so that I can support myself and my family adequately. Spinoza might argue that, if I think of the good things which could come my way if I got a certain job, and dwell positively on my qualifications for it, then I will conduct my interview in a hopeful, cheerful manner which will increase my chances. If, on the other hand, I am weighed down with worry and depression, then I will not do justice to myself in the interview and am less likely to get the job. In short, when approaching the problems of life with cheerful zest, or at least enjoying one's energy in making the attempt to get on top of them, one is more likely to succeed, than if one is too weighed down by worry. Clearly there is much in this.

But surely the prospect of evil of one sort or another is also a very powerful motivator. Fear of falling into the hands of some torturer is likely to affect us very strongly in what we do. To take a less drastic example from my own experience, I often only manage to get a lecture or paper prepared when I suddenly feel a sense of panic that the time is going to come and I shall have nothing ready to say. I would rather live without these feelings of panic, and it is much more sensible to arrange one's life so that one prepares well in advance for everything in a cool, sensible, and cheerful way, or perhaps drawn to what one hopes will be the pleasure of expounding one's own opinions at some length; however, panic at having nothing to say is for many of us a much stronger motivator, I suspect.

Is Spinoza perhaps thinking more of the contrast between what has been called intrinsic and extrinsic motivation?' Encouraging someone to do something by showing them that they will like doing it can indeed be more effective than threatening them with various ills. Health education is a case in point (see EIVp63c). Spinoza himself uses a quite homely example to illustrate the point that "through the desire that arises from reason we pursue good directly and shun evil indirectly" (EIVp63c), and that the former is preferable:

> This corollary can be illustrated by the example of the sick man and the healthy man. The sick man eats what he dislikes through fear of death. The healthy man takes pleasure in his food and thus enjoys a better life than if he were to fear death and directly seek to avoid it. (EIVp63c)

There is a lot of truth in this. All the same, fear can work as a very effective stirrer to action, and it does not seem always to lead to being overpowered by the pain of it. It is, of course, a quite different point that, self-evidently, it is more pleasant to feel pleasant emotions so that a wise man, granted Spinoza's general approach, will prefer to be controlled by them rather than by negative emotions.

6.

So much for psychology. But what of the ethics of the matter, the conduct one can expect from the free man as opposed to men in general? Well, although all men are motivated by the quest for pleasure and the avoidance of pain, the free man does so in wiser and more enlightened way than do the masses. And one implication of this, granted what we have just been saying, is that he will encourage himself to be motivated by positive emotions which are pleasurable rather than by negative emotions which are painful.

From this Spinoza deduces a series of propositions some of which most of us will find it easy to accept, but others of which are more troubling. In fact, there is sometimes something rather terrifying in Spinoza's stress on the supreme value of positive active pleasure and the desirability of moving beyond all painful emotions.

However, most of us will by and large welcome EIVp45: "Hatred can never be good." We may even welcome the strong challenge to major strands of certain forms of both Judaism and Christianity (especially in its Calvinist version) in EIVp53 and EIVp54, relished by Nietzsche from the point of view of his more extreme objection to what he saw as life-denying in Christianity. Thus: "Humility is not a virtue; that is, it does not arise from reason" (EIVp53); and: "Repentance is not a virtue, i.e. it does not arise from reason; he who repents of his action is doubly unhappy or weak" (EIVp54). But what of: "In the man who lives by the guidance of reason, pity [*commiseratio*] is in itself bad and disadvantageous" (EIVp50)? Here the apparent challenge to what may seem the most important aspect of both religions (and other world religions) is more troubling. Indeed, pity or compassion has been widely regarded as the very basis of a decent ethic. Schopenhauer is the Western philosopher who has most emphasized this, though his own personality, unless he has been badly misrepresented, is a poor advertisement for his philosophy compared with that of Spinoza for his. All the same, compassion presents itself to many of us as one of the most desirable things among human beings.

Spinoza does, indeed, allow that in most men—men who are not fully rational—the emotion of pity is desirable:

> Now I emphasize that I am here speaking of the man who lives by the guidance of reason. For he who is moved neither by reason nor by pity to render help to others is rightly called inhuman. For . . . he seems to be unlike a man. (EIVp50s)

But that hardly does justice to the role of empathy for which I argued above. Still, I would agree with Spinoza if the point is simply that to be effective in the world one must not get weighed down by the sorrows of others, any more than by one's own. Where one can do little or nothing about another's troubles, it may be better to get on with what one can do with one's own life. Moreover, when compassion persuades one that something needs to be done about another or others, it is probably true that once it has acted as an initial spur to action, it is better thereafter to get on with the job without feeling too much. So there is something to be said for avoiding pity as a clog upon action, but I would say that even in a man guided by reason it should have its place as a motivator. And in saying that it should have its place, I mean, in Spinozistic fashion, that it will have a place so far as one is rational.

But what should one think about oneself, and what should one do, when one does not feel pity and yet uneasily feels that one should? Perhaps one sees starving people on television, but is really so preoccupied with one's own life, that though one recognizes in a verbal way that it is a terrible thing, one's emotions are not moved. And perhaps, if they were, one would not do much more by way of giving to charity, say, than one does anyway on the basis of a cool ethical judgement of one's obligations. Is there a duty to cultivate feelings of compassion over and above a duty to do what they would motivate you to do? This is a tricky question, but I suppose that, in the end, one must be Spinozist enough to say that there is no point in feeling pity unless it is actually leading you to some effective action, and that as a mere negative drag upon one's own vitality it is pointless. (There is also the possibility of indulging in pity as a kind of pleasure. What is the correct Spinozist view here?)

7.

Let us consider now Spinoza's view that the supreme pleasure and value is that of active thinking. There are many places where

Spinoza speaks of our reason or understanding as 'the better part of us' (EIVapp §32), or of our true activity or virtue being reason itself (EIVp52d). Thus:

> We know nothing to be certainly good or evil except what is really conducive to understanding, or what can hinder understanding. (EIVp27)

> Now man's true power of activity, or his virtue, is reason itself which man regards clearly and distinctly. (EIVp52d)

One may be uneasy about this on two accounts; first, its acceptability as a view of human nature; second, its questionable basis in Spinoza's metaphysics. Quite a number of critics, including, for example, George Santayana and R.J. Delahunty, have thought this a real defect in Spinoza's view of human life.[8] Important as intellectual satisfaction is, they say, there are things worth doing other than understanding.

It is not an adequate answer to this charge to emphasize Spinoza's positive attitude to the graces of life in the beautiful scholium to EIVp45, for, as Delahunty emphasizes, these graces are essentially advanced as supportive of a life of adequate ideas. But perhaps we are taking the life of reason, devoted to adequate thinking, in too narrow a fashion? Is not the novelist or poet, and even the practitioner of non-verbal arts, such as painting and music, exercising his understanding in a broad sense? Are these activities not, at their best, forms of the intellectual love of God? After all, all the really worthwhile human activities do seem to involve thought as their core.

Yet, however widely we interpret 'reason', 'understanding', 'intellectual,' etc., there is a real problem for Spinoza in that he evidently takes such expressions as referring to something pertaining to human beings that distinguishes them from other finite modes. And there are many remarks setting up a sharp contrast between men and animals. But if the mind of a dog is God's idea of the canine organism in just the same sense as a human mind is God's idea of the human organism, what makes the *conatus* of the latter idea above all a striving to understand, which should not be equally true of the canine mind? Indeed, so far as I can see, the same should be true of God's idea of a flower or atom, since the reasons for regarding understanding things, and aspiring to the intellectual love of God, as primary targets of the *conatus* of the human essence, might seem to be applicable likewise to any mind, even if at a very different level of intellect. For the crucial superiority of the human mind over other finite minds is its greater complexity and its much subtler ways of interacting with the environment, rather than a total difference in character. (In this connection see EIIp13s, EIIIp4, EVp39,s.)

Spinoza does, indeed, emphasize that different sorts of creatures are susceptible to different sorts of pleasure, pain and emotion, referring in particular to the contrast between those of humans and of animals (see EIIIp57d). But the common features of animal bodies and human bodies, make it difficult not to suppose that there are analogues in the types of pleasures and pains experienced by each. Indeed if animals (not to mention humbler things) ever act at all, it seems that they must have some ideas of their situation in the world which are not totally inadequate (see EIIIdef2).

Clearly the basic Spinozistic system can make good sense of a striking contrast between men and animals (and likewise between animals and simpler physical things) on the ground that there is not the same complexity within them to allow of a similar degree of internal representation of the world at large. But still the basic conatus of any mind must be towards sustaining and promoting ideas which affirm the flourishing of its body, and of itself as the idea of its body. And this suggests that, even in animals, when this *conatus* is most fully satisfied, there may be some kind of analogue of that intellectual love of God which is the maximal satisfaction of the human essence. I have nothing against this metaphysically. But if so, the difference between men and animals must be one of degree rather than absolute. And it would seem that, insofar as there is a good deal in common between us and the animals, there must be a good deal in common in what constitutes our good. Thus, while the goods of animality ('bodily satisfaction' as it would ordinarily be called) should be recognized as having their own distinct value in human life (rather than as merely as a necessary background to the life of the intellect), some analogue to intellectual satisfaction should be allowed its place in animal life. Or, *if not*, more explanation as to *why not*, than Spinoza offers, is required.

One approach would be to point out that, for Spinoza, finite minds are, as it were, symbols by which the divine mind thinks about the physical or natural world. But these symbols vary a great deal in how much meaning they possess when considered apart from the total divine context. The symbols which are the minds at any one time of an individual with a highly developed intellect will be, as it were, complete sentences, while those of individuals with less developed intellects will be more like subordinate clauses, false or even short on meaning taken on their own, while those of the lowliest of creatures may be more like mere nouns, which, considered out of the context of the whole, as they figure for themselves, have quite minimal meaning.

This certainly casts some light on why the intellect is a more significant feature of human than of animal life or still lower types of physical existence. Still, there must be at least a minimum of intelligible wholeness, I think, to every mind if it is to have its own *conatus*. Therefore either 'intellect' must be understood in a sense so extended that every individual thing in the universe somehow aspires to think clearly and positively about itself, or the good of the human mind must incorporate aspirations to enriched consciousness of a non-intellectual kind which it shares with animals and perhaps even atoms (not stones, for these, one can reasonably say, are not genuine individuals with a *conatus* of their own).

8.

These reflections should help us understand the following proposition, on which recent commentators have looked somewhat dimly:

> Nothing positive contained in a false idea can be annulled by the presence of what is true, in so far as it is true. (EIVp1)

This is, in fact, essentially the view adopted by such absolute idealists as F.H. Bradley, Bernard Bosanquet, and H.H. Joachim in their doctrine of degrees of truth. They were therefore in a better position to understand it than those entirely in thrall to standard modern logic. It is the claim that every thought, as a mental response to the pressures of circumstance, is a partial registration of what is going on, and that this registration can always be included in a more effective, more comprehensive registration. It is possible to accept this doctrine while admitting that some sentences are absolutely false. For, in the first place, it is not supposed to apply to any old sentence a critic may think up, whether anyone affirms its truth or not, while in the second place, even affirmed sentences, which qua sentences have to be called simply false, can be regarded as registering something which is going on, even if it is very inadequately represented. And such false sentences, occurring in the divine mind as mere subordinate clauses, will be parts of something true, just as a false 'p' may be part of the true proposition 'The situation is rather like one in which 'p' is true'.

Actually EIVp1 seems bound to figure, in some form, in any type of pantheism for which the human mind is a component in the mind of God. For surely God must in some way make positive use of every ingredient of his mind, and this positive use can only be by subsuming it in some way within his own eternal knowledge, not merely as something known, but as part of his process of knowing.

NOTES

1. Quotations are from Spinoza, *The Ethics and Selected Letters*, trans. Samuel Shirley (Indianapolis: Hackett, 1982). The references within the quotes to previous propositions are generally omitted.

2. See my "The Significance of Spinoza's Determinism," *Mededelingen vanwege het Spinozahuis* 58 (Leiden: E.J. Brill, 1989).

3. But why as detached observers should we think it better that the whole should succeed than that the part should? Spinoza might appeal to what Menenius Aggrippa said to the Plebs when they threatened to rebel against the Senate, namely that each part only finds its real fulfillment when the other parts are working properly. See Shakespeare's *Coriolanus*, Act One, Scene One. Shakespeare is using a story from Livy's *History of Rome*.

4. "We can only have the highest happiness . . . by having wide thoughts, and much feeling for the rest of the world as well as ourselves. . . ." From the Epilogue to *Romola* by George Eliot, quoted in T.H. Green, *Prolegomena to Ethics* (Oxford: Clarendon Press, 1899), pp. 458-9.

5. See Frans van Zetten, "Russell and Spinoza: Free Thoughts on the Love of God," *Mededelingen vanwege het Spinozahuis* 65 (Delft: Eburon, 1991).

6. I say "on the face of it" to allow that Spinoza's doctrine of immortality might possibly make a difference here.

7. See D.L. Deci, *Intrinsic Motivation and Self-Determination in Human Behavior* (New York: Plenum Press, 1975).

8. R. J. Delahunty, *Spinoza* (London: Routledge and Kegan Paul, 1985), pp. 275-8; George Santayana, "The Ethical Doctrine of Spinoza" (first published 1886) in *The Idler and his Works*, ed. Daniel Cory (New York: George Braziller, 1957). See also my "Spinoza and Santayana: Religion without the Supernatural," *Mededelingen vanwege het Spinozahuis* 69 (Delft: Eburon, 1993).

Egoism and the Imitation of Affects in Spinoza

Michael Della Rocca

In the *Ethics*, Spinoza espouses a morality of self-interest. What one should do is what will benefit oneself. This egoism is evident in various places, including EIVp22c: "The striving to preserve oneself is the first and only foundation of virtue."[1] However, Spinoza's egoism is not a crude egoism which counsels one to ignore or ride roughshod over the interests of other people. On the contrary, Spinoza thinks that to the extent that one is virtuous, to the extent that one is better able to promote one's own interests, one will also have a deep concern for the interests of others. It is in our interest to have an interest in the welfare of others. Thus a Spinozistic egoist will, in fact, desire for others the good which he desires for himself (EIVp37).

This basic strategy is not novel in the history of philosophy.[2] What is distinctive is Spinoza's conception of the way in which self-interest generates a concern for others. Consider the standard Hobbesian basis for a concern for others: A rational, self-interested person will take into account at least some of the interests of others with a view to reducing potentially deadly competition for scarce resources and also with a view to effecting the division of labor required for meeting our various needs. On this view, we act on behalf of others because of what they will tend to do in return for us. If we act to satisfy the needs of others, or at least refrain from frustrating their needs, they will be more likely to do the same for us. On this view, the benefit in helping others is that those others will be more likely to bear us good will, or at least less likely to bear us ill will.[3]

Although Spinoza sometimes cites such a basis for having the interests of others at heart,[4] he emphasizes a quite different egoistic ground for concern for others. The reason Spinoza emphasizes is not that the others whom I help will be more inclined to help

---

I am grateful to Wallace Matson, Gerald Postema, and the participants in the 1993 Jerusalem Spinoza Conference for helpful comments on an earlier draft.

123

me or less inclined to hurt me; rather, the reason hinges upon the expectation that the people whom I help will be better able to do what is useful to themselves (simply because I have helped them). Spinoza contends that the fact that another human being, x, is better able to benefit himself, benefits me directly. The point is not that x's increased capacity for self-interested action aids me because it makes it more likely that x will continue to be able and willing to act with a view to benefiting me. Actually, the connection between x's self-interested action and mine is more direct. For Spinoza, the fact that x is better able to benefit himself is beneficial to me independently of any increase in the good will of x or any decrease of ill will. The reason why this is so, according to Spinoza, is simply that x is similar to me, or, as Spinoza says, similar to me in nature (EIVp30,31). By this Spinoza means at least that both x and I are human beings. It is precisely because x is similar to me in this respect that x's increased capacity for self-interested action is beneficial to me. For this reason, I have an interest in aiding x and making sure he retains and strengthens his capacity for self-interested action. It is the similarity between x and myself that makes it rational for me to be concerned about x's welfare.

This strategy for building concern for others into an egoistic ethical system is bold and exciting. If Spinoza succeeds, he will have grounded concern for others not in the standard and uncertain claims concerning the circumstances under which human beings are or are not inclined to help others, but in the perhaps more secure and simple claim that other human beings are similar to oneself. In this paper, I will investigate whether this bold strategy can work. First, I will describe the kind of concern for others that will, according to Spinoza, characterize a virtuous person. Second, I will examine Spinoza's first argument for the claim that we should have this particular concern for others simply because the others are similar to us. This argument is, unfortunately, unsuccessful. Although commentators have often criticized this argument, it has not been appreciated that its failure actually turns on a conflict between two views on the essence of individual things. I will show that this conflict is simply the most acute manifestation of a deep tension which permeates Spinoza's metaphysics. In light of this account of the failure of Spinoza's argument, I will then analyze and evaluate an alternative case that Spinoza makes for a rational concern for others. Like Spinoza's first argument, this alternative argument appeals to the fact that different human beings are similar to one another and not to the fact that the human beings whom we help will be more likely to be inclined to help us. But, unlike the first argument, the key element in the alternative argument is Spinoza's doctrine of the imitation of the affects, as articulated in Part III of the *Ethics*. Despite the fact that the doctrine of imitation is in need of further support and elaboration, I will argue that this alternative argument is, in some significant respects, superior to the first argument.

I

At EIVp37 Spinoza states that a virtuous person will promote the interests of others:

> The good which everyone who seeks virtue wants for himself, he also desires for other men; and this Desire is greater as his knowledge of God is greater.

Thus, a virtuous person will attempt to induce others to attain the same good that he seeks for himself. Before we see why the virtuous person would seek to help others in this way, we need to know exactly what good it is that the virtuous person seeks for himself. This requires explaining several terms that Spinoza uses.

For Spinoza, an individual is more active insofar as this individual is more nearly the complete cause or explanation of some effect. (See EIIIdef1,2.) Each thing is active to some degree and is capable of greater or lesser degrees of activity. In terms of this notion of degrees of activity, we can introduce Spinoza's notion of increase in power of acting:

x's power of acting increases to the extent to which x becomes less dependent on external things in the production of some effect.

A decrease in power of acting can be defined in a corresponding fashion:

For Spinoza, each thing strives to increase its power of acting and to prevent any decrease in its power of acting.[5] Although the notions of increase and decrease in power of acting apply to things in general, Spinoza gives special names to such transitions as they occur in human beings. He defines joy as a human being's transition to a greater power of acting and Sadness as a human being's transition to a lesser power of acting.[6]

Those things conducive to the joy of a person or, equivalently, those things conducive to an increase in his power of acting, are, according to Spinoza, *good* for that person. Further, those things conducive to sadness or to a decrease in a person's power of acting are *evil* for that person.[7]

Given the way in which the notions of good, evil, joy, sadness, and increase and decrease in power of acting are connected for Spinoza, we can see that when he claims that we strive to increase our power of acting and to prevent any decrease in our power of acting, he is claiming that we strive to bring about our own joy or what is good for us, and that we strive to prevent any sadness or evil from befalling us. This is evident from EIIIp28:

> We strive to further the occurrence of whatever we imagine will lead to Joy, and to avert or destroy what we imagine is contrary to it, or will lead to Sadness.

The notions discussed above underpin Spinoza's account of virtue. For Spinoza, a person's virtue is a function of his power of acting: the greater one's power of acting, the more virtuous he is. This is clear from EIVdef8:

> By virtue and power I understand the same things, that is . . . virtue, insofar as it is related to man, is the very essence, *or* nature, of man, insofar as he has the power of bringing about certain things, which can be understood through the laws of his nature alone.[8]

So far, we have seen two-way connections between virtue, the ability to do what is good for oneself and to prevent evil, and the power of acting. Bound up with all of these is the ability to have adequate ideas. For Spinoza, to the extent that we have adequate ideas, we are more active and to the extent that we have inadequate ideas, we are passive (EIIIp1). The reason Spinoza sees adequacy as bound up with activity in this way is part of a long and complicated story which I cannot go into here,[9] but the point to emphasize is this: Given the connection between adequacy and activity, and given the further connection between power of acting and virtue, it follows that a person's virtue is proportional to his ability to have adequate ideas.

Spinoza sometimes restricts the use of the term 'reason' to the capacity for having a certain kind of adequate idea—viz. adequate ideas of what he calls 'common properties' (EIIp40s2). But in Part IV he seems to be using the term 'reason' more broadly to cover adequate ideas in general (see especially EIVp27d). I will use the term 'reason' in this broader sense. According to this usage, we can see that the ability to reason goes along with the ability to have adequate ideas, and thus with the power of acting. Thus, drawing out the chain again, we can see that for Spinoza one's rationality or ability to reason is proportional to one's ability to have adequate ideas or to one's power of acting or to one's virtue. This is the way, then, in which virtue and reason are linked for Spinoza. A virtuous person will be a person highly capable of reasoning. Thus, Spinoza says:

> Acting absolutely from virtue is nothing else in us but acting, living, and preserving our being (these three signify the same thing) *by the guidance of reason* [*ex ductu rationis*], from the foundation of seeking one's own advantage. (EIVp24, my emphasis)

Spinoza holds not only that a virtuous person is rational, but also that one who seeks to be virtuous will seek to be rational and will seek the kind of understanding that is characterized by having adequate ideas. Spinoza's derivation of this latter claim (in EIVp26) is problematic.[10] The point to focus on, though, is that since an increase in understanding is bound up with an increase in activity, and since such an increase is good, an increase in understanding is therefore *also* a good. Further, it is a good that the virtuous person, qua virtuous, will recognize as a good. Since "[f]rom the laws of his own nature, everyone necessarily wants, or is repelled by, what he judges to be good or evil" (EIVp19), we can say that the virtuous person will seek the good of increased understanding.

It is important to note that in certain respects rationality and virtue are, within Spinoza's system, unattainable ideals for human beings. Since activity goes along with rationality and virtue, to be fully rational and virtuous (or, equivalently, to be such that one has only adequate ideas), one would have to be fully active and not subject to outside influences. But, as Spinoza emphasizes (EIVax and EIVp4), nothing within nature and, thus, no human being, is capable of such full activity. Such a status is reserved only for the one substance, God, and it is partly for this reason that Spinoza holds that all of God's ideas are adequate.[11]

It should now be clear what Spinoza means when he says in EIVp37 that a virtuous person will desire for others the good that he desires for himself. The good that a virtuous person desires for himself is increased understanding or increased exercise of reason. Thus, a virtuous person will desire that others possess the good of increased understanding or increased exercise of reason. He will, in effect, desire that others act in a way which best enhances the other persons' preservation and power, i.e., that they will act according to the guidance of reason. Now what a person desires, he will strive to bring about (EIIIp9s). Thus, a virtuous person will seek to bring it about that others be capable of understanding.

II

We can now see how Spinoza comes to include a concern for others in his ethical system. The question that immediately arises is: *why* should a rational person seek to make others more rational and virtuous? The reason stems from Spinoza's view that a rational person is beneficial to other people in general. By making another person more virtuous or rational, I am making her more beneficial to other people in general, including myself. It is for this reason that making her more rational is in my self-interest.

Fair enough, but this answer only generates another question: why are rational people advantageous to others? Spinoza has two very different answers to this question. The first answer is at work in EIVp35d and EIVp37d1 (which indirectly relies on EIVp35d), while the second answer appears in EIVp37d2. I will examine the first answer in this section and the second answer in the next.

At EIVp35d Spinoza says that a rational and virtuous person, like all others, aims at what he judges to be good. From the claims Spinoza relies on here,[12] it is clear that the good in question is what is good for the rational person himself. Since such a person is virtuous, he is active and thus acts on the basis of *adequate* ideas, which, for Spinoza, are all *true*.[13] Thus, what the virtuous person judges to be good (for himself) really is good (for himself).

So far this line of thought is clear; the next two steps, however, are dubious. Since a rational person does (or strives to do) what is in fact good for himself, that person does (or strives to do) what is good for human nature (this is the first dubious step). Thus he does (or strives to do) what is good for every single person (second dubious step). The steps in Spinoza's argument are apparent in this passage:

> [I]nsofar as men live according to the guidance of reason, they must do only those things which are good for human nature, and hence, for each man (EIVp35d).

In light of this interpretation, EIVp35d raises two questions:

(1) How does Spinoza get from the claim that a rational person does what is good for himself to the claim that he does what is good for human nature?

(2) How does Spinoza get from the claim that a rational person does what is good for human nature to the claim that he does what is good for each person?

In order to explain the steps Spinoza makes here, we must turn to EIVp31d. EIVp31 contains the claim that "[i]nsofar as a thing agrees with our nature, it is necessarily good." This claim, through its corollary, plays an important role in the overall proof of EIVp35. However, the interesting thing is how a certain conflation apparent in EIVp31d can help explain Spinoza's reasoning in that segment of EIVp35d that I have emphasized. In EIVp31d, Spinoza says that the claim that a thing does not act to preserve its nature is in conflict with the important claim from Part III: "Each thing, insofar as it is in itself, strives to persevere in its being" (EIIIp6).[14] When Spinoza says that each thing strives to persevere in its being, he means that each thing strives to preserve itself. This is clear from the glosses on the phrase "persevere in its being" which Spinoza gives in EIVp22, EIVp22c, EIVp26d and EIVp35c2. Thus, to persevere in one's being is to preserve oneself, and we can read EIIIp6 as saying that each thing strives to preserve itself. For Spinoza to see the claim that a thing fails to act to preserve its nature as directly in conflict with EIIIp6, he must be treating the nature of a thing as somehow equivalent to the thing itself. Spinoza here seems to be identifying or, perhaps, conflating a thing and its nature or essence.[15]

This identification is frequent in Spinoza. For example, in EIIp11 and EIIp13 Spinoza makes the point that what constitutes the human mind is nothing but a 'certain idea'. However, when Spinoza later discusses these propositions, he takes them as saying that what constitutes the *essence of* the human mind is nothing but a certain idea (see EIIIp3d, EIIIp9d, EIIIp10d). Consider also in this regard EIIp16c1, where Spinoza says that we perceive the nature of bodies external to our own. Immediately afterward and apparently in the same vein, he speaks of ideas of external bodies themselves (EIIp16c2).[16]

This conflation apparent in EIVp31d helps us begin to answer the two questions I raised earlier. The first was:

> (1) How does Spinoza get from the claim that a rational person does what is good for himself to the claim that he does what is good for human nature?

Given the conflation of an individual human being and his nature or essence, we can see how Spinoza might get from the claim that a rational person does what is good for himself to the claim that a rational person does what is good for his nature.

In order to answer our first question, we need to see how Spinoza gets from the claim that the rational person does what is good for his nature to the claim that he does what is good for human nature. We can see how Spinoza bridges this gap by noting that in EIVp35d he seems to consider human nature in general to be the nature of each human being. For Spinoza, a person who acts according to the guidance of reason will do what follows from the laws of his own nature (see EIIIdef2 and EIVp35c1). But in EIVp35d Spinoza seems to represent the rational person's acts as following from human nature. He says:

> [I]nsofar as men live according to the guidance of reason, they are said only to act (by IIIP3). Hence, whatever follows from human nature, insofar as it is defined by reason, must be understood through human nature alone (by IIID2), as through its proximate cause.

Here Spinoza shifts from talking about the activity of rational people to the acts that follow from human nature alone. But the acts of a rational person follow from his own nature alone. Thus, Spinoza seems to be equating the nature of an individual human being with human nature in general.

Given this further assimilation, we can now see how Spinoza gets from the claim that a rational person does what is good for *his* nature to the claim that he does what is good for *human* nature. If a rational person's nature simply *is* human nature, then in doing good for the former, he does good for the latter. So, putting it all together, we can say that in doing good for himself, the rational person does what is good for his nature, which, Spinoza seems to say is simply human nature. This account provides what is, I believe, a plausible answer to our first question.

We are now in a position to answer our second question as well:

> (2) How does Spinoza get from the claim that a rational person does what is good for human nature to the claim that he does what is good for each person?

In answering the first question, I noted first that in this section of the *Ethics* (and elsewhere) Spinoza seems to conflate a thing and its nature. I then applied the point that in EIVp35d Spinoza treats the nature of a particular human being as human nature in general. Now in order to answer the second question, we simply need to apply the same two points in the reverse order. Let us consider a rational person, *x*, and some other human being, *y*. As we have seen, *x* does what is good for human nature. Spinoza is, in this demonstration, comflating human nature with the nature of each individual human being. Thus, in particular, *y*'s nature is human nature in general. So, in doing good for human nature, *x* is, in particular, doing good for *y*'s nature. As has been emphasized, Spinoza often conflates a thing and its essence. Thus, *y*'s nature is somehow equivalent to *y* himself. So in doing what is good for *y*'s nature, *x* will be doing what is good for *y* himself. The same line of reasoning would apply to every other human being besides *y*, and so we reach the desired Spinozistic conclusion that a rational person will do what is good for each human being.

Here we can see how the usefulness of one rational person to others stems simply from the fact that all rational persons share the same essence. To explain the advantageousness to others, Spinoza does not appeal to any acts that the rational person will be inclined to perform specifically on behalf of others. Spinoza seems to be saying that whatever a rational person does for his own benefit will, merely by virtue of the overlap in essence, also be to the benefit of other human beings.[17]

Before turning to an evaluation of this argument, I would like to make a point about its scope that will be important later. The fact that, on Spinoza's view, rational people qua rational, *never* harm, and indeed *always* help others indicates that, for Spinoza,

131

the advantage provided by rational persons is not at all trivial. If Spinoza is right in claiming, for the reasons he gives in EIVp35d, that rational people are advantageous to others, then he is also entitled to claim that rational people are *highly* advantagous to others. In other words, the reason to be concerned for the welfare of others, which EIVp35d attempts to generate, is quite robust and not easily overridden. This helps us to understand Spinoza's claim in EIVp35c1: "There is no singular thing in nature which is more useful to man than a man who lives according to the guidance of reason."

We must now ask how good is Spinoza's argument in EIVp35d for the advantageousness of the rational person. The above interpretation of this argument gives a plausible account of the crucial part of the demonstration. Unfortunately, it also enables us to recognize, in a way that has not been done before, the precise character of what is wrong with Spinoza's reasoning. The two points driving Spinoza's argument—the claim that things are their essences and the claim that different human beings share the same nature or essence—conflict with one another. If x = the essence of x (where x is a human being) then the essence of x had better be unique. That is, it must be the case that the essence of x is not shared by another human being y. For if, in general, things are identical with their essences then, just as x = the essence of x so too y = the essence of y. But if x and y share the same essence then the essence of x = the essence of y. By the transitivity of identity it follows that $x = y$. Yet this conclusion contradicts the hypothesis that x is not identical to y, and that x and y are different human beings. So one cannot intelligibly maintain both that different human beings have the same essence or nature *and* that each human being is his or her essence. But this is precisely what Spinoza appears to be doing in EIVp35d.[18]

This mistake is not an isolated error on Spinoza's part. It reflects a deep tension in his metaphysics. The general point that the essence of a thing is simply that thing itself embodies a commitment to the uniqueness of essences—to the view that nothing shares its essence completely with another thing. For, as we have just seen, if one holds that distinct things share essences, then, on pain of contradiction, one cannot also hold that each of these distinct things is nothing but its essence. But, despite this commitment to the uniqueness of essences, Spinoza also expresses the opinion that, in many cases at least, distinct things do share essences. These conflicting commitments are pervasive in Spinoza.

What makes EIVp35d special and particularly interesting is that it is, perhaps, the only place where these two commitments collide head on, and where the conflict appears in a single strand of argument.

I want to illustrate briefly just how deep within Spinoza's metaphysics this conflict is. This will not only enable us to appreciate the character of Spinoza's first argument for the claim that rational people are beneficial to other people, but it will also illuminate the advantages of a different (but still Spinozistic) proof of this key claim.

A commitment to the uniqueness of essences emerges at various points in Spinoza's writings. The most telling occurrence is in his definition of that which pertains to the essence of a thing:

> I say that to the essence of any thing belongs that which, being given, the thing is necessarily posited and which, being taken away, the thing is necessarily taken away; or that without which the thing can neither be nor be conceived, and which can neither be nor be conceived without the thing. (EIIdef2)

Part of what Spinoza is saying here is that that which belongs to the essence of a thing cannot be without the thing. This indicates that, once the essence is given, the thing is given. If another thing could have the same essence, then, it seems, the essence could be given without the thing. But this would contradict the definition; therefore EIIdef2 indicates that essences are unique.[19] Spinoza's use of EIIdef2 in EIIp37d also yields this conclusion.[20]

Further evidence of Spinoza's commitment to the uniqueness of essences comes from the doctrine of *conatus* or striving—a topic closer to the main theme of this paper. Again, for Spinoza each thing strives to persevere in its being. This striving is simply the striving to preserve oneself. Thus, individual x strives to preserve x and individual y strives to preserve y. Since x and y are not identical it apparently follows that the *conatus* to preserve x is not identical to the *conatus* to preserve y. My conatus is not identical with your *conatus* simply because you and I are not identical. Of course, the *kinds* of things we strive for may be the same, but that only points to the qualitative similarity (or even qualitative identity) of your *conatus* and mine. It does not establish any numerical identity between your *conatus* and mine. But now recall that for Spinoza the striving or *conatus* of a thing is the essence of that thing (EIIIp7, cf. EIVp25d). Thus, the essence of x is the striving to preserve x and the essence of y is the striving to preserve y. Since the strivings in these cases are not identical, it follows that the essences of the two things are not identical. A similar conclusion would follow for any two objects. Thus we can say that Spinoza's *conatus* doctrine entails that no two things have the same essence, i.e., that essences are unique.[21]

Despite these manifestations of the view that essences are unique, Spinoza also seems to endorse the position that distinct things can share essences. Thus:

> The true definition of each thing neither involves nor expresses anything except the nature of the thing defined. From which it follows . . . that no definition involves or expresses any certain number of individuals, since it expresses nothing other than the nature of the thing defined. E.g., the definition of the triangle expresses nothing but the simple nature of the triangle, but not any certain number of triangles. (EIp8s2)

This passage certainly seems to allow a number of individuals to have the same nature or essence. Consider also this passage: "[Two men] can agree entirely according to their essence" (EIp17s).[22]

Thus, in some passages, Spinoza expresses a commitment to the uniqueness of essences and in other places he expresses a commitment to the opposite. The main problem with Spinoza's proof in EIVp35d of the claim that rational people are advantageous to others is that it expresses both commitments simultaneously. His failure to resolve this tension in his thinking about essences comes to a head in this important demonstration. Thus, Spinoza does not provide in EIVp35d an effective argument for the claim—crucial to his escape from a crude form of egoism—that rational people are advantageous to others. Is there a more successful argument for this claim to be found in Spinoza?

III

There is indeed such an argument—in EIVp37d2. This alternative argument has the advantage of *not* taking a stand on whether or not essences are unique. This is an advantage because no matter what stance one takes on this matter it will come into conflict with another of Spinoza's explicit claims.

The alternative argument does not rely upon the controversial claim that rational people share essences with other people but rather upon the much less controversial point that rational people are similar to other people. The claim here is that, qua human being, each human being is similar to other human beings and thus, in particular, that rational people are similar to other human beings. The fact that individuals are similar in this way carries no implications as to whether their essences do or do not completely overlap.

The notion of similarity among human beings is one that Spinoza relies on in this and other contexts. For our purposes, the most important of these other contexts concerns Spinoza's doctrine of the imitation of affects. Spinoza introduces the doctrine in EIIIp27:

> If we imagine a thing like us, toward which we have had no affect, to be affected with some affect, we are thereby affected with a like affect.

This imitation can arise in connection with each of the three main types of affect. When we feel sadness due to the sadness of another like us, what we feel is pity (EIIIp22s and EIIIp27s). When the imitation is "related to desire it is called emulation which, therefore, is nothing but the desire for a thing which is generated in us from the fact that we imagine others like us to have the same desire" (EIIIp27s). Spinoza admits that he knows no name for "the Joy that arises from another's good" (EIIIp22s). But, by whatever name, such joy would be another case of affect imitation.

The content of the imagining that Spinoza mentions in EIIIp27 can be construed in two ways:

(a) we imagine that a thing like us is affected with some affect

or:

(b) a thing is like us and we imagine that thing to be affected with some affect.

On the former reading, a key part of what we are imagining is that the object in question is similar to us. On the latter reading, this similarity need not be recognized. The former reading (where the indefinite description has, in effect, narrow as opposed to wide scope) seems preferable for both strategic and textual reasons. First a strategic reason: if we were to imitate the affects of things that are in fact similar to us regardless of whether we recognize them to be similar to us or not, then certain anomalies may occur. On this construal of EIIIp27, if x is a human being convincingly disguised as some non-human animal, for example, a bear, and x appears to y to be affected with some affect, then y will imitate that affect even though y does not regard x as a person and even though y does not in other cases imitate the affects of those things he takes to be bears. But whether y responds affectively in a certain way should not depend, it seems, on facts completely beyond y's ken—facts such as whether this object is indeed a human being, although it is convincingly disguised as a bear. Yet such an unacceptable dependence would be the case if we adopted the second (wide scope) reading of EIIIp27. This is the strategic reason for adopting the former (narrow scope) reading.

A textual reason for adopting this reading stems from Spinoza's views about a particular connection between affects. Spinoza believes that if we have an affect directed at a certain object x and if we regard y as similar to x then we feel the same affect toward y. In this case, Spinoza clearly says that the process involves 'perceived similarity'. Thus EIIIp16 says:

> From the mere fact that we imagine the thing to have some likeness to an object that usually affects the Mind with Joy or Sadness, we love it or hate it.

Given that this process involves 'perceived similarity' and not 'similarity *simpliciter*', it seems that Spinoza would also see the related process of affect imitation as involving perceived similarity and not 'similarity *simpliciter*'.[23]

Before showing how Spinoza's doctrine of imitation undergirds his alternative argument for a rational concern for others, we must note one further feature of that doctrine:

> If we imagine that someone loves, desires, or hates something we ourselves love, desire, or hate, we shall thereby love, desire, or hate it with greater constancy. (EIIIp31)

For Spinoza, affect imitation occurs not only when x's affect *engenders* a similar affect in y, but also when x's affect *strengthens* a similar affect in y. Affect strengthening plays a key role in EIVp37d2 as will be shown below.

Consider what the doctrine of imitation would entail about the effects a rational person would have on other people, at least on those who recognize their similarity to other rational persons. More particularly, the question is: what are the affects of a rational person that should thus be imitated by one who regards rational persons as similar? As Spinoza says in EIVp26 a rational person *desires* to understand, to have adequate ideas or, in other words, to be fully active. When this understanding is achieved the rational person will experience joy at the attainment of this good.

By focusing on the desire that a rational person has, we can present the alternative argument for the view that rational people are advantageous to others. According to the doctrine of the imitation of affects, a rational person, x, will inspire or confirm in another person, y, a similar desire to understand and be active.[24] It is certainly good for y that this desire be inspired or confirmed in her. This is because by desiring both understanding and activity, y will be pursuing her own interest most effectively. As we have seen, Spinoza sees understanding and the activity that goes with it to be good. Because of the recognized similarity between a rational person and others, the others will acquire the kind of desire that will most effectively lead to their own good (or at least they will be confirmed in this desire). For this reason, a rational person is advantageous to others. Thus, the doctrine of the imitation of affects provides an alternative Spinozistic proof of the claim that rational people are of benefit to other people.

To complete this case for Spinoza's enlightened egoism, we simply need to add the point that, since rational people are of benefit to others, it is in the interest of each person to induce or enhance rationality in others. Since a rational person is one who seeks to do that which is in his interest, a rational person will seek to induce or enhance rationality in others. The above argument is, I believe, simply an elaboration of EIVp37d2:

> The good which man wants for himself and loves, he will love more constantly if he sees that others love it . . . So . . . he will strive to have the others love the same thing. And because this good [viz., rational understanding] is common to all . . . and all can enjoy it, he will therefore . . . strive that all may enjoy it.

This argument would not apply to a human being who is steadfast in his desire for rationality, who has no need to have this desire confirmed. So it might seem as if there is an important gap in the argument for the claim that each human being has reason to promote the rationality of other human beings. However, there is really no gap here, for, on Spinoza's view, there could not be a human being of such steadfast rationality. As noted earlier, for Spinoza, each finite individual is subject to outside influences and therefore fails to be completely active and rational.[25] Thus, each human being has a need to strengthen his desire for rationality.

Like Spinoza's first argument, the argument in EIVp37d2 for a rational concern regarding other's rationality does not ground this interest in any good will (or lack of ill will) that rational others will bear to one another. Both arguments focus rather on a similarity between rational persons and others as the ground of the interest in the rationality of others. In EIVp37d2, it is to the extent that the rational others are (and are recognized to be) similar to one another that they confirm or create in one another the important desire for understanding and activity. The usefulness of the rational others lies not in their inclination to act on my behalf but simply in the example they set for me. Similarly, in Spinoza's first argument, rational persons are advantageous to one another simply because they are similar to one another; in fact they are similar to the degree they share the same nature or essence.

Thus, both proofs rely on some kind of similarity as the basis for generating interest in the rationality of others. But EIVp37d2 does not rely on either of the problematic pair of claims, i.e., that a thing is its essence and that distinct things can share the same essence, that undermine the argument at work in EIV35d and EIVp37d1. In part because it avoids this internal conflict, Spinoza's argument in EIVp37d2 is superior to the first argument for the view that it is rational to seek to promote the rationality of others.

IV

Although the argument in EIVp37d2 is superior, it is not without important problems. In this section, I will consider two such problems. First, the reason for concern for others that emerges at EIVp37d2 is rather thin and can easily be overridden. This makes it unclear whether or not Spinoza has really avoided a crude form of egoism. Second, Spinoza's argument (in EIIIp27d) for the doctrine of the imitation of affects has serious problems. These problems threaten to undermine EIVp37d2, which crucially invokes this doctrine. I will take up these difficulties in turn and conclude that although the second can be eased considerably, not so the first.

The first difficulty arises because Spinoza claims in EIVp37d2 that the rationality of others is beneficial to me because it will strengthen my own desire for understanding and activity. Thus, for Spinoza, I have a reason to promote the rationality of others. However, for all Spinoza says here, this reason may be relatively slight and often, if not always, outweighed by other, competing reasons. For example, my working to promote the rationality of others exacts a certain cost from me in time and effort. This cost may be greater than the benefit of my gaining a stronger desire to be active. Further, my increasing the rationality of others may be even more detrimental to me in certain cases, since by encouraging others to act on their own behalf, they may become more likely to monopolize the scarce resources I need for my own bene-fit.[26] Here again, the harm to me may well outweigh the benefit of my increased desire for activity.

There may, of course, be some cases in which my promotion of rationality in others is, overall, worthwhile to me, but there is nothing in Spinoza's argument in EIVp37d2 to guarantee that this is often or even ever the case. Thus, the rational concern for others that Spinoza derives from his doctrine of imitation is troublingly thin.[27] Perhaps there is a way to generate a more robust rational concern for others from the doctrine of imitation. Spinoza, how-ever, does not show how this can be done.

In this light, we can see that the first argument for a rational concern for others (the one at work in EIVp35d and EIVp37d1) aims for a stronger conclusion. As I noted, if that argument is cor-rect in showing that there is *some* reason to be concerned for the welfare of others, then it will also have shown that this reason is quite strong and not easily outweighed. This is because, according to that argument, rational people, qua rational, *never* harm and indeed *always* help others. This would generate a very strong rea-son to promote rationality in others, a reason much stronger, it seems, than the reason provided by Spinoza's application of the doctrine of imitation in EIVp37d2. Of course, as I explained, the earlier argument does not succeed in showing that there is any reason to be concerned with the welfare of others, and so, *a fortiori*, it does not show that there is a strong reason for this concern. My point, though, is that if the earlier argument works at all, it shows that the rational concern for others is quite robust. But this does not seem to be the case with EIVp37d2.

Let us turn to the second difficulty I mentioned at the begin-ning of this section. Here the outlook is considerably less bleak.

The problem arises from the fact that EIVp37d2 turns on the doctrine of imitation, yet the argument for this doctrine (in EIIIp27d) is unsuccessful. To show why, I will first analyze the demonstration. For Spinoza, when other bodies causally affect our body, we have an idea that represents that external body (EIIp16 and EIIp16c1). Spinoza claims that the idea that represents this external body involves the nature of our own body and of the external body as well. Spinoza goes on to say that if the external body is similar to our own and if the external body is affected in a certain way, "then the idea of the external body we imagine will involve an affection of our body like the affection of the external body" (EIIIp27d).[28] In other words, for Spinoza, our body will have an affection similar to that of the external body. In the particular case in which the affection of the external body is an affect, such as joy or sadness, our body will be affected by a similar affect. Thus, when the other individual (similar to us) has a certain affect (and its affect somehow acts on us), we will come to have a similar affect—we will imitate the other's affect.

This proof relies upon a notion of the involvement of the nature of a body in an idea. It is rather unclear what such an involvement amounts to.[29] But in order to see what is wrong with this demonstration, we do not need to unpack this notion. In evaluating Spinoza's proof, it is important to note that its main purpose is to show that when others are (or are perceived to be) similar to us and when we perceive them to have a certain type of affection, F, we become more like them in respect of this affection. The whole point of a doctrine of imitation is to show under what conditions one individual becomes more like a certain other individual.

Let's put this point together with the point that for Spinoza representation turns on a causal relation between my body and the represented object. These points together show that for Spinoza when x's being F acts on me (and thus when I represent x as being F) and when I myself am not F, I must become F or at least more F-like. Spinoza is implying here that a causal relation between my body (which antecedently is not F) and x's state of being F can occur only if my body comes to be in a more F-like state. But surely there is no reason to think this true. If I perceive someone to be bald when I have a full head of hair, I do not become more like the bald person in this respect than I was before. I do not shed a few hairs in sympathy.[30]

Causal influence of one object upon another does not require or bring about the kind of similarity that Spinoza has in mind here.

Spinoza does, of course, insist throughout the *Ethics* that causes and effects must have something in common.[31] In the relevant passages, though, he seems to be concerned simply with the anti-Cartesian point that no extended thing can interact with a thinking thing and vice versa. If the cause is extended, then the effect is extended, and if the cause is thinking then the effect is thinking. Nothing he says elsewhere in the *Ethics* would suggest that causes and effects must have the much higher degree of similarity that he apparently insists on in EIIIp27d.

I do not think that there is any way to make this demonstration succeed on its own terms. Nevertheless, we can find within Spinoza's system better support for the doctrine of imitation than that which EIIIp27d itself offers. Here we need to appeal to Spinoza's important doctrine of the association of ideas and other mental states within a single individual—a doctrine that plays an important role in the context of EIIIp27d, if not in the demonstration itself.

For Spinoza, the key to any kind of association of mental states lies in the following fact: if at a certain time I have two mental states, e.g., an idea of x and an idea of y, and if at a later time I again have an idea of x, I will at that later point come to have an idea of y as well. In general, if at one point two mental states occur together then, if at a later time I have one of the mental states, I will come to have the other as well.[32]

The doctrine of association plays a key role in a mechanism that may underlie affect imitation. Consider a case of the imitation of sadness. First note that what gives me the idea of another individual x as sad are her manifestations of sadness—perhaps her verbal expressions and other behavioral states. Let's say that in the past when I experienced sadness, I manifested pain in a way similar to that in which x is now manifesting pain. If so, the imitation of the affect of sadness might occur in the following way. In the past when I had the affect of sadness, I also had the idea of certain bodily manifestations of sadness. (In this case, the manifestations were those of my own body.) Given the doctrine of association, if I later come to have the idea of those manifestations or of similar ones, I will also come to have once again the affect of sadness. When I now see that x is sad, I see this by coming to have an idea of her bodily manifestations of sadness. Since these manifestations are similar to my own past manifestations of sadness, my idea of these manifestations will naturally give rise to an affect

141

of sadness. Thus the process of affect imitation would be complete. Similar accounts would cover the imitation of other affects.

Given this postulated mechanism for imitation we can understand why Spinoza restricts affect imitation to cases where the other individual is (or is perceived to be) similar to me. The bodily manifestations of pain or sadness in, say, a snake are quite unlike my own manifestations (and are perceived to be such). Thus the snake's affect of sadness will not tend to give rise in me to a corresponding affect of sadness. On the assumption that similar individuals manifest pain in similar ways, we can see why affect imitation occurs only between similar individuals (or individuals perceived to be similar).

This, I think, is a plausible way to account for affect imitation within the already established context of Spinoza's doctrine of association. I would, however, like to stress that Spinoza does not account for affect imitation in this way, nor does he emphasize, as I have, the bodily manifestations of pain in this context. I should also note that there are perhaps other ways of describing how the doctrine of association could explain affect imitation. But, to paraphrase what Spinoza says in a related context, even though there are other possible explanations, it is sufficient for me here to have given one potential explanation (EIIp17s). The fact that we can in a relatively natural way extend Spinoza's doctrine of association in order to account for the imitation of affects shows that the latter doctrine is more securely grounded in his system than the dubious proof of EIIIp27 would lead us to suspect.

V

Let us take stock. I have argued that Spinoza's first proof of the important claim that rational people are concerned with the welfare of others contains a deep conflict. But I have also shown how Spinoza's doctrine of the imitation of affects provides an alternative route to the same conclusion—a route that avoids this conflict. The fact that this alternative demonstration rests on the shaky ground of Spinoza's argument for the doctrine of imitation need not be seen as an irreparable defect. This is because independent Spinozistic support for this doctrine is available. A more serious defect in Spinoza's alternative argument is, as I have explained, that Spinoza seems to have no way to show that the doctrine of imitation provides a weighty or significant reason to be concerned with the welfare of others. Despite this failing, the alternative argument, by avoiding internal conflict, is superior to Spinoza's first argument.

I would like to close by pointing out a final advantage of the alternative proof. Unlike the first proof, the alternative proof highlights an important fact about human beings: we are incapable of being fully rational, of having only adequate ideas. Given such limitations, we can, perhaps, achieve a greater *degree* of rationality and virtue in our lives, but we can never reach complete rationality and virtue. Further, we must acknowledge that we may well have to rely on inadequate ideas even to reach a higher level of rationality and virtue. The alternative proof rightly emphasizes this fact because it relies on the doctrine of the imitation of affects. That doctrine is explicitly concerned with inadequate ideas: affective ideas are externally caused, i.e., caused from outside of the person whose ideas they are. Given Spinoza's account of adequacy, such ideas, therefore, count as inadequate.[33] The alternative proof, in effect, counsels us to exploit certain kinds of inadequate ideas (viz. the affective ideas gained through imitation) as a means for approaching the Spinozistic ideal of rationality and virtue. In light of the human limitations which Spinoza recognizes, we have no choice but to proceed in this way. The alternative argument, unlike the first argument, soberly acknowledges this important fact.

NOTES

1. See also EIVp20, EIVp22, and EIVp24.

2. For references and further discussion, see Edwin Curley, *Behind the Geometrical Method* (Princeton: Princeton University Press, 1988), Chap. 3.

3. On the connection between Hobbes and Spinoza, see Alexandre Matheron, *Individu et Communauté chez Spinoza* (Paris: Les Editions de Minuit, 1969), pp. 151-4.

4. See, e.g., EIVp35s: "Men . . . find from experience that by helping one another they can provide themselves much more easily with the things they require, and that only by joining forces can they avoid the dangers that threaten on all sides." See EIVp37s2 and Henry Allison, *Benedict de Spinoza: An Introduction* (New Haven: Yale University Press, 1987), p. 152.

5. Spinoza reaches this claim in EIIIp12d and EIIIp13d on the basis of his view that "Each thing, insofar as it is in itself, strives to persevere in its being" (EIIIp6). Relying on EIIIp6, Spinoza says in EIIIp12d that, if imagining certain things increases the mind's power of acting, then the mind strives to imagine those things. Elsewhere I argue that Spinoza's inference here from EIIIp6 is invalid. See Michael Della Rocca, "Spinoza's Metaphysical Psychology," in D. Garrett, ed., *The Cambridge Companion to Spinoza* (Cambridge: Cambridge University Press, 1996), sec. 1.

6. See EIIIdef.aff.2,3. In these definitions, Spinoza actually employs the term "perfection" instead of "power of acting." But, for him, these two notions are equivalent. See the explanation of EIIIdef.aff.3 and 4pref (GII 208-9).

7. See EIIIp39s, EIVdef1,2 and EIVp18d.

8. See EIVp23d.

9. See Michael Della Rocca, *Representation and the Mind-Body Problem in Spinoza* (New York: Oxford University Press, 1996), chap. 3.

10. See Jonathan Bennett, *A Study of Spinoza's Ethics* (Indianapolis: Hackett, 1984), pp. 304-5.

11. See EIIp32: "All ideas, insofar as they are related to God, are true." Spinoza regards truth and adequacy as coextensive (see, e.g., Letter 60), so we can say that all ideas are adequate insofar as they are related to God.

12. EIVp19 and, through this, EIVp18d and EIVdef1,2.

13. See note 11.

14. "Unaquaeque res, quantum in se est, in suo esse perseverare conatur." For the significance of the qualification "insofar as it is in itself" in EIIIp6, see Della Rocca, "Spinoza's Metaphysical

Psychology," section 1, and Don Garrett, "Spinoza's Conatus Argument," in John Biro and Olli Koistinen eds., *Spinoza: Metaphysical Themes* (Oxford: Oxford University Press, 2002).

15. Spinoza equates nature and essence in EIVdef8.

16. I believe that such a conflation of a thing and its essence is also behind Spinoza's tendency to identify a substance with its attribute or attributes. See, e.g., EIp4d, EIp10s, EIp14c2, EIp19, EIp20c2. Cf. Edwin Curley, "On Bennett's Interpretation of Spinoza's Monism," in Yirmiyahu Yovel, ed., *God and Nature—Spinoza's Metaphysics* (Leiden: E.J. Brill, 1991), vol. 1, pp. 35-51.

17. For a very different and intriguing interpretation of Spinoza's argument, see Diane Steinberg, "Spinoza's Ethical Doctrine and the Unity of Human Nature," *Journal of the History of Philosophy* 22 (1984), pp. 303-24. Steinberg seeks to avoid attributing to Spinoza the view, presupposed in my interpretation, that distinct human beings are distinct instances of human nature. On her interpretation, the only instance of human nature is mankind itself, a complex individual consisting of all human beings. I do not have the space here to do justice to this subtle interpretation. I simply want to note that Steinberg gives no satisfactory evidence for the view that Spinoza regards all of humanity as a single, complex individual. Steinberg does quote EIVp18s: "Man, I say, can wish for nothing more helpful to the preservation of his being than that all should so agree in all things that the minds and bodies of all would compose, as it were, one mind and one body; that all should strive together, as far as they can, to preserve their being; and that all, together, should seek for themselves the common advantage of all" (GII 223). However, this passage does not show that for Spinoza all human beings constitute a single individual, nor does it even show that for Spinoza all or even many human beings desire such unity. Spinoza is merely claiming that this unity would be a worthy object of desire. Evidence against Steinberg's interpretation comes from a sentence shortly before the passage just quoted. There Spinoza says, if "two individuals of entirely the same nature are joined to one another, they compose an individual twice as powerful as each one." The fact that this claim is a conditional indicates that Spinoza does not think that, in general, beings that have the same nature are joined together as an individual.

18. For a related point, see Bennett, *A Study of Spinoza's* Ethics, p. 302.

19. Both Bennett and Parkinson interpret EIIdef2 in this way. See Bennett, *A Study of Spinoza's* Ethics, p. 61; G.H.R Parkinson, "Being and Knowledge in Spinoza," in J.G. van der Bend, ed., *Spinoza on Knowing, Being and Freedom* (Assen: Van Gorcum, 1974), p. 29.

20. In this paragraph, I have adapted material from my *Representation and the Mind-Body Problem in Spinoza*, Chap. 5.

21. See Yirmiyahu Yovel, *Spinoza and Other Heretics*, vol. 1: *The Marrano of Reason* (Princeton: Princeton University Press, 1989), p. 163. Yovel

cites several passages from the *Short Treatise on God, Man and His Well-Being* that suggest the view that essences are unique. One should note that even if Spinozistic essences are unique they are not as fully packed as Leibnizian individual essences, which include all the properties a thing has. Spinoza clearly holds that not *all* properties of a thing are essential to it. See, e.g., EIIIp8 and EIIax1, after lemma 3 (GII 99:9-14).

22. A similar view is also present, though less explicitly, in the way in which Spinoza links the essence of a singular, changeable thing to the fixed and eternal things or laws of nature in TIE 101. The generality involved in these laws would seem to give rise to a corresponding generality in the essences of particular things—essences determined by these laws. See Curley's discussion of this passage in Edwin Curley, *Spinoza's Metaphysics* (Cambridge, MA: Harvard University Press, 1969), Chap. 2.

23. I consider several other problems in understanding Spinoza's doctrine of imitation in "Spinoza's Metaphysical Psychology," pp. 247-51. These need not be taken up here.

24. Again this holds only if *x* sees that *x* is similar to *y*.

25. Similarly, it might be said that for Spinoza no human being completely *fails* to be active and rational. All human beings have some causal powers (EIp36) and so are active to some degree. Further, they all have at least some adequate ideas (EIIp38, EIIp47). Thus, each human being experiences to some extent the joy of activity and understanding, and everyone, to a corresponding extent, *desires* understanding. (See EIIIp37 for the connection between joy and desire.) If this is correct then, for Spinoza, when a rational person seeks to promote rationality in others, it is always a matter of *confirming*, instead of *engendering*, rationality in those others.

26. See Bennett, *A Study of Spinoza's* Ethics, p. 301 and C.D. Broad, *Five Types of Ethical Theory* (London: Routledge and Kegan Paul, 1930), pp. 43-4.

27. A similar problem arises in Hume's moral philosophy. See Gerald Postema, "Hume's Reply to the Sensible Knave," *History of Philosophy Quarterly* 5 (1988), pp. 23-40, especially pp. 36-8.

28. Given the causal element in Spinoza's account of representation, this kind of involvement presumably occurs only when our body is affected not simply by the external body, but in particular by the relevant affection of the external body.

29. I have discussed this issue in *Representation and the Mind-Body Problem in Spinoza*, Chap. 5.

30. For this kind of criticism of EIIIp27d, see Bennett, *A Study of Spinoza's* Ethics, p. 281, Broad, *Five Types of Ethical Theory*, pp. 37-8. For a more favorable account, see Matheron, *Individu et Communauté chez Spinoza*, pp. 154-5.

31. See, e.g., EIp3 and EVpref.

32. In "Spinoza's Metaphysical Psychology," I show how this general view is at work in EIIp18d. This general claim holds, of course, only *ceteris paribus*. One would need to take into account here phenomena such as forgetting and confusion. See TIE 81-83.

33. Similar points apply to the doctrine of the association of mental states. See EIIp18s, where ideas are said to be associated in an order that is not that of the intellect.

The Affects as a Condition of Human Freedom in Spinoza's *Ethics*

Ursula Goldenbaum

The shock and the indignation that greeted Spinoza's *Ethics* at the time of its publication are hard to understand in our time. While Spinoza's philosophy has been accepted since the end of the eighteenth century, this acceptance came at the price of taking the edge off of its central anti-teleological program. Furthermore, this was accompanied by a kind of Christianization of his philosophy by the majority of its recipients. In this way, while Spinoza's system was integrated into the history of philosophy as one of the great systems,[1] its author was misinterpreted as a thinker who stood in the long tradition of those who sought ways to subordinate affects to reason, and who understood human freedom as the freedom from affects, i.e., as the reign of reason over affects.[2] Contrary to this, the achievement of Spinoza was, in my opinion, to show that human action is always and necessarily determined by affects. Even the free man's acts are caused by affects—albeit affects that are actions rather than passions. Because of this it cannot have been the concern of Spinoza to provide a program for subordinating affects to reason in general, but rather to provide a program for optimizing affects so as to find out the possibilities of human freedom, virtue, and happiness.

At first glance, it looks well in line with tradition when Spinoza announces in the Preface to Part IV of the *Ethics* that he wants to investigate the cause of human bondage, i.e., the inability to master and restrain the affects, and to further examine the good and evil of the affects. When he says that because of its bondage the human being, "though he sees the better for himself, he is still forced to follow the worse" (EIVpref, GII 205:11-12), it seems to be only a new variation on the struggle of reason against the affects. The attempt to sharply distinguish affects from reason, and the conception of the human being as a mean between God and animals, etc., are typical signs, be they in ancient philosophy or modern anthropology, of such an attitude.[3] Examining the aims of Spinoza's *Ethics*, one finds much that corresponds with the history of mainstream ethical theory. We find happiness in the cognition of God, we find that cognition itself leads us to freedom and happiness, good affects lead us to friendship, to harmony in a commonwealth, and to more and more cognition. Meanwhile, bad affects will divert us from cognition and lead us into conflicts with people and thus conflicts within the commonwealth.[4] In particular, the great significance of cognition, and the rules for the practice of mastering and restraining the affects clearly show us a real correspondence between Spinoza and the tradition, as correctly pointed out by past readers.

Yet, in a way different than Descartes, Spinoza was aware of his being in accord with the tradition regarding the aforementioned points, and did not consider this accordance to be accidental. It is to be expected that people, through experience, would have long known how to deal with the passions (EVpref, GII 280:23-25)—though they might not always put that knowledge to use. Spinoza not only explicitly appreciated all of the wise men, "who have written many admirable things about the right way of living, and given men advice full of prudence" (EIIIpref), but also considers himself much indebted to their works and efforts.

Nevertheless, in the Preface to Part IV of the *Ethics*, Spinoza promises to outline something new, which previously had been insufficiently investigated. His contemporaries also understood it to be new—indeed, to be too new, to be a revolution in moral thinking.[5] This new approach was to base an ethics upon a general theory of affects; that is, not only upon human passions, but upon all of the affects in nature. This general theory of affects specifies their powers, their origins, and their modes of functioning in the whole of nature. With Spinoza, the notion of affect itself acquires a new content that, when compared to that of the human passions, has a constitutive significance for Spinoza's whole system. "But no one," he says, "has determined the nature and the powers of the Affects, nor what, on the other hand, the Mind can do to moderate them" (EIIIpref). Spinoza sees the reason for this theoretical insufficiency in the fact that philosophers did not seek the causes of powerlessness and instability in the common forces of nature, but rather in "I know not what vice of human nature, which they therefore bewail, or laugh at, or disdain, or (as usually happens) curse" (ibid.). These philosophers, who have

> written about the Affects, and men's way of living, seem to treat, not of natural things, which follow the common laws of nature, but of things which are outside nature. Indeed they

> seem to conceive man in nature as a dominion within a
> dominion [*imperium in imperio*]. (ibid.)

This conclusion is the consequence of the view that human beings have an absolute freedom, that man "has absolute power over his actions, and that he is determined only by himself" (ibid.).

It is this anthropomorphic position that is the main subject of Spinoza's criticism. Against this position, Spinoza offers his anti-teleological program of a general theory of affects and of an ethics based on this general theory. The human being is, like all other individuals, necessarily a part of nature. Both the body and soul of the individual human being depend upon other things and individuals in nature. At the same time, the human being is *potentia agendi et patiendi*, and so it cannot always be the adequate cause of effects, but must also necessarily be passive. For Spinoza, this integration within the common forces of nature is, in principle, the cause of human bondage, an inevitable incapacity to master and restrain the affects. And this, above all, is the subject of Part IV of the *Ethics*. Yovel calls Spinoza's philosophy a philosophy of immanence:

> This principle views this-worldly existence as the only actual being, and the unique source of ethical value and political authority. All being is this-worldly and there is nothing beyond it, neither a personal creator-God who imposes His divine will on man, nor supernatural powers or values of any kind. The laws of morality and politics, too, and even religion, stem from this world by the natural power of reason; and recognizing this is a prelude and precondition for human emancipation.[6]

The scandal caused by the *Ethics* was a result of just this principle of immanence. This principle seems to require the notion of human slavery, i.e., of the impossibility of escaping nature, and one's relations with other natural individuals, so as to acquire absolute freedom (see EIVp4). But Part IV of the *Ethics* also deals with the possibility of human freedom—a limited freedom, yet one that can be increased. This aspect of Part IV is often overlooked in the treatment of Spinoza's notion of freedom, because of its title, "Of Human Bondage." However, only the first eighteen propositions deal with the causes of human slavery. By the sixty-sixth proposition Spinoza has pointed out the way to freedom, a freedom within the limits of the human being as a part of the common forces of nature.

In addition to the principle of striving for self-preservation, the general principles of Spinoza's explanation of a (limited) human freedom are: 1) the division of affects into passions and actions; 2) the differentiation of affects according to their origin in the transition from greater or lesser perfection; and 3) the notion of perfection itself.

Actions are affects of which the individual is the adequate cause, i.e., the individual determines the effect. Passions are those affects of which the individual is only a partial, hence inadequate cause, and the effect thus depends more on other natural causes. Because every individual as a part of nature also partakes of its power to act, of its *potentia agendi*, every individual is able to act. But insofar as individuals are a part of nature, they are also acted upon. The essence of natural individuals is therefore *potentia agendi et patiendi*. In every operation of self-preservation this *potentia agendi et patiendi* will be kept or even increased, or in the case of failure, reduced or destroyed. Spinoza calls this increase or reduction a transition to greater or lesser perfection (EIVpref, GII 208-9).

The striving for self-preservation and the transition to greater or lesser perfection find its expression in affects that Spinoza reduces to three general types; desire (the striving for self-preservation with self-consciousness), joy, and pain. With Spinoza, all affects of desire and joy are good in principle because they are expressions of an increased power of acting and of increased perfection. The fact that all affects of desire and joy are good in principle (including the passions of joy and desire)[7] is often overlooked, although it is of great importance for Spinoza's anti-normativistic ethics.

Because of the importance of an anti-teleological understanding of perfection, already defined in Part II of the *Ethics*, Spinoza dwells at length on this topic at the beginning of Part IV, stressing above all that there is no absolute perfection for the individual. Perfection is nothing other than reality itself (EIIdef6). We can recognize different degrees of perfection only as the result of comparing either different states of a single individual at different times or comparing different individuals regarding their *potentia agendi et patiendi*. In the same way, Spinoza explains his view of good and bad: "they also indicate nothing positive in things, considered in themselves, nor are they anything other than modes of thinking, *or* notions we form because we compare things to one another" (EIVpref, GII 208:7-11).

Starting from these theoretical foundations, i.e., from the total immanence of human beings in nature, Spinoza develops his ethical program in Part IV, pointing out the possibilities for acquiring human freedom, virtue, and happiness. In spite of the previously mentioned agreement between Spinoza and the tradition on various particular ethical values, the fact that Spinoza, in the spirit of immanence, founds his ethics on the general theory of affects has far-reaching consequences for the contents of his ethics. In particular, it has a consequence for the method of determining human ethical values.[8] Thus, within Spinoza's ethics, sensuality and the body are viewed positively and become serious subjects of scientific and philosophical investigation. The principle of immanence, i.e., the renunciation of every non-natural principle of explanation, involves an unceasing examination of the human being in its relation to other individuals, as well as of the series of his/her own internal states.

Below, I will call attention to the following continuities in Spinoza's theory of affects, which provide a possible transition from passions to actions, and thus to freedom, virtue, and happiness: 1) the gradual continuity from the animal to the human being; 2) the continuity of body and soul based on their substantial identity;[9] and 3) the continuity of passive and active affects.

1) The general principles of Spinoza's theory of affects—i.e., everything that concerns perfection, the striving for self-preservation, and the relation of body and soul—are valid for all individuals in nature. Animals can be spoken of differently with regard to joy and pain but, insofar as they are all subject to the natural law of *conatus*, and, striving for self-preservation, achieve greater or lesser perfection, they must also be understood as active and passive with regard to the affects. The difference between animals and human beings lies only in the lesser complexity of animal bodies and, consequently, in a lesser capacity for affecting or being affected by other individuals, and so in a smaller power of thinking.

Although Spinoza wrote his *Ethics* for human beings, the principles on which it is based are taken from his general theory of affects, which itself relies upon his conception of the whole of nature in which all individuals constantly affect and are affected by other individuals. This view is the opposite of Descartes', who denies that animals have sensations at all. This, because Descartes

153

needs to postulate a general difference between body and soul as a premise in his argument for the immortality of the human soul.[10] In opposition to this, Spinoza understands the difference between animals and human beings as only a gradual and continuous one. This is confirmed by Spinoza's view that all individuals in the world are "animata."[11]

2) Another case of continuity concerns the affections of the body and the ideas of these affections in the soul. This follows from Spinoza's view of the substantial identity of the body and soul and from his definition of affects as "affections of the Body by which the Body's power of acting is increased or diminished, aided or restrained, and at the same time, the ideas of these affections" (EIIIdef3). Spinoza does not admit of any break between affects that only concern the body and affects that only concern the soul. This is another basic difference between Spinoza and the tradition.[12] This means that in the soul there are ideas of all the affections of the body—passions as well as actions—and vice versa. Therefore, the affects of the soul cannot be better than the affects of the body.

One significant consequence of this view is that the body is rendered completely innocent, or rather it is liberated from sin. The affections of the body, like their ideas in the soul, can be both passions and actions, as can the ideas of these affections in the soul. In Part IV of the *Ethics*, body and sensuality receive a moral justification and, as such, become serious subjects of philosophical attention. Spinoza clearly intends exactly this in the following passage (often quoted by his detractors):

> The Affects, therefore, of hate, anger, envy, etc., considered in themselves, follow from the same necessity and force of nature as the other singular things. And therefore they acknowledge certain causes, through which they are understood, and have certain properties, *as worthy of our knowledge* as the properties of any other thing, by the mere contemplation of which we are pleased. Therefore, I shall treat the nature and the powers of the Affects, and the power of the Mind over them, by the same Method by which, in the preceding parts, I treated God and the Mind, and I shall consider human actions and appetites just as if it were a Question of lines, planes, and bodies. (EIIpref; my emphasis)

Because of the principle of immanence, i.e., the integration of the human being into the common forces of nature, man is not only a very needy being, because of the highly complex composition of his body and soul, but also (and perhaps because of this) a being with many affections caused by many individuals. These affections provide individuals with more occasions and causes for thought and for the formation of adequate ideas: "The more the Body is rendered capable of these things [affecting and being affected], the more the Mind is rendered capable of perceiving" (EIVp38d). Therefore the body, and in particular its well-being and highest possible perfection, are the conditions for the perfection of our soul. As such, the body deserves good care:

> The principal advantage which we derive from things outside us—apart from the experience and knowledge we acquire from observing them and changing them from one form into another—lies in the preservation of our body. That is why those things are most useful to us which can feed and maintain it, so that all its parts can perform its function properly. (EIVapp XXVII)

Furthermore, by no means is the body to be supplied only with what is absolutely necessary:

> Indeed, the human Body is composed of a great many parts of different natures, which require continuous and varied food so that the whole Body may be equally capable of doing everything which can follow from its nature, and consequently, so that the Mind may also be equally capable of conceiving many things. (ibid.)

Physical wellbeing and its increased perfection are for Spinoza the preconditions of an individual's increased capability for being affected and of affecting, and therefore of thinking.

The wellbeing of the body, the power of affecting and of being affected, is thus the basis for increased perfection, which finally allows one to attain freedom, virtue, and happiness. The perfection of the body expresses itself in the affects of joy and desire. The path to freedom and virtue cannot be found through renunciation *via* the diminution of sensual joy and joy in general, but only through the optimization of joy. The constant increase of pleasure and joy is the means to achieve freedom, virtue, and happiness. In this sense should we understand Spinoza's justification of sensual pleasure in *Ethics* IV, not accidentally stated on the occasion of a defense of laughter:

Nothing forbids our pleasure except a savage and sad superstition. For why is it more proper to relieve our hunger and thirst than to rid ourselves of melancholy? My account of the matter, the view I have arrived at, is this: no deity, nor anyone else, unless he is envious, takes pleasure in my lack of power and my misfortune; nor does he ascribe to virtue our tears, sighs, fear, and other things of that kind, which are signs of a weak mind. On the contrary, the greater the Joy with which we are affected, the greater the perfection to which we pass, i.e., the more we must participate in the divine nature. To use things, therefore, and take pleasure in them as far as possible—not, of course, to the point where we are disgusted with them, for there is no pleasure in that—this is the part of the wise man. It is the part of the wise man, I say, to refresh and restore himself in moderation with pleasant food and drink, with scents, with the beauty of green plants, with decoration, music, sports, the theater, and other things of this kind, which anyone can use without injury to another. (EIVp45c2s)

The more perfection we attain—hence the more we participate in the nature of God—the more pleasure we enjoy. There is no pleasure that does not concern both body and soul simultaneously since there is no break between the two. Of every affection of pleasure in the body, be it passion or action, there is an idea in the soul, and to every emotion in the soul there corresponds an affection of the body. Relying on these findings, Spinoza works out a strategy for gaining ever-greater perfection, freedom and virtue by optimizing the affects. This rehabilitation of body and sensuality is directed not only against the tradition of anti-sensual ethics, with its concomitant contempt of the body, but also against an attitude in libertinism, which sees the only pleasures as sensual ones, precluding the participation of the soul. This latter view is, in fact, only the other side of the traditional understanding, i.e., only a kind of reversal of Christian ethical values. Thus, for example, Sade does not renounce the notion of sin in his arguments for libertinism.[13]

When an individual, in its necessary striving for self-preservation, achieves a greater perfection and is thus affected by pleasure, it also gains a greater power of acting and of suffering, of affecting and of being affected, of thinking and of knowing. The more an individual's striving for self-preservation is realized, the richer are its affects, and thus, the more it is able to know. Therefore "it should be noted that in ordering our thoughts and images, we must always . . . attend to those things which are good in each thing so that in this way we are always determined to acting from an affect of Joy" (EVp10s). It is impossible to renounce a pleasure that is a passion solely through rationality. This can only happen through a greater affect of pleasure, which is an action. The consequence for Spinoza is that "nor do we enjoy it [blessedness] because we restrain our lusts; on the contrary, because we enjoy it, we are able to restrain them" (EVp42).

This rehabilitation of sensuality and of the body in Spinoza's theory of affects has deep significance for his ethics, an ethics formulated in opposition to traditional ethics. Before and after Spinoza, the body and sensuality are considered to be the cause of bad passions and the opposite of freedom. Only in eighteenth century aesthetics[14] and nineteenth century psychology was Spinoza's account of sensuality and of the body taken up.[15]

3) The third continuity is Spinoza's view of actions and passions as affects in general. Whereas in the *Short Treatise on God, Man and His Well-Being* Spinoza still speaks only about '*lijdings*' or 'passions' (GII 56) in the *Ethics* the new notion of affect as the genus of the two species of affect, namely, action and passion, is introduced. The introduction of this notion indicates Spinoza's new view, which no longer accepts an absolute difference between human operations based on inadequate ideas and others based on adequate ones. They are rather to be recognized in their continuity. Passions, like actions, are affects—affections of the body and the ideas of them in the soul—and both are expressions of the striving for self-preservation, and of the resulting transition to more or less perfection. Both concern the body as well as the soul. The difference between passions and actions is that the latter, qua adequate causes, better enhance an agent's self-preservation. As a result, painful affects, as expressions of unrealized striving for self-preservation, can only be passions. The affects of desire and of pleasure, on the other hand, as expressions of a realized striving for self-preservation, can be a result of operating from an inadequate as well as from an adequate cause. As such, they can be passions or actions.

I think we can understand this by its analogy to Spinoza's view of inadequate and adequate ideas. In an inadequate idea there is nothing that is positively false; similarly, no passions are, in themselves or in their entire nature, bad or wrong. Only with an eye toward the possible betterment of affects in an individual—in terms of his striving for self-preservation—can we find anything bad in passions. Inadequate ideas are, in Spinoza's view, not only defective and representative of the lowest kind of knowledge, they are, at the same time, indispensable for gaining new ideas. Inadequate ideas are the result of the affections of an individual caused by other individuals, and without these affections we cannot gain any new ideas. The more affections we have the more possibilities we gain for cognition.[16] Our integration in the whole of nature, in a great number of affection-causing relations with other individuals, is thus not only a defect, but also a chance to be in relation with more and more individuals, and thus, with the whole of nature and with God. This is especially evident in light of the following:

> Again . . . it follows that we can never bring it about that we require nothing outside ourselves to preserve our being, nor that we live without having dealings with things outside us. Moreover, if we consider our Mind, our intellect would of course be more imperfect if the Mind were alone and did not understand anything except itself. (EIVp18s)

The possibility of relationships with many other individuals, of affecting them and of being affected by them, is the other side of the neediness and of the finiteness of the human being. The human being not only depends on other things, but he can, by a richness of relations with other individuals in nature, also secure the preconditions necessary for him to be in relation with the whole of nature. In this way, the human being exceeds his individual finiteness and so forms adequate ideas.

Konrad Hecker shows this aspect in an outstanding way when he writes that the essence of any individual implies a determinate reference not only to other entities as alternative forms of the structure of the infinite entirety in general, but also to the other entities as those particular forces that stand in a determinate correlation with the individual. Since the relationship is valid in both directions, the correlation can be understood in two ways: 1) the other entities/forces represent the almost infinite power that the individual is lacking for its existence; 2) the other entities/forces lack the power of this individual and hence they lack the absolute complete power that yields the existence of the whole.[17] Thus, it is fully consistent when Spinoza says that the more we are able to know singular things the more we are able to know God (EVp24).

What has been said here about the continuities of inadequate and adequate ideas is also valid for the relation of passions and actions. Spinoza considers the affects that are passions to be a kind of striving for self-preservation that we depend on at all times and that can be considered bad only in the sense that we can have better affects. Of course, there are many passages in the *Ethics* where Spinoza evaluates human passions in a very negative way. But this evaluation only occurs where the passions are compared with the greater possibilities of action in the individual. Therefore affects, including passions, are the basic condition for any individual striving for things necessary for his self-preservation: "For each one governs everything from his affect; those who are torn by contrary affects do not know what they want, and those who are not moved by any affect are very easily driven here and there" (EIIIp2s, GII 143:34-144:2). All affects, passions as well as actions, are the precondition of life, the expression of a more or less perfect self-determination. Even the passions come into being as expressions of the striving to preserve one's own existence. All affects are thus the condition for the heightening of perfection toward freedom, virtue, and happiness. Although passions are not able to lead us there, they are, especially as affects of pleasure and desire, the first steps on the way, the first increase of the perfection of an individual. Passions would be "of no use if men could be guided by reason" (EIVp59s). But that is plainly an illusion. This interpretation of the significance of the passions in Spinoza's theory of affects is confirmed by Spinoza's view of suicide, which he equates with the death of even the smallest passion of the individual, of every kind of striving for self-preservation (see EIVp20s).

It is just this continuity between passions and actions that is the basis for Spinoza's explanation of how an individual can pass from one to the other. Just as, at first, inadequate ideas are the only material for forming adequate ideas, so the passions are the only material for forming actions, since they are not of a different kind altogether. To make the transition from passions to actions we do not have to exceed the limits of our nature at all; we still remain part of the common forces of nature. But the possibility of action lies in the powers of the affects themselves. "No affect can be restrained by the true knowledge of good and evil insofar as it is true, but only insofar as it is considered an affect" (EIVp14). The affects of pleasure—coming into being by a passage to a greater perfection—both as passions and as actions, play an especially significant role in Spinoza's strategy of acquiring freedom and virtue:

> So if a man affected with Joy were led to such a great perfection that he conceived himself and his actions adequately, he would be capable—indeed more capable—of the same

actions to which he is now determined from affects which are passions.

> But all affects are related to Joy, Sadness, or Desire . . . and Desire . . . is nothing but the striving to act itself. Therefore, to every action to which we are determined from an affect which is a passion, we can be led by reason alone, without the affect, q.e.d. (EIVp59d)

Consequently, the essence of Spinoza's strategy is a non-teleological principle of perfection.[18] What enables individuals to become more perfect is the power of preservation and the striving for self-maintenance. Therefore, the affects as a whole, including the passions, are for Spinoza's ethical strategy the precondition and the means for the increase of perfection toward freedom and virtue.

The other side of this view consists in the understanding of the human being as a being that is constantly being affected. The free man, too, is determined to act by affects that correspond with adequate ideas, with reason. This is confirmed by Spinoza's notion of intuitive cognition, a notion connected with adequate ideas on the one hand, yet also connected with an affect of pleasure on the other. This pleasure that comes into being by the third kind of cognition is connected at the same time with the affect of love, whose object is God. For "*Love is* nothing but *Joy with the accompanying idea of an external cause*" (EIIIp13s), and "from this kind of knowledge there arises the greatest satisfaction of Mind there can be . . . Joy; this Joy is accompanied by the idea of oneself, and consequently . . . it is also accompanied by the idea of God as its cause" (EVp32d). Because we can enjoy greater pleasure in the state of freedom and of intuitive cognition than we can in passions, we can master these passions (EVp42).

Already in Part IV of the *Ethics* Spinoza meets the challenge of showing how individuals can achieve freedom, virtue, and happiness. Furthermore, Spinoza meets this challenge while maintaining his view of immanence and thus, without exceeding the limits of nature. It is a conception of the immanence of all things (including human beings) in the whole of nature—which implies continuity between animals and human beings, between body and soul, and between passions and actions. It is in nature thus conceived that we can become more and more perfect, and more and more affected by actions instead of passions. And, notwithstanding the passages in Part V of the *Ethics* concerning the existence of the human soul without its body and the notion of an absolute perfection, which apparently contrast with this view, in Part V

Spinoza still explicitly confirms the view of Part IV. For in EVp41 he maintains that:

> Even if we did not know that our Mind is eternal, we would still regard as of the first importance Morality, Religion, and absolutely all the things we have shown (in Part IV) to be related to Tenacity and Nobility.

> Dem.: The first and only foundation of virtue, or of the method of living rightly . . . is the seeking of our own advantage. But to determine what reason prescribes as useful, we took no account of the eternity of the Mind, which we only came to know in the Fifth Part. Therefore, though we did not know then that the Mind is eternal, we still regarded as of the first importance the things we showed to be related to Tenacity and Nobility.

NOTES

1. See Manfred Walther's introduction to his "Spinoza als Kritiker der Neuzeit? Bestimmungen der Aktualität Spinozas in der neueren Literatur," *Philosophische Rundschau* 28 (1981), p. 274.

2. Above all, the works of Dilthey are exemplary for this view of Spinoza's *Ethics*. He even claims "that the whole of Spinoza's actual ethics, the aim of his work, is based on the Stoa" (Wilhelm Dilthey, "Die Autonomie des Denkens, der konstruktive Rationalismus und der pantheistische Monismus nach ihrem Zusammenhang im 17. Jahrhundert," in *Gesammelte Schriften*, vol. 2, *Weltanschauung und Analyse des Menschen seit Renaissance und Reformation. Abhandlungen zur Geschichte der Philosophie und Religion* [3rd edition, Leipzig & Berlin: Teubner, 1923], p. 285). Regarding Spinoza's theory of affects Gertrud Jung even holds the opinion that it seems to be "a foreign body artificially implanted" in his system, and thus its origin is to be sought outside his system in the history of the theory of affects. See G. Jung, "Die Affektenlehre Spinozas," *Kant-Studien* 32 (1927), p. 137.

3. For example, Aristotle remarks: "A further confirmation is that the lower animals cannot partake of happiness, because they are completely devoid of the contemplative activity. The whole of the life of the Gods is blessed, and that of man is in so far as it contains some likeness to the divine activity; but none of the other animals possess happiness, because they are entirely incapable of contemplation" (Aristotle, *Nicomachean Ethics*, trans. H. Rackham, in Aristotle, *Works*, Loeb Classical Library [London: William Heineman, 1982], Book 10, vol. 19, pp. 623-5). On the history of the view of the human being in the position between animals and God, from ancient philosophy to modern anthropology, see Kuno Lorenz, *Einführung in die Philosophische Anthropologie* (Darmstadt: Wissenschaftliche Buchgesellschaft, 1992), pp. 21-49.

4. The consonance of Spinoza with the tradition in many singular ethical values, especially with Christianity, was used by the editors of Spinoza's *Opera posthuma* for his justification. See the *Praefatio* to *B.d.S.: Opera posthuma*, eds. Jarig Jelles and Jan Rieuwertsz (Amsterdam: Rieuwertsz, 1677), p. 17.

5. Blyenbergh's letters to Spinoza impressively document the spirit of the time insofar as he takes himself to be an unprejudiced man:

> So I can only suppose that if man is such as you describe him, the ungodly by their actions serve God as much as do the godly by their actions, and so we are made as dependent on God as the elements, plants and stones, etc. Of what use then, is our understanding? Of what use our power of keeping our will within the limits of our understanding? Why is this order impressed upon us?
>
> And see too, on the other side, of what we deprive ourselves, namely anxious and earnest considerations to make ourselves perfect accord-

ing to the law of God's perfection, and according to the order which He has impressed on us to make ourselves perfect. We deprive ourselves of prayer and sighing to God, from which we have so often felt that we derive an extraordinary increase of strength. We deprive ourselves of all religion, and of all the hopes and all the joys which we expect from prayers and religion.

For, surely, if God has no knowledge of evil, it is still less credible that He should punish evil. What reasons are there, then, why I should not eagerly commit all villainies (if only I can escape the condemnation of the judge)? Why not enrich myself by horrible means? Why not do whatever pleases us indiscriminately, and whatever the flesh prompts us to do?" (Letter XX from William Van Blyenbergh, January 16, 1665, p. 162)

With Leibniz the question of an absolute perfection and of an absolute good is of important significance for the argumentation of the freedom of God, and so in many passages he criticizes the position of Hobbes and Spinoza as an arbitrary view. See, e.g., his self-published essay about the principle of continuity: "Principium quoddam generale . . ." in G.W. Leibniz, *Gesammelte Werke*, vol. 3, *Mathematik*, ed. C.I. Gerhardt (Hildesheim: Olms, 1860), vol. 6, p. 134.

6. Y. Yovel, *Spinoza and other Heretics: The Adventures of Immanence* (Princeton: Princeton University Press, 1989), p. ix.

7. Thus, e.g., Birnbacher's very interesting article about Spinoza's view of remorse, in his study of Spinoza's theory of affects, overlooks the passions of pleasure and desire. See Dieter Birnbacher, "Spinoza und die Reue," *Zeitschrift für Philosophische Forschung* 38:2 (1984), p. 226.

8. See note 6.

9. "In deducing the other affects from the three main affects Spinoza gives almost exclusive attention to the passions of the mind/soul and to the connections among them (although they are connected '*a priori*' with the passions of the body). He gives almost no definitions of any passions of body and mind together, or of body alone. Therefore he tries to neglect certain body-like phenomena which [usually] have been dealt with within the field of affectivity—phenomena such as trembling, turning pale, sobbing, laughing, and so on—because they concern only the body, without any connection with the soul" (Herman de Dijn, "Inleiding tot de Affectleer van Spinoza," *Tijdschrift foor Filozofie* 39:3 [1977], p. 404).

10. The complete title of Descartes' *Meditations* reads as follows: "Meditations on First Philosophy, in which are demonstrated the existence of God and the distinction between the human soul and the body" ("Meditationes de prima philosophia, in quibus Dei existentia, et Animae humanae a corpore distinctio, demonstratur"). In his "Preface to the Reader," Descartes explains the significance of this difference between body and soul by pointing out that it provides a possibility of hope for another life, for the destruction of the

body is without consequence for the soul. (See Descartes, *Meditations*, in *The Philosophical Writings of Descartes*, trans. J. Cottingham, R. Stoothoff, and D. Murdoch [Cambridge: Cambridge University Press, 1984], vol. 2.)

11. See: EIIIp57s, EIVp37s1 (GII 237:7-11).

12. Aristotle takes all those pleasures to be worse than others "which man shares with the lower animals," but above all "pleasures of touch and taste." See Aristotle, *Nicomachean Ethics*, Book 3, p. 177. Descartes, who still believed in the doctrine of animal spririts, also assigned the affects to the soul or to the body, depending on their origins. See Descartes, *Passions of the Soul*, in *The Philosophical Writings of Descartes* (Cambridge: Cambridge University Press, 1985), vol. 1, art. 25, 212, pp. 337-8, 404.

13. Cf. László F. Földényi, "Der Tod und die Marionette," in D.A.F. de Sade, *Justine und Juliette*, eds. S. Zweifel and M. Pfister (Munich: Matthews & Seitz, 1990), vol. 1, p. 291.

14. In eighteenth century Germany, even the Wolffian philosopher Baumgarten, in his aesthetic theory, still had great problems justifying his intention of investigating sensuality with regard to its cognitive capacities. "On the one hand you ran the risk of being criticized because of vanity and foolishness; on the other hand the subject of observation was judged inferior and considered unworthy of science and philosophy. Therefore Baumgarten offers excuses for his bold action and has to some degree a guilty conscience" (A. Nivelle, *Kunst- und Dichtungstheorien zwischen Aufklärung und Klassik* [Berlin: De Gruyter, 1960], p. 14). Mendelssohn explicitly followed Spinoza in this regard. See his letter to Lessing, August 11, 1757, in Moses Mendelssohn, *Gesammelte Schriften*, Jubiläumsausgabe (Stuttgart: Frommann-Holzboog, 1974), vol. 11, p. 149.

15. "I frankly confess my dependency on the teachings of Spinoza. I was not prompted to mention his name directly, because I didn't take my assumptions from studying him, but from the atmosphere produced by him [sic]. And because I was not at all interested in any philosophical justification" (Freud to Bickel, June 28, 1931; in *Spinoza in neuer Sicht*, eds. L. Sonntag and H. Stolte [Meisenheim am Glan: Anton Hain Verlag, 1977], p. 169).

16. EIVp38, EIVp39; see also EIVappXXVII.

17. Hecker wrote that:

> die Wesenheit eines jeden Einzeldings . . . schon in ihrem konstituierenden Sinngehalt als endliche Organisationsmacht einen bestimmten Verweis [impliziert] nicht nur auf andere Wesenheiten als alternative Ausprägungen der Struktur des unendlichen Ganzen überhaupt, sondern auf die anderen Wesenheiten als jene partikularen Mächte, die kraft ihres bestimmten Zusammenhangs jene beinahe unendliche Macht repräsentieren, die der einzelnen Wesenheit als einzelner zum Existieren fehlt und—da dieses Verhältnis ja in beiden Richtungen gilt—der zugleich die Macht dieser

einzelnen Wesenheit noch zu ihrer absoluten, das Dasein des Ganzen setzenden Machtvollkommenheit fehlt" (Konrad Hecker, "Spinozas Ontologie der Körperwelt," *Zeitschrift für philosophische Forschung* 31:4 [1977], pp. 614-5).

18. In a critical letter to Mendelssohn regarding Rousseau's *Discourse on Inequality* and its notion of perfection, Lessing developed a similar principle of a non-teleological perfection: "I only know, that I connect a completely different concept with it [i.e., *perfectibilité*]—not a concept from which one could deduce what you deduced from it. You take it to be an effort to make oneself more perfect; and I understand it only as a characteristic of a thing, by which it can become more perfect—a characteristic possessed by all things in the world, and which [is] absolutely necessary for the world's continued existence. I think that the creator had to make everything that he created capable of becoming more perfect, if it was to remain in that perfection, in which he created it" (Lessing to Mendelssohn, January 21, 1756, in M. Mendelssohn, *Gesammelte Schriften*, vol. 11, pp. 33f).

Spinoza on Human Desire and the Impossibility of Utopia

Menachem Brinker

I

Spinoza's political philosophy is usually recognized as the first classical model of enlightened liberal thought, recommending a complete separation of church and state. He insisted on the absurdity of any intervention of the state in the beliefs of its citizens by showing its futility. Beliefs are formed in the mind of the individual by the necessary action of the supreme laws of nature, in connection with the individual's place in 'the order of nature'. Therefore, it would be irrational to expect that a state could directly influence the mental attitudes of its citizens by either punishments or rewards. Punishment or reward can influence the overt behavior of subjects (or citizens) in a commonwealth. But by themselves they cannot prevent individuals from holding beliefs that are harmful to the authorities. They cannot make them hold beliefs that are desirable to the rulers.

Beliefs and evaluations concerning the state itself, its laws and its rulers can only be changed in an indirect way. The state or its rulers can always change the life-situations of the citizens within the commonwealth. And as all opinions and beliefs are formed in the minds of individuals by their place in the order of nature—the human commonwealth being but one manifestation of the all-embracing order of nature—any change in the commonwealth that influences one's fate will also have bearing upon one's beliefs.

A large part of Spinoza's liberal political philosophy stems from these simple rational assumptions. A state that makes its citizens happy and satisfied with their lot will induce them to have a grateful attitude towards the laws and their enforcers. On the other hand, a bitter citizen will never act favorably toward the state. The state can fully control his behavior by threatening him with severe punishment for any rebellious activity. It cannot, however, force him to love the state, its rulers, or its laws.

Spinoza makes it very clear that the real strength of a state does not consist in its ability to endure, its ability to fight enemies, or even in its ability to avoid civil war within the commonwealth. In his famous comparison of the Turkish state with the ancient Roman republics, he praises the ancient republics and condemns the Turkish state, despite the fact that the latter was able to achieve external victories, longevity, and internal quiet much more effectively than the ancient democracies. He goes on to condemn the social order that is achieved by fear alone, by distinguishing peace from slavery. He sums up the comparison with the memorable words: "For peace, as we said before, consists not in mere absence of war, but in a union or agreement of minds" (*Political Treatise* 6:4, p. 317).

All this leaves us with little doubt as to Spinoza's view of the *good* and the *bad* state. The good state achieves its stability and maintains order through the hopes of positive rewards and benefits that will redound to the subject living in harmony with other citizens. The bad state achieves the maintenance of order through the fear of punishment instilled by the ruler (or rulers) in the hearts of his (or their) subjects. The first advances real peace, unity, and harmony; the second is actually based upon slavery.

Our emotions of 'gratitude', 'hope', and 'fear' are all related to our evaluations of actual and possible states of affairs that may influence our own welfare. Hence, there is a possibility of a third kind of state. When looked upon objectively by a shrewd observer there is but little reason for its citizens to be satisfied with it. Yet, the rulers of this state succeed in manipulating public opinion to such extent that its citizens are unable to judge their real situation. They deem it a good one and mistakenly feel gratitude towards their leaders. Spinoza indicates this possibility very briefly in mentioning "he who has another under his authority attached to himself by past favor, so that the man obliged would rather please his benefactor than himself, and live after his mind rather than after his own" (TP 2:10, p. 295). It seems to me that he has also this kind of state in mind when he mentions Machiavelli as he who demonstrated "what means a prince, whose sole motive is lust of mastery, should use to establish and maintain his dominion" (TP 5:7, p. 315). However, unlike Machiavelli, Spinoza does not develop the idea of this state. He assimilates this kind of state to the explicitly bad state. Though the prince of this state does not instill terror in the hearts of his subjects, Spinoza treats him, i.e., the "one who holds someone under his authority" by "past favor," in the same way he would treat the one who does so by "taking from the subjects arms and other means of defense" or the one "who holds the subjects under his authority by inspiring them with fear" (ibid.).

Spinoza's position on this specific issue points to the difference of conception between Machiavelli's *Il Principe* and his own *Tractatus Politicus*. From the perspective of the prince, whose sole aim, in Spinoza's words is "to establish or maintain his dominion" (ibid.), there is no difference between the good state and the successful manipulative one. The *Political Treatise* is written from the subject's point of view, and from this perspective, there is all the difference in the world between the really good state and the only seemingly good, i.e., the manipulative state. To summarize this first point we may say that Spinoza maintains a qualitative binary opposition between the good and the bad states. The two are clearly distinguished one from the other. Though there may be degrees of goodness and badness in different commonwealths, the basic opposition cannot be blurred.

II

Spinoza wrote the *Political Treatise* with the expressed hope of influencing political life. He had hopes for the restoration of liberalism in Holland. There are grounds to assume that his hopes were not limited to his own country. Moreover, these hopes overcome a certain contradiction in his thought. At the end of the introduction Spinoza states that those who "persuade themselves, that the multitude of men distracted by politics can ever be induced to live according to the bare dictate of reason, must be dreaming of the poetic golden age, or of a stage-play."[1] Yet what else did Spinoza take upon himself in writing the *Political Treatise* other than indicating to his readers the 'bare dictate of reason' in the political sphere? Realism brought him to distinguish sharply between the goodness of the commonwealth and its fate. The internal merit of the good state is not tied to its external success. Still, like Machiavelli and in distinction to optimistic democrats, Spinoza believed that a prince or a government can fool all the people all of the time. True, Spinoza recommends political arrangements that will guarantee that those who administer public affairs will not "act treacherously or basely," whether guided "by reason or passion."[2] However, he himself has shown that avoidance of revolts and violence can be achieved through terror or manipulation as well as through honest and humane means.

We must conclude, therefore, that the 'dictates of reason' as well as the evaluations of different political communities in Spinoza's treatise were not meant to reach only the ears of the prince or other rulers. His hopes of influencing political affairs were based upon making some of the subjects (or citizens), the enlightened part of the community, aware of the virtues of a veritable good commonwealth. Thus, we may ask, what are the reasons that prevented Spinoza from assuming even the possibility of a gradual improvement of all commonwealths? What caused his certainty that the good state cannot achieve limitless stability and perfection? What prevented Spinoza from believing in the idea of political progress based upon rational education of an ever-growing part of the public? In order to understand this issue we must leave the *Political Treatise* and return to Spinoza's anthropology in the third and the fourth sections of the *Ethics*. Only those sections of the philosophical anthropology, to which Spinoza attributes *a priori* evidence, can explain his positive denial of the mere possibility of the perfect state.

Spinoza does put forth the image of a perfect commonwealth. A perfect commonwealth will achieve constant obedience to the law on the part of both subjects and rulers through free agreement and unity of minds. Thus, law enforcement will be unnecessary as all rivalry, antagonism, and conflict will be cancelled. This will be a commonwealth governed by an all-embracing solidarity. But according to Spinoza's anthropology, it is precisely such a commonwealth that is not just highly improbable but logically impossible.

Let me begin by emphasizing that no anthropological explanation for Spinoza's sceptical attitude towards the idea of an enduring perfect commonwealth is needed. In his view, knowing the real circumstances of a particular political commonwealth is a matter of experience, which cannot be deduced from general principles. History books tell us of states that endured for long periods of time and others that collapsed shortly after their birth. Any political body is a finite mode within nature, composed in itself by the actions of other finite modes. Like any other finite mode in nature, a commonwealth is an individual whose coming into being, persistence, and passing away must be explained according to the causal nexus, the circumstances that surround it. This nexus is no less individual than the particular mode itself. Any inquiry into the fate of real existing states will have to follow the particular conditions that caused their rise, persistence, and decline. We cannot deduce their fate from any general feature like their belonging to one type of government or another (aristocracy, monarchy, or democracy). This impossibility is obvious. We cannot understand these forms of government as Aristotelian 'essences' since this will lead us to ignore the principle that all finite modes ought to be explained by their proximate causes. The fate of a good or a bad state cannot be deduced from its internal merit or lack of merit alone any more than the fate of an individual can be deduced solely from his own virtue. In both cases we must take into account the specific circumstantial context. This is enough to induce scepticism concerning the realization of a stable commonwealth.

Spinoza's explicit mockery of utopian expectations is tied to his denigration of those authors who write on political matters as preachers. He blames them for their refusal to examine whether their descriptions of the perfect state fit what we know about human nature from our own experience. Hence, he thinks that experiential non-philosophical knowledge is enough to cause a sceptical attitude towards utopias and their dreamers. Yet, in distinction from general scepticism, asserting the *impossibility* of a perfect commonwealth requires more than historical experience. It requires a philosophical description of human nature. In what follows, I shall try to demonstrate that the impossibility of a perfect commonwealth is deduced by Spinoza from his view of human nature.

III

Spinoza finds that human beings resemble one another in their most basic drives. It is precisely this resemblance that brings them to oppose one another, and causes all rivalries, conflicts, and wars among them.

Hatred is the emotion man necessarily entertains towards anything that causes him pain (i.e., a loss to his *conatus*). His endeavor to persist in his being is in constant need of objects that cannot be possessed by several individuals at one and the same time. It is inevitable, therefore, that emotions of envy, hatred, rivalry, and aggression will play a central role in man's psychic life (EIIIp32). The arousal of such emotions is not limited to the possession of material goods. The loss of a beloved woman to another man will arouse envy and aggression in the heart of the loser (EIIIp32,s). When one reads carefully the all-important Proposition 32 and its Scholium in *Ethics* III, one understands that, due to the laws of association and the basic resemblance of human beings to one another, we may come to desire anything the other possesses. We imagine that we too could possess and enjoy this object. Even if we never felt desire toward such an object before, we feel it now and this feeling creates in us a new need. We also understand that in Spinoza's anthropology desires are not defined by needs. On the contrary, the objects men come to desire define their needs.

Conceived in this way no abundance of nature, no social or politically just order will ever quench the source of ambition, rivalry, aggression, and antagonism among men. The irrationality of these passions is derived from the fact that they are dependent on the imagination in two ways. First, the extent of our envy towards the other fits our image of the extent of enjoyment the other derives from the object he holds in his possession. Second, this image itself is dependent upon the image the other has of the object's utility as a source of pleasure. The force of these emotions of sadness, envy, and hate has therefore very little to do with real needs as conceived from the privileged point of view of adequate knowledge.

This double dependence on imagination is characteristic also of pity. Here too the intensity of one's emotion depends on one's image of the extent of suffering to which the other is disposed and this image in turn depends on the other's image of the harm or damage caused to him. But pity cannot moderate envy or hatred, as we are not free to pity those we hate.

The same basic resemblance between people that motivates them to rivalry brings them also to sympathize with one another in situations in which nothing causes them to envy one another. This highly interesting idea also may be explained negatively. We can imagine a community in which the desires of all people are aimed towards different satisfactions. In this community people will pursue different objects. There will be no place in this community for envy, rivalry, or aggression. True, in such a community there will also be no place for intense sympathetic relations between people and no real solidarity will be formed between different individuals or groups. However, Spinoza's point is that such a society is inconceivable since we know well that human nature, and indeed the nature of all finite modes, is the same everywhere. The rest, i.e., the destiny of every specific individual, must be explained within its specific causal context. This causal context will always include the same basic drives and emotions as part of the explanation. Hence, the impulse towards competition, envy, and rivalry is derived directly from human nature and not from a contingent factor of nature or social life. "Desire," which is "the essence of man,"[3] strives towards infinity of satisfactions achieved through the use and consumption of an infinity of objects. It is not triggered by an adequate understanding of the real utility of these objects to the one who desires to use them or consume them. The "quantity" of the emotions of which Spinoza speaks (love, hate, jealousy, etc.) is fitted to the "quantities" of pains or pleasures obtained or avoided according to our image and not to any pre-established need.

True, rivalry is especially strong when the rivals imagine the desired object to be necessary to their survival. It will be relatively weak when men have other means of satisfying a need that they regard as a basic need. But the existence of alternative objects to satisfy this need cannot uproot the arousal of aggression, as our desires are not limited to the challenges of survival or self-preservation. Aggressive drives are aroused by a specific image of an object that gives birth to a specific envy, and a specific desire. Our desires are not limited by types and they do not follow a given list of needs. These desires are individual, specific, and infinite. This is why aggressive drives cannot be uprooted. The only possible way to fight them is to set against their intensity opposing drives and desires that also follow from human nature and from the resemblance of all human beings. Here, there is, at least, the hope of restraining the behavioral results of the negative emotions. There is, at least, the hope of decreasing the number of situations of open aggression and war between men.

IV

The basic resemblance of human beings to one another is not just responsible for the socially-negative emotions. Already on the level of blind associations of ideas—where people are driven by passions whose causes are unknown to them—there are emotions that bind them together. The soul loves to contemplate whatever may increase its power. Hence the joy it takes in contemplating the happiness of others and the sadness it suffers while contemplating their sufferings, in all cases in which "negative" passions are not involved. But these sympathetic feelings rarely occur unalloyed with stronger negative feelings. They dominate our soul only when we are wholly indifferent to the other or have no relations to the object or state of affairs that brings him pleasure or pain.

As the states of joy or sadness of others are usually tied to our interests and relate to objects that cannot be shared by several people at once, sympathy has very limited influence upon one. Lust, love, envy, hatred, or rivalry will usually replace pure sympathy and poison it at its roots. Spinoza draws a very sharp distinction between the resemblance of human beings to each other and "their agreement in nature." Resemblance can be the cause of "agreement in nature" as well as the cause of "opposition" or "contrariety in nature." Pure sympathetic feelings will usually be only a transition towards the more intense emotions of "agreement" or "disagreement" (opposition) "in nature." Very often people differ from one another "in nature" due to the fact that one possesses something that the other lacks. No more is needed to create "a difference in nature" (EIVp34d,s).

Yet, there is one privileged state of affairs in which the basic resemblance among men leads systematically to an "agreement-in-nature" between them. This occurs when they cultivate desire towards an object that can be possessed by several men at one and the same time. There is only one object of this sort, reason. Systematic, non-accidental agreement of nature between men requires, therefore, that they introduce elements of reason into their psychic life (EIVp35, EIVp36). Reason is an ensemble of adequate ideas. It is also an ensemble of useful methods for the knowledge of the veritable value of things. In both senses of the word, reason is not a passion and cannot act on passion (EIVp7, EIVp14). Nevertheless, human beings find out that to preserve their being they must employ reason. Reason's actual deployment in reaching adequate ideas causes joy, and this joy is an active emotion that may overcome passions (EIIIp53). In this way, the most elementary and modest applications of reason may change the former drives of men. It may replace mistaken groundless fears and expectations with fears and hopes that better correspond to the true value of things. The joy that accompanies reason in its activity enables it to uproot harmful passions without itself becoming an emotion. Thus, Spinoza succeeds in making reason an active force in human destiny, while maintaining the truth, so important to his naturalistic ethics, that only emotions can cancel other emotions. The joy the soul takes in its operations will bring it to pursue more and more adequate ideas and these may gradually liberate a man from the state of bondage to the passions to the sublime freedom in the intellectual love of God.

The first lesson that reason teaches man concerning social matters is the knowledge of the perils involved in constant and continuous rivalries and, correspondingly, the merits of cooperation for mutual benefits. Spinoza ascribes a calculus of pain and pleasure to all men. To a certain extent everybody—even the most ignorant person—calculates his steps by measuring the possible advantages and disadvantages of any act. A complete enslavement to transient passions would be, in Spinoza's system, a tremendous miscalculation due to total ignorance. Such a complete enslavement to passions will be rare even among members of the multitude. That is why, according to Spinoza, the worst can never happen to human societies. Because of the constant presence of this calculus there is no place in Spinoza's philosophy for a Hobbesean state of nature, that is, for social situations of total antagonism where everybody fights everybody else.

Indeed it is possible to claim that according to Spinoza the same drives that characterize man's aggressive attitude to everything and everybody who stands in his way, will produce by itself secondary structures of solidarity and cooperation among men. If Peter, Paul, and Bill are fighting each other, there must be at least a provisional cooperation between Peter and Paul to destroy Bill, or a similar cooperation between Paul and Bill to destroy Peter. Of course, such cooperation will be shaky and full of suspicions. But the reality of cooperation in this state of affairs will be no less conspicuous than the reality of the general antagonistic background. Even the history of the Mafia recognizes periods of relative stability. International relations where there is no law, because there is no authority to enforce a law, seem to Spinoza an embodiment of the hypothetical Hobbesean state of nature. Yet we may assume that even in this instance, in the 'jungle' of inter-state relationships, the calculation of risks versus hope will prevent a war of all against all from becoming an actual state of affairs.

A commonwealth of course is something different. It is based on necessities of cooperation that are institutionalized. Wise men may know from their own reflection the benefits of cooperation and the less wise will introduce into their calculations the risks involved in breaking laws. These relatively less rational people will not look like the wise men for further occasions for cooperation. They will entertain larger 'quantities' of negative passions like envy and hatred. However, they will be deterred from overt expressions of their aggressive drives in their actual behavior because of the risks involved.

As already remarked, a Spinozistic utopian commonwealth will be the one in which nobody has to restrain hostile drives because of fear of punishment. People will restrain these drives due to their conscious awareness of the benefits of such restraint. Aware of the basic decency of the rulers, people will be ensured that their obedience to the laws will not be exploited to give the rulers an unfair advantage. When all the citizens of the state will be rational in this way, threats, and indeed even the enforcement of law, will become unnecessary. In such a state all hostile passions will be immediately, 'automatically', converted to positive social emotions. The joy in rational activity that results will accompany adequate conception and generous conduct. Of course, in this utopian commonwealth there will be no place for what Spinoza calls the 'multitude'. But does the omnipresence of the multitude follow necessarily from the nature of God?

V

We saw that Spinoza recognizes one desire in human life for which no restraint is ever necessary. The desires for true knowledge and adequate understanding of things cannot produce competition, envy, rivalry, or hatred among men. The reason for this is that many people can share the object of this specific desire at one and the same time (EIVp36, EIVp37d1). Moreover, the more prevalent adequate understanding of things is, the better are the chances of every man to get hold of it and to widen his own understanding. In order to get together for the pursuit of this specific 'object' no overcoming of hostile emotions is needed. All one needs is to desire knowledge and be ready to acquire it, with gratitude, from whoever he can.

Spinoza knows, of course, that knowledge is power, yet he believes that the pursuit of knowledge can never become part of the world of competition, envy, rivalry, and hatred. He never even mentions reason as the gift or property of an individual that can motivate envy or pride. By definition alone, reason aspires to increase communion and to decrease opposition among men. True knowledge is neither an individual's possession nor is it a mere instrumental tool. Reason is always a way of using knowledge for its own end, i.e., for the sake of the joy of understanding itself. Spinoza admits the occasional risks sometimes entailed in diffusing knowledge. After all, these risks were part of his experience. But these risks do not derive from its nature as knowledge. They derive from those that do not treat it as knowledge, namely, the multitude. There is nothing to fear from the diffusion of knowledge among men of reason who can understand it and use it properly. (I am following here the logic of the argument in the *Ethics*. Some of Spinoza's other writings, and especially his letters reflecting his own personal experience, draw a less idealistic picture of this issue.)

Here there is a sharp and non-gradual dichotomy. The pursuit of reason is ontologically different from the pursuit of all other objectives. Like the mystical union with God in some religious doctrines, reason is here the exact contrary of all terrestrial possessions. It induces pure cognition beyond the domain of envy and rivalry. Only here does the basic resemblance of people bring them to a full "agreement and harmony in their nature." Spinoza implies the presence of this unique power of reason in its restraining power. He shows that anytime that people are asked to restrain themselves and cancel the opposition (or contrariety) in their nature they are actually asked to stick to what is common or "in agreement in their nature" (EIVp35c1,c2). Every moderation or restraint of antagonistic passions is based on the activation of the power of reason. Hence, in restraining themselves people aspire not only to cancel their opposition (negating the negation), but also to exhaust and affirm positively that which is common to their nature: reason.

VI

Harmonious and ideal interpersonal relations may therefore exist insofar as people pursue reason and live according to its dictate. Spinoza clearly envisages a place for such a community within the general community or the commonwealth. We may now ask what prevents the general community from becoming such a philosophical community.

This brings us to the distinction Spinoza draws in so many different places between the philosophers and the multitude. I think that the philosophical meaning of this distinction has too often been taken for granted by Spinoza scholars. The assertion that only a limited number of people can live according to the dictates of reason cannot be deduced from any proposition of the *Ethics*. It is a datum of experience and not a necessary derivation from the nature of God. Spinoza relates to the existence of the multitude as to a generalization formed from the experience of all past sages. It is therefore a kind of Platonic true *doxa*, and not just Spinoza's subjective impression. But, as I argued earlier, an impression held by so many sages may justify scepticism with regard to the possibility of the perfect state. This impression cannot serve, however, as a sufficient ground for the assertion that a whole commonwealth composed of people who follow the dictates of reason is logically impossible.

It is my view that the impossibility of such a commonwealth, according to Spinoza, derives not from the nature of the multitude, but from human nature itself. It is possible to show that even in a commonwealth composed of Spinozistic philosophers, envy and rivalry will be inevitable, and will have to be restrained by the enforcement of the law. As the highest ideal to which all men of reason aspire, the intellectual love of God is located between the Platonic contemplation of the idea of the good and the Aristotelian contemplation of the unmoved mover. On the one hand, it is not comprised of random isolated moments of exultation. Having achieved this state, a man will aspire to achieve it again and again, and will also have a better chance of achieving it again as repeated cognitions of the third kind, advancing thereby the emergence and development of a philosophical disposition. On the other hand, intellectual love of God is not a constant or stable condition. One occurrence of cognition does not guarantee another one. It is no accident that Spinoza emphasizes the "quantity" (i.e., the plurality), of acts of adequate cognition, as a characteristic of the wise man.[4]

The term "love of God" itself points to finitude and fragmentariness. God himself, as substance, is unable to love anything. As he cannot pass from inferior to higher states of being he cannot experience joy or happiness and cannot relate lovingly to the cause of his joy. Only finite modes are prone to these transitions and only *qua* finite modes can God love himself (Evp36). Yet finitude, which is the necessary condition of all intellectual love of God, is also defined as the being that cannot sustain itself and is constantly dependent upon other finite modes.

The philosopher's achievement of the intellectual love of God consists, therefore, of many repetitive acts of ascent from the 'general order of nature' and 'human bondage' through reason and science to *scientia intuitiva*. The emotional motivation of this ascent is especially strong when the starting points are his own affections. Hereby he experiences, in addition to the joy of adequate cognition, the joy of liberating himself from his enslavement to passions. This additional joy could not accompany him while contemplating through *scientia intuitiva* non-human objects like a star, a tree, or an animal.

Even if he converts every affection to an action and every muddled impression into an adequate idea he cannot avoid 'falling' again into the 'common order of nature'. There, by the necessity of substance, new fragmented impressions, new inadequate ideas are formed in his mind. To remain forever attached to the third kind of knowledge, the philosopher has to give up his finitude, i.e., his life. Hence the philosopher must be infected like everybody else with hatred, rivalry, and envy before he converts them into the objects of adequate knowledge, which brings joy. This conversion is not a solitary act but a never-ending continuous process. Philosophers can constitute a perfect community without any kind of antagonism only when they study together. Since they must exist also outside the study-room, they cannot fail to experience the same urges that other people experience.

There is no full analogy between two distinctions Spinoza draws: The distinction between possessions that can and those that cannot be shared is not parallel to the distinction between the philosopher and the multitude. The first distinction is qualitative and sharp. Reason is an absolutely unique kind of possession. The last distinction is quantitative and relative. In many respects, the philosopher is part of the multitude.

At the conclusive part of Spinoza's political theory there is no room for sharp oppositions. Relative ranking of the commonwealth gets the upper hand. As we saw, even a society of ignorant people cannot exist with full antagonistic relations between each of its members. Similarly, a society of philosophers cannot exist where all antagonistic passions evaporate into thin air and full solidarity takes their place.

For the wise man life is a continuous transition from the preoccupation with possessions that cannot be held by many individuals to a preoccupation with the one and only possession that can be shared universally, namely, knowledge. But this process of transition is never complete. The philosopher cannot achieve perfection once and for all but must struggle for it again and again all his life. The same reasons that prevent him from achieving a constant and stable state of beatitude also prevent the human commonwealth from achieving a permanent state of perfection. Utopia is, therefore, not just highly improbable—it is logically impossible.

NOTES

1. Spinoza, *Political Treatise*, Introduction, 5, p. 289.

2. Ibid., Introduction, 6, p. 290.

3. "... when [this striving] is related to the Mind and Body together, it is called Appetite. This Appetite ... is ... nothing but the very essence of man ... *desire* can be defined as appetite together with consciousness of the appetite" (EIIIp9s).

4. See, for example, the language used in Evp10s, dealing with the wise man's ability "to direct *most* of his actions according to the command of reason" (GII 289:13-14, my italics), and the language he uses after the explanation of the nature of the third kind of knowledge ("a Body capable of *a great many things*" [Evp39, my italics]), as well as his description of the wise man as being *more* active and *less* passive (Evp40).

Dr. Fischelson's Dilemma: Spinoza on Freedom and Sociability

Daniel Garber

Isaac Bashevis Singer's memorable character, Dr. Nahum Fischelson, the Spinoza of Market Street, nicely illustrates an interesting problem in Spinoza's philosophy. Dr. Fischelson is striving to be like Spinoza's free man, striving to exemplify the model of a more perfect human nature that Spinoza presents in the *Ethics*. This, he thinks, entails a life alone, a life lived as much as possible without having to depend on the help of others, the imperfectly rational masses that live their lives in the bondage of the passions and in ignorance of the supreme pleasures of the pure intellectual love of God. But in the end, Dr. Fischelson finds this impossible to do; in his frailty, he needs others, and eventually he marries Black Dobbe, the woman who took care of him when he fell ill. In his marriage bed, Dr. Fischelson sees his strength return, and he finds himself more powerful than when he was alone. Going to the window, he murmurs, "Divine Spinoza, forgive me. I have become a fool."[1]

Dr. Fischelson would certainly seem justified in seeing Spinoza's ethical thought as centered in the idea that we should seek to become as perfectly rational and as free from the passions as we can become. In the *Treatise on the Emendation of the Intellect*, among the earliest of Spinoza's words to survive, he writes:

> [Since] man conceives a human nature much stronger and more enduring than his own, and at the same time sees that nothing prevents his acquiring such a nature, he is spurred to seek the means that will lead him to such a perfection. . . . This, then, is the end I aim at: to acquire such a nature. (TIE 13,14 GII 8)

Earlier versions of this paper were read at Notre Dame University, the University of Michigan, and Purdue University. I would like to thank audiences there for helpful comments. I would also like to thank the students in my Spinoza seminar in Fall 1992 at the University of Chicago. And finally, my greatest debt is to the other participants in the Jerusalem Spinoza Conference, whose presentations and discussions caused me to rethink a number of basic issues connected with this paper.

A similar view (though, as we shall later see, not absolutely identical) is found in the Preface to Part IV of the *Ethics*, where Spinoza writes that "we desire to form an idea of a man, as a model [*exemplar*] of human nature which we may look to," and defines the good as "a means by which we may approach nearer and nearer to the model of human nature that we set before ourselves" (EIVpref, GII 208).[2]

It is not implausible to associate the model of human nature Spinoza has in mind here with the free man discussed in Parts IV and V. The free man is, for Spinoza, the man free of passions, "one who lives according to the dictate of reason alone" (EIVp67d). Spinoza identifies rationality (having adequate ideas) with acting as opposed to being acted upon (EIIIp3). Furthermore, for Spinoza, to act is to be the adequate (complete) cause of our behavior (EIIIdef2). And so, it would seem to follow, if the person who has the character for which we strive is perfectly rational, then he is the adequate cause of all he does; everything that happens to him is a consequence of his nature and his nature alone. What need could such a person have for others? To put it another way, from the perspective of EV, the free man would seem to be so totally absorbed in his contemplation of God and the world *sub specie aeternitatis* that there would be no room for relations with other finite creatures. In this way, Spinoza's *Ethics* would seem to lead us out of society and relations with other human creatures, and into ourselves and our relations with God alone.

But there is another, seemingly different side of Spinoza's thought. Despite what Dr. Fischelson seems to think, Spinoza often claims that reason leads us not to isolate ourselves from one another, but rather to join ourselves to others in friendship and society. At the end of EIII, for example, he writes of the person strong of character, one of whose two salient qualities is what Spinoza calls nobility, *generositas*, "the Desire by which each one strives, solely from the dictate of reason, to aid other men and join them to him in friendship" (EIIIp59s). In this way sociability and rationality seem linked in Spinoza's conception of the model of human nature: the perfectly rational character is perfectly sociable as well. Perhaps Dr. Fischelson has simply made a mistake, and ignored those sections of Spinoza's *Ethics* (and other writings) which emphasize that people are, by their nature and rationally, social.

This is what I shall call Dr. Fischelson's Dilemma. Our rational need for other people seems to conflict with other demands of complete rationality. If what we seek is perfect rationality, perfect freedom, then we would seem to be drawn into ourselves and our relation with God, and drawn away from other humans, while if reason draws us into society, then we would seem to be drawn away from exemplifying the model of a human nature better than our own. Perhaps the servant girl Black Dobbe was not the perfect soul-mate for the learned Dr. Fischelson. But so far as I can see, he had no reason to apologize to the 'Divine Spinoza' for seeking the companionship of other humans; textually speaking, it isn't entirely clear exactly what the complete Spinozist is *supposed* to do. In this paper I would like to explore this apparent tension in Spinoza's thought.[3]

Freedom and Community

A good place to begin unraveling Spinoza's complex thought is by examining the concepts and arguments that underlie what I have called Dr. Fischelson's Dilemma: first, Spinoza's conception of freedom; then, his arguments for community in the *Ethics*.

Spinoza defines the free man as follows: "I call him free who is led by reason alone" (EIIIp68d). But to be led by reason alone is to behave by virtue of having adequate ideas, and adequate ideas alone. And so, immediately after giving this definition of the free man, Spinoza continues: "Therefore, he who is born free, and remains free, has only adequate ideas" (EIIIp68d). Now, among adequate ideas Spinoza includes both common notions, and the adequate ideas that we can have of the formal essence of certain attributes of God; in this way, adequate ideas form the foundation of both the second and the third kinds of knowledge. Insofar as Spinoza argues that "the greatest striving of the Mind, and its greatest virtue is understanding things by the third kind of knowledge" (EVp25), that is, understanding things through the adequate ideas of the formal essence of certain attributes of God, one can be free in the full sense and have only adequate ideas, and yet fall short of the kind of beatitude that is the ultimate goal of Spinoza's program, as outlined in Part V of the *Ethics*. Still, the model of a human nature better than our own that Spinoza presents to us in Parts IV and V of the *Ethics* would seem at the very least to *include* this freedom, even if freedom isn't the whole story. And it is from Spinoza's conception of freedom that one horn of Dr. Fischelson's apparent dilemma derives.

A free man is one who has adequate ideas and adequate ideas alone. Now, by EIIIp3, "the actions of the Mind arise from adequate ideas alone; the passions depend on inadequate ideas alone." So, the individual whose behavior derives from adequate ideas (reason) therefore acts rather than is acted upon; the free man is thus free from all passion. Furthermore, by EIIIdef2, "we act when something happens, in us or outside us, of which we are the adequate cause, i.e. . . . when something in us or outside us follows from our nature."[4] And so, for the free man, all of his behavior derives from his own nature, and not from anything outside of his nature. (This, of course, is very close to the definition of freedom Spinoza gives earlier on in EIdef7.) Consequently, as Spinoza uses the term, being perfectly free is equivalent to being perfectly rational, which is equivalent to acting rather than being acted on, which is equivalent to being such that all of one's behavior follows from one's own nature.

From this follows one extremely important consequence. Because all the behavior of the perfectly rational individual derives from his own nature, because he only acts, and cannot be acted upon. He is, in a sense, causally isolated from the rest of the world: he can act on other things, but other things cannot act on him. In particular, he cannot be harmed by things external to himself. As a consequence, Spinoza's free man must be immortal, incapable of dying, for death can only come from an external cause.[5] It is no wonder that "a free man thinks of nothing less than of death" (EIVp67), his immortality gives him that luxury! But if the perfectly free man cannot be harmed from the outside, he cannot, it would seem, be helped either; a passion is a passion, whether harmful or helpful. But, of course, the free man needs no help. Such a person is causally self-sufficient; his nature is the source of all of his affects, and he is incapable of being acted upon, for good or for bad, from the outside. Following this to its extreme, it would seem that the perfectly free individual would not even need external supports for his continued existence, needing neither food nor water nor air. Once we have attained this state, it would seem that we must be perfectly self-sustaining, completely detached and causally isolated from the world around us.[6] And with causal interaction ruled out, what possible *social* interaction can there be between the free man and anyone else?

Yet, Spinoza clearly holds that we do seek the society of others, and are rational in doing so. In EIIIp59s, at the very end of his 'geometrical' exposition of the passions, and before his systematic summary of them, he writes:

> All actions that follow from affects related to the Mind inso-
> far as it understands I attribute [*refero*] to Strength of
> Character [*Fortitudo*], which I divide into Tenacity
> [*Animositas*] and Nobility [*Generositas*]. For by Tenacity I
> understand the Desire by which each one strives, solely from
> the dictate of reason, to preserve his being. By Nobility I
> understand the Desire by which each one strives, solely from
> the dictate of reason, to aid other men and join them to him
> in friendship. [trans. modified]

Spinoza returns to this notion of strength of character again at the
end of EIV, after he has characterized the perfectly free and rational character. He writes:

> These and similar things which we have shown concerning
> the true freedom of man are attributed [*referuntur*] to
> Strength of Character, i.e. (by EIIIp59s) to Tenacity and
> Nobility. (EIVp73s; cf. EVp41s; trans. modified)

In this way, the model of human nature that Spinoza puts before
us is sociable; the free man seeks to join himself to others and
seeks to do good for others. Insofar as our actions follow from our
understanding, that is, insofar as we are rational and act freely,
we will exhibit this same nobility, this *generositas*; we too will seek
others.

This same spirit of community is quite evident in Spinoza's
propositions concerning the nature of the free man. "A free man
strives to join other men to him in friendship" (EIVp70d). "Only
free men are very useful to one another, are joined to one another
by the greatest necessity of friendship" (EIVp71d). "A man who is
guided by reason is more free in a state, where he lives according
to a common decision, than in solitude, where he obeys only himself" (EIVp73).

Sociability thus seems quite basic to the character of Spinoza's
free and rational man. In EIV, Spinoza offers an argument to
establish why this is so, why human beings should seek out the
company of other humans. Indeed, he seems to offer at least two
somewhat different arguments.[7]

First there is the argument Spinoza offers in the explicit
sequence of propositions and corollaries. The argument proper
begins with EIVp30, where he argues that "no thing can be evil
through what it has in common with our nature." This follows in
a straightforward way from considerations Spinoza advanced
early in EIII, where he argues that a thing can only be destroyed
by something external to it and contrary in nature (see EIIIp4,

EIIIp5). Spinoza then argues that "insofar as a thing agrees with our nature, it is necessarily good" (EIVp31), concluding directly that "from this it follows that the more a thing agrees with our nature, the more useful or better it is for us" (EIVp31c). The argument continues with a demonstration that the more we are subject to passions, the less like one another we are. This leads Spinoza to conclude that "only insofar as men live according to the guidance of reason, must they always agree in nature" (EIVp35), and finally that "there is no singular thing in Nature that is more useful to a man than a man who lives according to the guidance of reason" (EIVp35c1). Furthermore, he argues, "the good which everyone who seeks virtue wants for himself, he also desires for other men, and this Desire is greater as his knowledge of God is greater" (EIVp37). And so, Spinoza concludes, "the rational principle of seeking our own advantage teaches us the necessity of joining with men" (EIVp37s1).

On one hand, the argument is clear enough. But it also seems problematic. I find it very difficult to follow Spinoza's argument that the more rational we are, and the less we are subject to the passions, the more we agree in nature. It seems to me that whatever passions we may be subject to, our natures should remain exactly the same; if they agree when we are rational, they should agree when we are less so. But I do follow Spinoza's argument for the claim that things that agree with our nature are good, and it seems to me to be simply fallacious. Having established that that which agrees with our nature cannot be evil for us (EIVp30), Spinoza attempts to show that that which agrees with our nature cannot be indifferent with respect to our nature, but must be positively good (EIVp31). Spinoza writes:

> If [the thing which shares its nature with us] . . . is neither good nor evil, then . . . nothing will follow from its nature that aids the preservation of our nature, i.e. . . . that aids the preservation of the nature of the thing itself. But this is absurd (by IIIP6). Hence, insofar as it agrees with our nature, it must be good. (EIVp31d)

As I understand it, the argument goes like this. Everything strives to preserve itself, that is, its own nature, by EIIIp6. And so, if I share a nature with something, and it strives to preserve its nature, it will strive to preserve mine too. But the argument is quite evidently problematic. When one looks back at EIIIp6, the proposition doesn't say quite what Spinoza represents it as saying. It reads:

> Each thing, as far as it can by its own power, strives to perse-
> vere *in its being.* (EIIIp6; emphasis added)

That is, each thing strives to maintain *its own existence*, and that alone. There is nothing in this proposition to suggest that Spinoza thought that an individual strives to preserve anything that happens to share its nature; what is preserved is *being*, not *nature*. And so one cannot infer that everything that agrees with our nature is necessarily good (that is, good for us). And with that crucial proposition called into doubt, Spinoza's official case for human sociability would seem to be in some difficulty.

In addition to this explicit development of human sociability, there is a somewhat less official version in the *Ethics*, which is echoed in other texts. Consider the following passage which introduces the formal discussion of sociability that we have just examined:

> There are . . . many things outside us which are useful to us, and on that account ought to be sought. Of these, we can think of none more excellent than those that agree entirely with our nature. For if, for example, two individuals of entirely the same nature are joined to one another, they compose an individual twice as powerful as each one. To man, then, there is nothing more useful than man. Man, I say, can wish for nothing more helpful to the preservation of his being than that all should so agree in all things that the Minds and Bodies of all would compose, as it were, one Mind and one Body . . . and that all, together, should seek for themselves the common advantage of all. (EIVp18s)

This view is presented even more lucidly in a passage from chapter V of the *Theologico-Political Treatise*:

> A social order is very useful, and even most necessary, not only to live securely from enemies, but also to spare oneself many things [*ad multarum rerum compendium faciendum*]. For if men were not willing to give mutual assistance to one another, they would lack both skill and time to support and preserve themselves as far as possible. Not all men are equally capable of all things, nor would each one be able to provide those things which, alone, he most needs. Everyone, I say, would lack both powers and time, if he alone had to plow, to sow, to reap, to grind, to cook, to weave, to sew, and to do the many other things to support life, not to mention now the arts and sciences which are also supremely necessary for the perfection of human nature and its blessedness. For we see that those who live barbarously, without an organized community, lead a wretched and almost brutal life,

> and that still it is not without mutual assistance, such as it is,
> that they are able to provide themselves with the few
> wretched and crude things they have. (GIII 73)[8]

The argument here is rather straightforward and depends not at
all on the formal machinery of the *Ethics*. According to this argument, we need others to supply our own lacks of strength and
ability, and to help us do the things that we need to have done in
order to sustain our lives. Others can help us to defend ourselves
against our enemies, to plow, to sow, to cook, and to make shelter,
in short, to do all of the things we need to do but could not do by
ourselves. Such help is, of course, necessary for the preservation of
life.[9] But more than that, Spinoza suggests that it is also necessary
for the attainment of knowledge and blessedness. In freeing time
for thought and intellectual investigation, the organization of individuals into a society can free time that will allow us to approach
the state of reason, freedom, and blessedness that, for Spinoza, is
the goal of human life. To the extent that we are rational (in the
ordinary, everyday sense of the term, if not in Spinoza's), we will
recognize this and seek the company of others. And insofar as we
want others to join us, we will try to get others to see the rationality of this point of view, and get them to want to join with us in a
society of mutual benefit. To the extent that they resist this, and
behave in ways that undermine common action, they are behav-
ing irrationally (again, in the ordinary sense, if not in Spinoza's).
Spinoza is probably wrong to suggest, as he does in the passage
quoted from EIVp18s, that two individuals of the same nature
make up a new individual of the same nature but twice as powerful; taken literally, that must be false. But in another sense it is
true. For when two people are working together, in harmony with
one another, they do in a sense form a larger body of sorts, though
not of the same nature, and increase the ability each of them alone
has to do work. (Here, perhaps, one sees the influence of Hobbes
and the idea of his *Leviathan*, a literal body politic composed of its
citizens.) To this extent Spinoza has interesting reasons for believing that the more rational we are, the more we do and should seek
out the company of other people, and the more rational they are,
the more they should seek out our company.[10]

And so we seem stuck in what I earlier called Dr. Fischelson's
Dilemma. Perfect freedom and rationality seem inconsistent with
what is also a rational need for other people; if we seek perfect
freedom, then it seems that we must give up other people, and if
we seek to unite with other people, then it appears that we cannot

attain the true freedom and rationality that, Spinoza says, we must seek. What then are we to do?

Master and Apprentice: a Preliminary Solution

As I noted earlier, Spinoza seems to suggest that the perfectly rational and free individual is also perfectly sociable. If this can be sustained, then it would seem that Spinoza is caught in a direct contradiction. For then the free man would have to be joined to others in community, and, at the same time, causally isolated from them and everything else. If that is the case, then no wonder Dr. Fischelson is somewhat confused!

But looking back over the arguments for community discussed above, it would seem that those arguments depend strongly on our own imperfection and inadequacy; it is precisely because we are the imperfect and limited creatures that we are that we need the help of other people. Were we capable of sustaining ourselves, without the help of things outside of us, then we would not need the help of others, nor would it even be in our interests to encourage others to become more rational. But this is precisely the definition of someone who is perfectly free, perfectly rational: such a person is causally self-sufficient, and capable of sustaining himself without the help of external things. And so, it would seem, such a person should not need the help of others.

Furthermore, even though Spinoza does seem to assert from time to time that the perfectly free and completely rational individual is social, a closer look shows that he has no real arguments to that conclusion.

Consider, first, the statement Spinoza makes in EIVp70d: "A free man strives to join other men to him in friendship." This is supported with a reference to EIVp37. But that proposition says: "The good which everyone who seeks virtue wants for himself, he also desires for other men." Now, by EIVdef8, virtue is simply the ability to bring about things "which can be understood through the laws of his nature alone." So, it follows, the perfectly virtuous man is the same as the perfectly rational and free man. But it is clear that EIVp37 is intended to hold not for the *perfectly* rational or virtuous man, but only for the person who *seeks* virtue, and is thus less than perfectly virtuous and rational.

Consider next the statement Spinoza makes in EIVp71d: "Only free men are very useful to one another, are joined to one another by the greatest necessity of friendship." Spinoza supports this statement by appeal to EIVp35 and EIVp35c1. According to

EIVp35, "only insofar as men live according to the guidance of reason, must they always agree in nature"; EIVp35c1 says that "there is no singular thing in Nature that is more useful to man than a man who lives according to the guidance of reason." Both propositions do, indeed, hold of perfectly free and rational people. However, neither *assert* that perfectly rational people are 'joined to one another by the greatest necessity of friendship'. It is perfectly consistent with those propositions that while perfectly rational individuals are in principle useful to one another they are, as a matter of fact, only of practical use to less perfect individuals insofar as free men have no *need* of external help.

Finally, consider Spinoza's statement at EIVp73: "A man who is guided by reason is more free in a state, where he lives according to a common decision, than in solitude, where he obeys only himself." When we look at the demonstration Spinoza offers for this proposition, it is clear that it applies not to the completely free individual, but to the person who "*strives* to preserve his being" and "*strives* to live freely" (EIVp73d, emphasis added).

And so, even though Spinoza concludes in the scholium that immediately follows EIVp73 that "these and similar things which we have shown concerning the true freedom of man are attributed [*referuntur*] to Strength of Character," including Nobility, "the Desire by which each one strives, solely from the dictate of reason, to aid other men and join them to him in friendship" (EIIIp59s), it seems as if he is not really entitled to say this.

If it cannot be shown that the perfectly free man is social, if the free man stands outside society, then in a sense, there is no real dilemma. We *seek* to *become* free, but insofar as we *actually* are *less* than free, it is rational for us to be social. We are social to the extent that we are imperfectly rational; when we attain perfect rationality, we can stand outside of society altogether.

What gives the view the appearance of a dilemma for Dr. Fischelson is, perhaps, a misunderstanding about the role that the free man plays as an exemplar of our behavior. Let us return to Spinoza's ideal model of human nature that I referred to at the beginning of the paper, and reflect a bit on the way or ways that model might function in directing our behavior. There is little guidance on this in the *Treatise on the Emendation of the Intellect*. However, the parallel passage in the *Ethics* is somewhat more suggestive. Spinoza writes that "we desire to form an idea of a man, as a model [*exemplar*] of human nature which we may look to." The word 'model,' '*exemplar*' in Spinoza's Latin, is very significant here. In late scholastic usage, the term 'exemplar' is commonly used in connection with the mental model or plan an architect or craftsman uses when constructing a building or a machine; in this sense, 'exemplar' is often taken to be synonymous with the term 'idea'.[11] Spinoza acknowledges this conception of the term earlier in the very same Preface to Part IV of the *Ethics* where the ideal model of human nature is presented. There he uses the term model (*exemplar*) in connection with a model we have in our minds against which we judge the perfection or imperfection of things as they are in the world, a model that may or may not be the same as that which the artisan used for the thing in question, if there is an artisan at all. (We shall return to this question later and examine the texts in some detail.) Admittedly, in this particular text, Spinoza does not explicitly call the model the artisan uses an exemplar; but the context strongly suggests that Spinoza was well aware of the close connection between the traditional use of the notion of an exemplar and the production of an artifact by an artisan.

In calling the type of human nature we seek a model or exemplar in this sense, Spinoza suggests one obvious way in which that conception of a more perfect human nature might function in guiding our behavior. Just as the sculptor shapes her clay to fit the image of the exemplar that she has in her mind for the statue she is trying to make, the person seeking freedom shapes his own behavior to exemplify the properties of the free and perfectly rational man, the exemplar he uses in shaping himself. Understood in this way, the model of human nature Spinoza sets before us would seem to function as a model to imitate, a model that provides direct examples for us to follow.

But plausible as this is, it is not unproblematic; indeed, this conception of the way the model functions leads us directly into a version of Dr. Fischelson's Dilemma. There may be no direct contradiction between freedom and sociability, insofar as it is only the imperfectly free and rational individual who is called upon to be social. But if we are supposed to *imitate* the perfectly free man, then our situation is, in a way, just as bad. Properly understood, the perfectly free man whom we are supposed to imitate is a rather unsociable fellow, absorbed with himself and his apprehension of God. Insofar as we are called upon to imitate the free man, we must reject society. But even while we are striving to become the free man, we continue to be finite and imperfect creatures. And as finite, imperfect creatures, it is rational for us to seek others of our kind. We thus seem caught, again, in a direct contradiction. What are we to do?

A way out of this version of the dilemma can be found if we reflect a bit on other ways of understanding how the ideal human nature might function to guide our behavior. Let us think more generally about the way in which a goal might guide our behavior, not only in acquiring a particular character, but in acquiring any state at all. One might try to attain some particular state by trying as much as possible to act as someone would if he or she were actually in the state in question. Understood in this way, an ideal model would be something to *emulate*, a standard in the sense that it provides direct guidance as to how we should act in a range of situations: act as if you were already in the state in question. For example, if you wanted to become the sort of person who is calm in the face of chaos, you might actually attain the state in question by imitating those who are in that state, by trying to be calm in situations in which we are surrounded by chaos. (Though here we might find some specific techniques for actually accomplishing this end, thinking calm thoughts, carrying worry balls, etc.) Similarly, if you want to be a good writer, what you have to do is practice writing, or if you want to be a good squash player, you have to practice squash, and try to do what your models of good writing or good squash do. This is the conception of the ideal model as an exemplar that we discussed above.

But there are other circumstances in which this is not the appropriate way in which to behave, circumstances in which we ought not to emulate those in the state we seek to be in, if we hope to attain our goal. Suppose that I am a member of a Renaissance workshop that produces paintings and I want to become a master painter. What this entails (as I understand it) is having one's own shop, in which one supervises the production of paintings of various sorts by apprentices and assistants at various levels. Now, to learn how to paint one must practice painting; here, as with some of the other examples, one attains the state we seek to be in by emulating the activity in question. But it is a bit different when we think about attaining the social status of master within the hierarchy of the workshop. Here it seems evident that it would be inappropriate to emulate the behavior of the master. The beginning apprentice who orders other apprentices around—'You there, fill in that sky; you, paint some apples on that tree; let's see some wings on that angel on the left'—will soon be out of a job, and never become a master. The apprentice who wants to become a master, whose goal it is to become a master must emulate the behavior not of the master, but of the ideal apprentice; by doing what the master asks to the best of one's abilities, one climbs the ladder and becomes a master. And so, in order to attain the desired state, one must perform activities of a very different sort (activities appropriate to an apprentice) than those appropriate to the state in which we aspire to be (that of a master).

I think that the situation is similar with respect to the person seeking perfect rationality and perfect freedom. The perfectly free individual has certain characteristics, including complete causal self-sufficiency, characteristics that, I have argued, make it unnecessary for him to seek the help of others, or even to be able to benefit from the help of others. Such is not the case for us imperfectly rational and imperfectly free finite creatures; unlike our perfectly rational betters, we *need* the help of others, and need it quite desperately. But to attain the state of blessedness toward which we aim, should we try to *emulate* the behavior of the perfectly free individual? I think not. It is here that Spinoza's argument for the necessity of community enters. Imperfect individuals that we are, we need the help of others, not only for the necessities of continuing life, but also for the time and leisure necessary to become the more rational creatures we seek to be. If I want to become free, I shouldn't necessarily act as if I already am free. Rather, I should act like a good *apprentice for freedom*. While it is reasonably clear to me that Spinoza is not completely aware of this way of thinking of his project, he does use a locution suggestive of it. In the context of a discussion of the elimination of the passions as a means for attaining freedom and blessedness, Spinoza talks of one who acts from the "love of freedom [*libertatis amore*]" (EVp10s). This suggests to me a distinction between someone who *is* free, and someone who loves freedom and *seeks to become* free. Freedom and rationality may be my goal, but to get there, I must acquire the character of the lover of freedom, and, among other things, engage in certain sorts of social behavior that I need to become rational, but which I will no longer need once I become completely rational.[12]

And this, I think, gets us at least part of the way towards a resolution of the apparent contradiction between the different characterizations Spinoza offers of the character we should all seek. The goal we set before us is perfect rationality and perfect freedom; this is the character that we ultimately would like to acquire, the character that will give us the greatest happiness and what

Spinoza calls blessedness. But in order to acquire *that* character, we must in our imperfect state acquire another character, that of lovers of freedom and rationality. It is here, I think that the notions of strength of character and nobility enter; in order to attain our goal, we must be strong of character, noble, and able to enter into the community of other human beings. This is the character of the good apprentice for freedom.

A Ladder to Nowhere: the Impossibility of Perfect Freedom

We must distinguish between the character that is our aim and goal, and the character that we must emulate in order to attain that goal. It was Dr. Fischelson's error, and perhaps Spinoza's as well, to confound the two senses in which the model of a better human nature can serve as a guide for our behavior. The perfect freedom and rationality that we ultimately seek may exclude our relations with other finite creatures, but in order to attain that state, we must enter into relations with them; in our imperfect state, we are of necessity social creatures. Sociability, for Spinoza, thus would seem to be a temporary state, to be set aside when we attain perfect rationality, a ladder that we climb to reach the state of blessedness, a ladder that we can then kick away once we get to that state of intellectual love of God.[13] On this view, Dr. Fischelson has simply jumped the gun, and prematurely adopted the behavior to which he will ultimately become entitled.

But matters are actually a bit more complicated that this would suggest. Spinoza is quite clear that we can never attain this state of complete freedom and rationality.

The free man has many fine qualities, to be sure; in addition to being immortal and causally self-contained, he "thinks of nothing less than death" (EIVp67), he avoids danger (EIVp69) and he "always acts honestly, not deceptively" (EIVp73), among others. But one of his less attractive characteristics (from our point of view, at least) is the fact that in the strictest sense, the free man is impossible. It is not clear that Spinoza always thought so. When the notion of the model of human nature is first introduced in the TIE, Spinoza asserts that the investigator should see that "nothing prevents his acquiring such a nature" (GII 8), suggesting that this perfect character is genuinely attainable.[14] But by the time Spinoza wrote the *Ethics*, his view seems to have changed. EIVp4 reads:

> It is impossible that a man should not be a part of Nature, and that he should be able to undergo no changes except

those which can be understood through his own nature alone, and of which he is the adequate cause.

From this Spinoza draws a direct corollary:

> From this it follows that man is necessarily always subject to passions, that he follows and obeys the common order of Nature, and accommodates himself to it as much as the nature of things requires. (EIVp4c; paraphrased in the *Political Treatise*, chap. I, sect. 5)

In short, the perfectly free and rational man is an impossibility.

Central to the demonstration of this proposition and its corollary is the single axiom that Spinoza gives in EIV:

> There is no singular thing in nature than which there is not another more powerful and stronger. Whatever one is given, there is another more powerful by which the first can be destroyed. (EIVax1)

From this axiom an important proposition follows directly:

> The force by which a man perseveres in existing is limited, and infinitely surpassed by the power of external causes. (EIVp3)

And so however powerful we might be, there is always something more powerful than we are, something capable of destroying us. Closely connected are two of the four postulates Spinoza gives in the short treatise on physics following EIIp13. Spinoza writes:

> III. The individuals composing the human Body, and consequently, the human Body itself, are affected by external bodies in very many ways.

> IV. The human Body, to be preserved, requires a great many other bodies, by which it is, as it were, continually regenerated. (EIIpost3, EIIpost4)

Here, it would appear, the claim is more general. Spinoza is explicit in claiming that the bodies external to us can not only harm us, but can sustain us as well; the external causes that affect us include not only the boulder that can crush us, but also the air and food necessary for our survival.

It is important to see that these are no arbitrary assumptions, made merely to be able to get the conclusions that Spinoza seeks.

They are closely connected to the very definition of finitude, one of the first definitions Spinoza presents in EI:

> That thing is said to be finite in its own kind that can be limited by another of the same nature. For example, a body is called finite because we always conceive another that is greater. (EIdef2)

Note here that for something to be finite, we must simply be able to *conceive* of a thing that limits it. Consequently, it does not *follow* from the fact that something is finite that there *actually exists* in nature something which is greater than any individual and which limits it; this is why Spinoza must posit the existence of external causes more powerful than we are by axiom and postulate. But given the general position Spinoza takes that there are no unactualized possibles, it would be very surprising for him *not* to posit their real existence. If such causes were conceivable but non-existent, then there would be finite things for which it is in the strictest sense impossible that a limit could exist; something decidedly odd, if not absurd.

This sets the strategy of the demonstration of EIVp4, the proof of the impossibility of a perfectly free and rational person. Spinoza writes:

> If it were possible that a man could undergo no changes except those which can be understood through the man's nature alone, it would follow (by IIIP4 and P6) that he could not perish, but that necessarily he would always exist. (EIVp4d)

But for the reasons I just gave, a finite creature is always subject to perishing through another more powerful finite creature. So if we are to be imperishable, as our perfect freedom and rationality entails, then we must be infinite creatures. But we are not.[15]

It is thus our very finitude that puts us in this position and makes it impossible for us to be perfectly self-sustaining. To the extent to which we are finite, it is thus impossible for us to realize the model of human nature, the perfect character to which we aspire. Or, to put it a different way, the idea of a perfectly free and rational person is incoherent; perfect freedom and rationality conflict with the finitude implicit in human personhood.

The impossibility of the perfectly free man raises an obvious question for Spinoza's enterprise. If it is impossible, strictly speaking, for us to be perfectly free, how can such an idea function as a regulative ideal in Spinoza's ethical thought? If a perfectly free and rational person is like a round square, how could we possibly aspire to become such a thing? If we know that we can never be masters, do we then lose all motivation for being good apprentices? If we know that the ladder leads ever upwards, without ever leading anywhere in particular, why should we keep climbing?

"A Model of Human Nature Which We May Look To"

Dr. Fischelson is doing his best to follow what he takes to be Spinoza's advice, and seeks to become the free man Spinoza describes at the end of Part IV of the *Ethics*. Earlier I suggested that Dr. Fischelson may be in error in taking the free man as an exemplar on which to model himself, and suggested that, if he ever wants to attain that state, perhaps he should adopt the character of the perfect apprentice for freedom. But the impossibility of perfect freedom suggests to me that Dr. Fischelson's mistake may be more basic still. In the *Treatise on the Emendation of the Intellect* it is clear that the model of human nature is intended as a goal toward which we direct ourselves. We are, Spinoza says, "spurred to seek the means that will lead [us] to such a perfection" (GII 8). But in the TIE there is no reason to think that Spinoza thought perfect freedom an impossibility either: "man conceives a human nature much stronger and more enduring than his own, and at the same time sees that nothing prevents his acquiring such a nature" (GII 8). But when in the Preface to Part IV of the *Ethics* Spinoza introduces the model of human nature, it isn't so clear what role it plays in the program.

In the Preface to *Ethics* IV Spinoza presents the model of human nature in the more general context of a discussion of how evaluative terms get their meaning. He begins with a discussion of the notions of perfect and imperfect. When a builder builds a house, it is called perfect or imperfect to the extent to which the thing built does or does not correspond to the conception in the mind of the author, i.e., the exemplar (GII 205). This, of course, is the literal meaning of the Latin word '*perfectus*', which normally means 'complete'. "But," Spinoza continues,

> after men began to form universal ideas, and devise models [*exemplaria*] of houses, buildings, towers, etc., and to prefer some models of things to others, it came about that each one called perfect what he saw agreed with the universal idea he had formed of this kind of thing, and imperfect, what he saw

agreed less with the model he had conceived, even though its maker thought he had entirely finished it. (GII 206)

The next stage takes place when people form such universal ideas of natural things, and use them (improperly, of course) to make judgments about the perfection and imperfection of natural things:

> Nor does there seem to be any other reason why men also commonly call perfect or imperfect natural things, which have not been made by human hand. For they are accustomed to form universal ideas of natural things as much as they do of artificial ones. They regard these universal ideas as models of things, and believe that nature . . . looks to them, and sets them before itself as models. So when they see something happen in nature which does not agree with the model they have conceived of this kind of thing, they believe that Nature itself has failed or sinned, and left the thing imperfect. (GII 206)

As Spinoza had argued earlier, such universal ideas are the result of a sort of confusion; unable to hold in the imagination the determinate ideas of a multitude of different individual men, say, we form a single universal idea, characteristically different from one person to another, that captures what strikes us as common to all (see EIIp40s1). In this way, Spinoza argues, "perfection and imperfection . . . are only modes of thinking, i.e., notions we are accustomed to feign because we compare individuals of the same species or genus to one another" (GII 207). Judgments of perfection and imperfection are relative to the universal ideas an individual forms on the basis of the particular individuals with which he is acquainted and the ways in which they strike him. Spinoza suggests that the notions of good and evil must be understood in a similar way:

> As far as good and evil are concerned, they also indicate nothing positive in things, considered in themselves, nor are they anything other than modes of thinking, *or* notions we form because we compare things to one another. (GII 208)

It is in this context that Spinoza introduces his account of the notions of good and evil in connection with human beings:

> But though this is so, still we must retain these words. For because we desire to form an idea of man, as a model of human nature, which we may look to, it will be useful to us

> to retain these same words with the meaning I have indi-
> cated. In what follows, therefore, I shall understand by good
> what we know certainly is a means by which we may
> approach nearer and nearer to the model of human nature
> that we set before ourselves. By evil, what we certainly know
> prevents us from becoming like that model. Next, we shall
> say that men are more perfect or imperfect, insofar as they
> approach more or less near to this model. (GII 208)

What is interesting here is that unlike the sort of models that he discussed earlier in the Preface, this model does not seem to differ from person to person; it seems to be a single model of human nature that we can all, as humans, agree upon. Similarly, insofar as it represents what we all strive for and never attain, it is obvious that it cannot be derived in any straightforward way from the confused perceptions of a multitude of individual men. Where, then, does it come from? And why do we adopt it as our standard for good and evil?[16]

It is significant that Spinoza says that we *desire* to form the idea in question. But why do we desire to form an idea of a human nature for us to strive for? Spinoza's discourse is very obscure on this question. My suggestion is this. Basic to Spinoza's view is that reason itself, the adequate ideas we posess, lead us to desire and strive for more and more adequate ideas. Spinoza writes: "What we strive for from reason is nothing but understanding; nor does the Mind, insofar as it uses reason, judge anything else useful to itself except what leads to understanding" (EIVp26). The process begins with knowledge of the second kind, knowledge based on common notions. But, Spinoza argues, knowledge of the second kind leads us higher to the knowledge of things through God, to knowledge of the third kind: "The Striving, or Desire, to know things by the third kind of knowledge cannot arise from the first kind of knowledge, but can indeed arise from the second" (EVp28). Furthermore, Spinoza argues, "the more the Mind is capable of understanding things by the third kind of knowledge, the more it desires to understand them by this kind of knowledge" (EVp26). In this way reason, the adequate ideas we have impel us to desire more and more adequate ideas, and lead us to greater and greater levels of activity and freedom.

How does this lead us to the model of human nature at issue here? Reason presses us to acquire more and more adequate ideas. But insofar as we want to understand this in terms of the notions of good and evil, we must conceptualize it in terms of some idea or another of human nature—that, Spinoza argues, is simply what the terms good and evil *mean*. If we are to apply the term 'good' to the acquisition of adequate ideas, then we must have in mind some idea of human nature, a model, an *exemplar* such that the acquisition of adequate ideas brings us closer to it and the acquisition of inadequate ideas puts us further away. And so we create one, and the one we create is the idea of a person all of whose ideas are adequate, that is, Spinoza's free man. In what sense do we *desire* to create such an idea? Desire, Spinoza tells us, is just conscious appetite, and appetite is what we call will when we consider it in relation to the mind and body together, and not just the mind (see EIIIp9s). So to say that we desire to create the idea of this human nature simply is to say that it is a conscious creation of the mind. And although we may have universal ideas of 'man' that differ from person to person insofar as we have different experiences of different people, this model of human nature is something we all share; it is, in a sense, a creature of reason itself.

But even though it is reason that leads us to form the idea in question, and even though it is reason that pushes us to do that which will put us closer to the model of human nature, that model itself is an inadequate idea insofar as it represents something that cannot be realized. Bernard Rousset calls it a "rational and ideal common notion."[17] Spinoza's own comments on that idea suggest the kind of idealization he may have in mind. Spinoza discusses the case of the man born perfectly free in EIVp68, one of the series of propositions in which he draws a picture of what exactly the free man is like. In the Scholium to that proposition, Spinoza faces the fact that strictly speaking, the notion of a free man is incoherent. He writes:

> It is evident from P4 that the hypothesis of this proposition [i.e., that some person is born perfectly free] is false, and cannot be conceived unless we attend only to human nature, or rather to God, not insofar as he is infinite, but insofar only as he is the cause of man's existence. (EIVp68s)

Spinoza's language is obscure here, but I suspect he means something like this: We might attend only to human nature, that is to the individual finite thing, taken in isolation from the greater things capable of destroying him. Though in reality he is limited by them, we can attend only to his nature, and ignore those other things for the purposes of argument. Regarded in such a way, the individual remains finite insofar as we can still *conceive* of something greater than him that limits him, but insofar as we feign that such limiting things don't exist, we can consistently consider the possibility of a finite thing that is causally self-contained. In this way we might regard the perfect (finite) individual in the way that Galileo regarded a ball rolling down a frictionless inclined plane, disregarding the friction that would inevitably slow the rolling ball down, or the way in which Descartes regarded a body in rectilinear motion without end, disregarding the surrounding plenum which inevitably would slow it down. Though we can never build a frictionless plane, or (if we are Cartesians) throw a ball through a vacuum, it may still be interesting to contemplate what things would be like under those admittedly impossible circumstances. The case is a bit more difficult with respect to the perfectly rational man. While we can describe coherently a frictionless plane or an empty (or unresisting) space, it is not altogether clear to me that we can describe a perfectly rational man under the conditions of the idealization. Will he need to eat? To breathe? Will he be able to see or to hear? But however problematic it may be, this at least furnishes one strategy for conceiving a model of human nature to which we are supposed to aspire, impossible though it may be. Or, at least, Spinoza seems to have thought so.

We can now return to the question that initiated the discussion in this section. How can we use the free man as a model of human nature toward which we are to aspire, as a regulative ideal to guide our behavior, if the free man is an impossibility? The answer is, I think, that we cannot. Even though the free man may well have been a regulative ideal in the TIE, his role in the mature philosophy of the *Ethics* is quite different. In the *Ethics*, it is *reason itself* that impels us to become more and more rational; in that process, it is just the *adequate* ideas we have that move us, not the *inadequate* idea that is the model of human nature. In that way, the model of human nature is not an idea that regulates our behavior in the strict sense. It is, rather, a way of representing to ourselves what we do and how we behave in such a way that terms like good and evil, perfect and imperfect, can be applied to human beings in an objective way.[18]

Dilemma Dissolved

Earlier I suggested that Dr. Fischelson was mistaken in wanting to *imitate* the free man, Spinoza's model of human nature, rather than simply doing that which would lead him to *become* more and more *like* the free man. But this discussion suggests that his error may go deeper still, insofar as he takes this model seriously at all as a regulative ideal, something that actually serves to guide his behavior. Rather than looking to the idea of the free man, and seeking to become like him, Dr. Fischelson should simply have been guided by his reason, his adequate ideas, to become more and more rational.

And what then becomes of the question of sociability in this perspective? When we realize that the free man is an idealization, something impossible that cannot be realized in the world, then we realize that our need for society is not temporary, not a provisional state until we attain the freedom to which we aspire, but a permanent and inevitable feature of human existence—as inevitable as our imperfection (with respect to the examplar of human nature) and incomplete rationality. Though we seek greater and greater rationality, we will never attain complete rationality and so we will never be without need for others. Despite the fact that our need for society is an 'imperfection' with respect to the exemplar of the perfect human nature, we should always keep in mind that imperfection is only relative to an exemplar, and that the exemplar in this case is radically inadequate, representing to us an impossibility as if it were possible.

Dr. Fischelson is obviously troubled by his need for other people. At the end of the story, contrite over having given in to his need for other humans, he asks 'Divine Spinoza' for his forgiveness. Were the Divine Spinoza around to hear such a plea, he would consider it completely inappropriate, I should think. At the end of EIV, Spinoza writes:

> We shall bear calmly those things which happen to us contrary to what the principle of our advantage demands, if we are conscious that we have done our duty, that the power we have could not have extended itself to the point where we could have avoided those things, and that we are a part of the whole of nature, whose order we follow. (GII 276)

Given the impossibility of ever attaining the state of complete freedom, and given our inevitable finitude and consequent need for others, Dr. Fischelson shouldn't regret his need for other people. That he does is a measure of the extent to which he depends upon inadequate ideas. Rather than asking Spinoza for his forgiveness, Dr. Fischelson should thank him for what he has demonstrated: 'Divine Spinoza, I thank you for having helped me to see my inevitable finitude, my inevitable need for others of my own kind, my inevitable humanity'.

NOTES

1. I.B. Singer, *The Spinoza of Market Street* (Philadelphia: Jewish Publication Society of America, 1961), p. 24.

2. It isn't uncontroversial that Spinoza actually held this conception of ethics and the notion of the good in his mature thought; see, e.g., Jonathan Bennett, *A Study of Spinoza's Ethics* (Indianapolis: Hackett, 1984), p. 296. Nor is Spinoza's version of this view without complications; see, e.g., E.M. Curley, "Spinoza's Moral Philosophy," in M. Grene, ed., *Spinoza: A Collection of Critical Essays* (Garden City, NY: Anchor Books, 1973), pp. 354-76. We shall discuss some of these complications later in this essay.

3. Although I will only be concerned with this question as it comes up in Spinoza's system, it seems to be an instance of a more general problem in Judeo-Christian thought, insofar as we are enjoined both to devote ourselves to God, and to love our neighbor as ourselves. On this, see Robert Merrihew Adams, "The Problem of Total Devotion," in Robert Audi and William Wainwright, eds., *Rationality, Religious Belief, and Moral Commitment* (Ithaca and London: Cornell University Press, 1986), pp. 169-94.

4. Spinoza defines an adequate cause as one "whose effect can be clearly and distinctly perceived through it" (EIIIdef1). It seems close to what others have called a total cause.

5. This kind of immortality, of course, is not the same as the eternity that will be a main theme of *Ethics* V. Immortality is simply existence continued indefinitely, while Spinoza conceives of eternity as "existence itself, insofar as it is conceived to follow necessarily from the definition alone of the eternal thing" (EIdef8).

6. The idea that something depends on an external support is somewhat problematic here; it is not clear just how it relates to the question of the causal relations between the free man and things outside of him. I take it that, at very least, if A depends on B in this sense, B must cause something in A beneficial to A's continued existence.

7. There is a third kind of argument implicit in the text. The two arguments I discuss below emphasize the rational foundations of community. But Spinoza can also be read as showing how certain affects, like pity and sympathy, work to unite individuals with one another. However, Spinoza never offers a full-blown argument of this sort for community; at best it constitutes a suggestion in the text. The role that the passions in particular and the affects more generally play in sociability is one of the central themes of Alexandre Matheron, *Individu et communauté chez Spinoza* (Paris: Les Editions de Minuit, 1969), esp. chaps. V-VII. Similarly, in his essay in this volume, Michael Della Rocca argues for a Spinozistic conception of community based on the doctrine of the imitation of the affects in Part III of the *Ethics*.

8. The translation here is taken from Edwin Curley's yet unpublished but widely circulated translation of the TTP.

9. It is interesting to observe here that in contrast with the official argument, which makes others useful to the extent that they are *like* us, this argument makes others useful to the extent that they are *unlike* us, and can make up for our defects.

10. It is interesting to note here that in the early *Short Treatise*, Spinoza argues for a somewhat different view; see KVII 5 (GI 63). There he claims that we should avoid loving other finite creatures, humans included: "For they are weak, and one cripple cannot support the other. And not only do they not help us, but they are even harmful to us." But this may not represent a complete rejection of sociability. A few pages later (KVII 6 [GI 67]), Spinoza appeals to the model of human nature, the perfect man, and says that we should strive to attain that state and bring others to that same state as well, "for only then can we have from them, and they from us, the greatest benefit." The point may be that while imperfectly rational men are to be avoided, perfectly rational men are of the greatest use to us. In this way, the doctrine may be closer to the doctrine of the *Ethics* than it looks at first.

11. D'Abra de Raconis characterizes the notion of an exemplar as follows in his popular scholastic textbook:

> An exemplar, or idea (for these two things are the same), is that which the craftsman copies with the intention that he be able to work in accordance with the laws governing an art. This is taken in two senses. First, in a general sense, [it can be taken] for whatever exemplar you like, and thus it includes both external and internal [exemplars]. An external [exemplar] is that which the craftsman sets out for the eyes to imitate; an internal [exemplar] is that which the craftsman forms in his soul. Secondly, 'exemplar' is used in a more specialized sense only for the interior exemplar. (*Tertia pars philosophiae seu Physica, auctore C.F. D'Abra de Raconis* [Lyon, 1651], p. 94; my translation)

It was a standard question in scholastic textbooks whether the 'exemplar cause', the relation between the exemplar and the object created in accordance with that exemplar, constituted a kind of causality separate from the Aristotelian four causes. See D'Abra, *Physica*, pp. 93-8, and Eustachius a Sancto Paulo, *Summa philosophiae quadrapartita: Physica* (Cambridge, 1648), p. 138 for representative discussions.

12. In his elegant discussion of EIVp72, Don Garrett makes a similar distinction between that which the perfect man would do and that which one would do in the process of becoming a perfect man. See D. Garrett, "'A Free Man Always Acts Honestly, Not Deceptively': Freedom and the Good in Spinoza's *Ethics*," in Edwin Curley and Pierre-François Moreau, eds., *Spinoza: Issues and Directions* (Leiden: E.J. Brill, 1990), pp. 221-38, esp. pp. 229-30. Garrett, though, is con-

cerned with the apparent conflict between the claims that one must act so as to preserve one's being—that acting deceptively sometimes is necessary to preserve one's being—and the claim that a free man always acts honestly.

13. It is interesting to note that in the *Short Treatise* Spinoza uses a similar analogy. He compares reasoning to a stairway that can bring us to a true knowledge and love of God. See KVII 26 (GI 109-10).

14. It is also possible that the model he had in mind in the TIE is different from the one he later seems to adopt in the *Ethics*, and thus that the nature he thinks we can acquire is different from the one he later declares impossible to exemplify. But I doubt it. See, e.g., KVII 26, roughly contemporaneous with the TIE, in which Spinoza goes on at length about true freedom.

15. In the demonstration of the proposition, Spinoza offers a positive argument for why an immortal thing must be infinite. I'm not sure that such an argument is needed to establish the proposition. Since everything is either infinite or finite, establishing that a thing that exists cannot be finite should suffice to establish that it must be infinite.

16. In the discussion that follows, I am deeply indebted to the discussion in Curley, "Spinoza's Moral Philosophy" (see n. 2 above), esp. pp. 364 and *passim*, and to Bernard Rousset, *"Recta Ratio,"* in this volume.

17. See Rousset, *"Recta Ratio."*

18. In this way I find myself approaching Bennett's view of the central passage from the Preface to Part IV of the *Ethics*. Bennett suggests that the discussion of the "model of human nature" in EIVpref is "a relic of a time when Spinoza planned to make the concept of a favored model of mankind do some work for him in the body of Part 4" (Bennett, *A Study of Spinoza's* Ethics, p. 296), and that, as a matter of fact, the model does no real philosophical work for him. Though he may have taken the view more seriously in the *Treatise on the Emendation of the Intellect* than he does in the *Ethics*, I disagree with Bennett's view that the model of human nature does *no* work in the *Ethics*. If I am right, it still functions to ground judgments of good and evil, perfection and imperfection. However, I do agree with Bennett that it doesn't do the philosophical work that it would appear to do, insofar as it it isn't, strictly speaking, a guide for our behavior.

Hilaritas and Acquiescentia in se ipso

Laurent Bove

According to Spinoza, *hilaritas* (cheerfulness or joy) is a pleasure that expresses a perfect affective equilibrium of the body's parts (and, in fact, all the parts of our being), which are, in this affect, identically and equally affected.[1] But Spinoza, at EIVp44s, quickly adds that *hilaritas* "is more easily conceived than observed." Spinoza further points out that:

1) While this particular affect of pleasure only occurs in practice very rarely and fleetingly, it is, nonetheless, the adequate expression of the presupposed structure of all existence whatsoever in that it is enclosed within the essential love of self and / or the *conatus* itself, which develops and affirms it in a certain proportion of motion-and-rest.

2) *Hilaritas* indicates a direct practical and affective route (that of balanced pleasure) for the production of adequate ideas; this is the route to our freedom, a dynamic shift from passive affects to active ones.

3) Consequently, *hilaritas* is also, and above all, the adequate expression of the presupposed ethical existence *par excellence*, namely, *acquiescentia in se ipso*. This is the ethical end that draws its origin from reason, and from the essential equilibrium that this "contentment" encloses, and that, by EIVp52s, is the "highest good we can hope for." Moreover, according to EIVapp4, "for the man who is guided by reason, the final goal, that is, the highest desire whereby he strives to control all the others, is that by which he is brought to an adequate conception of himself and of all things that can fall within the scope of his intelligence."

4) Positioned at the heart of Ethics IV, *hilaritas* is a fair indication that the ethical end aimed for is, inasmuch as it can be, *acquiescentia in se ipso* of man in his totality—equally and positively affected in all the parts of his body and mind.

It is through this straight and practical route of the dynamism of the affect of *hilaritas,* and of the vital equilibrium which it simultaneously supposes and expresses (one which experience shows us to be too rare, but reason and Spinozistic philosophy nevertheless claim to be necessarily and immanently present in any activity whatsoever, particularly in ethical practice), that I will now begin to examine the structural underpinnings of reason and human freedom as expressed in Part IV of the *Ethics.*[2]

The Pleasant Passion of Children

Why, above all, does Spinoza affirm that *hilaritas* "is conceived more easily than observed?" EIVp42 affirms that cheerfulness cannot be excessive and it is always good. In EIIIp11s, Spinoza had defined cheerfulness as an affect of pleasure related simultaneously to the soul and the body when all the parts of a man, in his body as well as his mind, are equally affected. EIVp42d specifies that in this affect:

> [T]he body's power of activity is increased or assisted in such a way that all its parts maintain the same proportion of motion-and-rest towards one another. Thus cheerfulness is always good, and cannot be excessive.

We understand, then, the rarity, indeed the transience, of *hilaritas;* a state which supposes a perfect equilibrium of our being. This equilibrium is, at first sight, not due to this being's own power, since even if *hilaritas* is a pleasure, it is a passive pleasure. Rather it seems to be due to 'fortune,' i.e., to fluctuating yet favorable external causes, which establish a perfect equality of change within the parts of our soul and body. This means that with *hilaritas* we are only the 'partial' cause of our affects (EIIIdef1; EIVp2d). As with the passive affects, the 'force' and 'increase' of *hilaritas* "must be defined not by human power but by the power of things external to us" (EIVapp2; EIVp5). From EIVax, EIVp2-4, EIVp4d,c and EIVapp30 we learn how rare this situation of equilibrium is in a being endowed with many capacities for being affected, and which is in constant commerce (*commercium;* EIVp18s; GII 222) with an external world in which "things do not act with the object of affecting us with pleasure," and which "is not adjusted to suit our needs" (EIVapp30). If this affect is rare, it is however, not impossible. We could even say undoubtedly that we have all already experienced it. It is Spinoza's ethico-political project to alter external circumstances in such a way that the greatest possible number of people should be able to experience it, for this is the road to freedom. Let us return, first of all, to EIIIp57s:

> [A]lthough each individual lives content with the nature wherewith he is endowed and rejoices in it, that life wherewith each is content (*gaudium*) and that joy are nothing other than the idea or soul (*anima*) of the said individual, and so the joy of the one differs from the joy of another as much as the essence of the one differs from the essence of the other.

Let us, then, take the case of children, whose capacities to be affected and to affect are reduced since children "cannot talk or walk or reason" (EVp6s). Because a child's soul has not been in existence long enough it has "practically no consciousness of itself, of God, or of things" (EVp39s). Its only appetite is for its mother's milk and the physical, affective warmth of its environment. Due to its native weakness and its "very small number of capacities" to be affected or to affect, the child is in an extremely unstable "equilibrium," highly dependent on the fluctuations of external causes (EVp39s).[3] Yet a child can easily reach the desired state of equilibrium, because its needs—nourishment, well-being, and love—are easily met (EIIIp32s). The child, because it demands little, thus experiences a joy that will maintain itself for as long as circumstances will allow. But this joy is experienced within a dynamic of the *appetitus* in a regimen of near total heteronomy. We could say of the newborn what Spinoza says of the ignorant, that is, that as soon as he ceases to be passive (with sadness or with pleasure), he ceases to be (EVp42s).

Although the equilibrium of the body can be effectively realized by external conditions, Spinoza nonetheless notes in EIVp42d that what characterizes the pleasure of *hilaritas* is that the same proportion of motion-and-rest among the body's parts is maintained throughout. This proportion of motion-and-rest by which the body experiences a certain measure of plenitude is not, in itself, created by external causes, even if it is sustained by them (EIVp39). Besides, cheerfulness is always good and cannot be excessive, for the proportion of motion-and-rest conserved in this affect is already itself, in itself, and through itself, beneficial; that is, balanced, good, and without excess. Thus, it is not the conservation merely of the same proportion that causes cheerfulness, but the conservation of a good equilibrium of all the parts of our being. Let us suppose a proportion of motion-and-rest that would be a pleasant imbalance. This is the case of *titillatio* that Spinoza defines in EIVp43d as follows:

> Titillation is pleasure which, in so far as it is related to the body, consists in one or more of the body's parts being affected more than the rest. (See its definition in Sch.Pr.11,III). The power of this emotion can be so great as to surpass the other activities of the body (Pr.6,IV) and to stay firmly fixed therein, and thus hinder the body's ability to be affected in numerous other ways.

Let us suppose, then, a pleasant imbalance in a body in which the power to act would yet be increased equally among all its parts. Rather than *hilaritas*, this would always produce *titillatio*, carried out on a superior degree of the body's power to act, due to the prior unbalanced structure, even if the latter was maintained along with all its proportions.

Cheerfulness, therefore, already supposes a state of equilibrium good in itself. Furthermore, it presupposes a particular affect (and/or desire) without excess, intrinsically tied to the state of equilibrium of our body and of our whole being. This affect is not the expression of the transition from a lesser perfection of our body's power to act to a greater perfection. This is a pleasure, "if we may still use this term," as Spinoza says of blessedness in EVp36s, a pleasure in a certain kind of tranquility, as with the Epicureans. It is constitutive, active, and of the same type as the feelings of freedom, love, or glory, experienced along with the third kind of knowledge. In fact, this affect of tranquility which accompanies the idea of self (however barely conscious it should be) is already blessedness itself, but not yet adequately thought nor lived out in the autonomy of desire. This is the love of ourselves, the first principal form of adequateness, or the equilibrated affect of the self by itself that necessarily encloses the *conatus*. This love of self contains the minimum of reflexivity which is the singular self-determining of Nature in its affirmation in us and through us. This is a "natural love" (KVapp2:6), necessarily balanced and without excess, since it affirms our singular essence in all our existence. This love also affirms the characteristic proportion of motion-and-rest in and through which this singular essence actualizes itself. And this equilibrium in the tranquility of the love of self is now immanent to the power of acting itself, to the real moment of the real in its productive affirmation. This state of motionlessness is active and fecund.

Let us return to the particular case of the child. There is in the child a contentment, or a sense of well being proper to its nature, that is, to its singular proportion of motion-and-rest. This is a condition of its plenitude, of its adequateness for itself which expresses itself perfectly in the equilibrium of its affects in its body as well as its mind. Contrary then, to the usual reading of EIIIp11s and EIVp42, which systematically treats cheerfulness and melancholy (two affects distinguished from titillation [or pleasure] and from pain, and that are related to man inasmuch as all the parts of his being are 'equally affected'), these two affects do not have a balanced relationship. If cheerfulness is by nature an affect of equilibrium without excess and therefore always good, melancholy, despite the equilibrium of the body's parts in the moment of depression, is by nature unbalanced and excessive. It would be in this sense the opposite of a *titillatio*, yet likewise, still an increase in all of the body's parts; that is, an anguish excessive by nature to which all the body's parts are radically subjected. This subjection diminishes the power to act of our whole being, and likewise of all its parts, so that no further resistance should be possible. In becoming constitutive—but this is the very limit of life and its possibility—the sadness of melancholy becomes a veritable instinct for death. The pleasure of *hilaritas* is, on the contrary, positively constitutive, in the sense that it is attached not only to an actual growth in power to act, but also, and above all, to an active tranquility immanent to the moment of affirmation. Thus this essential tranquility, which is the preservation, in this increase of power, of the same balanced proportion and equilibrium of the being in its affirmation, is in itself by nature without excess, like the love which accompanies it. And here at this point we already have the pleasure of blessedness.

Acquiescentia animi and Adequate Knowledge

As we have seen, a direct route leads from a balanced love of self to blessedness. *Hilaritas* marks in some way an important milestone on this route, a practical condition of the transition. Even though it is modified by external causes and organized and made favorable in some way by good encounters (as in the case of childhood), it still supposes an essential balance the very essence of which expresses itself in a particular proportion of motion-and-rest. This means that although the intervention of external causes which act in our favor is necessary for *hilaritas*—this is our passivity—this sole intervention is not sufficient to explain the unique character and power of this affect. It must still encounter our actual essential activity, i.e., that of the *conatus* itself, which—once a certain degree of perfection of our being is reached, based upon the fact that our bodies already have numerous capacities to be affected and to affect—will make these fortunate circumstances the occasion of a true constitution of internal contentment whose origin is reason. Thus, "the force of the desire that arises from pleasure must be defined by human power together with the power of an external cause" (EIVp18d). This is a case *par excellence* of *hilaritas* increasing its force. The dynamic of *hilaritas* is in itself the practical, direct, and chief route for the achievement of an *acquiescentia in se ipso* that takes its origin and its solid equilibrium from reason itself. That is, from the autonomous power of our singular life. For, if cheerfulness is a passive pleasure, it is thus the expression of a powerful joy to live fully in all our actions, of an *acquiescentia animi*, of an adequateness of self and of life, of a fundamental confidence which, as soon as it can accompany itself with the idea of God as a cause in the second as in the third type of knowledge, will become an active affect, blessedness. This dynamic of the pleasure of joy, as yet a passive activity, can lead us to adequate knowledge (EIVp45c2s, EIVapp31, and EIVp59d1). Let's read EIVp45c2s:

> [T]he more we are affected with pleasure, the more we pass to a state of greater perfection; that is, the more we necessarily participate in the divine nature. Therefore it is the part of a wise man to make use of things and to take pleasure in them as far as he can. . . . For the human body is composed of many parts of different kinds, which are continually in need of fresh food of various kinds so that the entire body may be equally capable of all the functions that can follow from its own nature, and consequently that the mind may be equally capable of simultaneously understanding many things.

And EIVp59d1:

> [I]n so far as pleasure is good, it is in agreement with reason (for it consists in this, that a man's power of activity is increased or assisted), and it is a passive emotion only in so far as a man's power of activity is not increased to such a degree that he adequately conceives himself and his actions (Pr.3,III and Sch.). Therefore if a man affected with pleasure were brought to such a degree of perfection that he were adequately to conceive himself and his actions, he would be capable, indeed, more capable, of those same actions to which he is now determined by passive emotions.

Thus cheerfulness—which is always good and without excess—is the passive affect *par excellence* that agrees adequately with reason. Through this affect, reason can begin to express itself. This occurs

in the very process of life's self-arrangement, a process of composition and organization which is that of reason itself. This process
affirms pleasure and actively resists external forces that tend to
suppress the state of cheerfulness, that is, the perfect affective
equilibrium among all the parts of our being. This is both the
dynamic of perfection and reason's rising through pleasure. This
is "so that men may thus endeavor as far as they can to live in
accordance with reason's behest, not from fear or dislike, but
motivated only by the emotion of pleasure" (EIVapp25). Similarly,
"we should always concentrate on that which is good in every single thing (Cor.Pr.63,IV and Pr.59,III) so that in so doing we may be
determined to act always from the emotion of pleasure" (EVp10s).
Neither passivity nor a decrease in power can flow from this
dynamic self-arrangement, which only really occurs in the case of
autonomy that accompanies the idea of God as cause of our
affects. Even if it is still extrinsically passive, as in the case when a
man's power to act has not yet reached this critical point or
threshold when he conceives himself and his own affects adequately, cheerfulness is not, however, essentially passive. His relative passivity is in some way a passive activity, since only activity
can flow from his own bodily and conceptual dynamics. Thus, if
unfavorable external causes do not obliterate cheerfulness, then
cheerfulness is indeed the immanent active route to the production of adequate ideas, the first being common notions. But how is
it that cheerfulness is a productive power of common notions?

We could say that cheerfulness is taken simultaneously (in particular due to the equilibrium and the equality it supposes) as an
affection of the body in all its parts, and as the idea of this affection. Now, at a certain level of perfection (or of richness of its
capacities to be affected and to affect) when the human body, as in
the case of cheerfulness, is affected by external causes equally in
all its very numerous parts, this means that it also affects itself; for
it is affected by something that is common to all its parts and/or
something that is also common with all the other bodies. The
body's extrinsic passivity is therefore immediately correlative with
a real activity which, absolutely speaking, is that of reason. For
reason truly comes to be at this point, since "that which is total in
the thing"—i.e., the plenitude itself of the affection—"is *ipso facto*
total (or adequate) in the idea."[4] Now, according to EIIp38, "Those
things that are common to all things and are equally in the part as
in the whole, can be conceived only adequately." The affections,
therefore, since they permit individuals to harmonize with each

other, should thus be considered in their activity; they express the common properties that are deduced from the very essence of the bodies under consideration. Thus, EIIp39 reads:

> Of that which is common and proper to the human body and to any external bodies by which the human body is customarily affected, and which is equally in the part as well as in the whole of any of these bodies, the idea also in the mind will be adequate.

And the corollary reads:

> Hence it follows that mind is more capable of perceiving more things adequately in proportion as its body has more things in common with other bodies. (EIIp39c)

Knowing, as we are reminded by EIVp32d, that things which agree in nature agree in power rather than in weakness or in negation, we thus find in EIIp37, EIIp38, and EIIp39, the justification of this ethics of quantity, later developed in EIVp38, EIVp45s, EIVapp27, and then in EVp24, EVp26, and EVp39,s.

Cheerfulness, which indicates a process wherein no affect is contrary to our nature (EIVp30) or obstructs our thought (EIVp26,27), thus expresses the dynamics whereby clear and distinct ideas are formed and deduced from one another (EIIp40s2, EIIp47s). Consequently, following EVp1 and EVp10d, for as long as our cheerfulness maintains itself and increases, "we have the ability to arrange and associate affections of the body according to the order of the intellect."

All human development supposes that the dynamics of *hilaritas* should not be perturbed by external forces, and that this cheerfulness is already capable of resisting these perturbations. Furthermore, it presupposes that this dynamics of perfecting the body as well as the mind can in the end arrange itself in an autonomous manner, that is, rationally. For the active motionlessness of *hilaritas*, that is, *cupiditas*, or the very essence of man insofar as it is by nature balanced and without excess (EIVp61d), makes possible, in the ethical endeavor, an autonomous and rational conduct for life. For, as Spinoza says in EIVp21d, "the desire to live happily . . . is the very essence of man." External causes are thus only occasional causes in the fortunate manifestation of *hilaritas*, but the force of this manifestation is in itself an activity, that of *cupiditas*, which at a certain level of perfection of being will be able, by itself alone, to produce clear and distinct ideas—and thus transform *hilaritas* to *beatitudo*.

A Dynamic Balance: Return and Productivity

However, we must insist that Spinoza, like the materialists of antiquity, always thought that "one will not triumph over internal enemies before having vanquished the enemies from outside."[5] Blessedness thus serves as a preliminary to the material arrangement of the conditions of existence, conditions necessary if not sufficient for its establishment.

Similarly, Spinoza's ethico-political project is clearly a matter of arranging, as much as one can, for the possibility of *hilaritas*. This is already projected in the first pages of the *Treatise on the Emendation of the Intellect*. The demands of adulthood are certainly much greater that those of childhood, but the problem for both of them is the same. In order to construct a man, with "human nature much stronger than [one's] own" (TIE 13), it is necessary thus "to establish such a social order as will enable as many as possible to reach this goal with the greatest possible ease and assurance" (TIE 14-5). If it is going to be necessary, as indicated by EVp39d,s, to direct the body's perpetual changes toward this ethical end, it is also necessary to direct the mass of social institutions that concern bodies and their internal as well as mutual equilibrium toward this same end. From this point of view, we can better understand the necessity of Spinoza's political program in the TIE:

> Furthermore . . . attention must be paid to moral philosophy and likewise the theory of the education of children; and since health is of no little importance in attaining this end . . . the whole science of medicine must be elaborated. And since many difficult tasks are rendered easy by contrivance, and we can thereby gain much time and convenience in our daily lives . . . the science of mechanics is in no way to be despised. (TIE 15)

School (moral philosophy and the theory of education), the medical services (medicine), and the work world (mechanics) are three institutions that are directly concerned with the life and death of men, the very existence of *conatus*. Still more precisely, these institutions concern bodies, their 'equilibrium,' and the 'convenience of daily lives'. We thus understand better the socio-historic determination these 'corporeal capacities'—which Spinoza grants an essential role—play in the practical life of humans as the basis of the mind's modification and production of true ideas. One calls to mind the love or friendship that other men, either by reason or under the influence of a 'true faith,' can feel for us, and which, for a child, are sources of equilibrium and well-being since they are, even before one has taken the route of reason, truly effective remedies against the passive affects.[6] Moreover other men, and external causes in general, far from always being favorable to our being, open us up to a violent struggle for predominance between reason and the affections and between the affections themselves. This same logic of the affects applies as well to the predominance of one affection over another (in *titillatio*), as to the predominance enforced by reason over the affections.

Reason is thus presented in *Ethics* IV in an extrinsic manner as the form of an *imperium* and its dictates (*dictamina*). However, these forms only order that which nature affirms in and through its own self-arrangement; reason itself cannot realize this directly because of our own weakness and/or the passive affections of our body which is subjected to external forces. But the number one rule prescribed by reason is the love of self (EIVp18s).[7]

We must recall that the love of self (*amour de soi*), which is an essential equilibrium, is not a self-love (*amour-propre*), which implies a structural imbalance since it is necessarily both imaginary and marred with pride or false modesty. The love of self is, on the contrary, balanced as nature itself, or as "desire considered absolutely." It cannot exceed in affirming itself, since it is an affect of the self for itself, a positive determination intrinsic in and by our nature:

> So if this desire could be excessive [as Spinoza might say for
> a desire having its origin in reason], human nature, consid-
> ered absolutely, could exceed itself, that is, it could do more
> than it could do, which is a manifest contradiction. (EIVp61d)

Thus, when Spinoza in EIVp18s first posits the dictates of reason which "demand nothing contrary to nature," and which require one to love oneself, he is essentially thinking of a love of self which is a balanced love of being or of its perfection. He is not thinking of self-love, which is necessarily an unbalanced love towards an image of oneself. Thus the ethical endeavor, i.e., conduct "under the dictates of reason," presents itself in *Ethics* IV as a spontaneous strategy for the affirmation of bodies or of the dynamic centrifuge of immediate love of self; but in part it also counters this strategy, or, more precisely, counters its extrinsic forms of actualization which, left to their own imaginary mechanisms, have led each man to become the worst possible enemy to himself and to those like him.

The ethical endeavor, therefore, presents itself as the dynamic continuation of an equilibrated love of self, i.e., as a strategy according to a double movement: The first is a return to a state of equilibrium made normal by the essential proportion of motion-and-rest. This is a strategy of resistance in the double sense of the prefix 're' of 'resist': the return to self or subsistence, and the repetition of being, its persistence or perseverance. But this is an active resistance, for it dynamically opposes (*opponere*) that which, in undermining the essential proportion of motion-and-rest, tends to break the equilibrium grounded in *hilaritas*. This is to say that if there is effectively a 'return,' nostalgia (sadness, pain) is not its mover. The second movement, which is also a consequent of the first, is a dynamic and productive affirmation (for tranquility is active!) of new desires, new pleasures, and new ideas, according to which the proportion itself can modify itself positively by increasing the capacity of our body and mind to affect and to be affected. Thereby not only the radical change from the state of infancy to that of adulthood is defined ("Do we deal with the same person?" Spinoza asks himself in EIVp39s), but also the ethical endeavor itself, being a true ethics of accumulation (EIVp20), of quantity (EIVp38) and of an indefinite productivity (end of EVp39s). Let us reconsider these two aspects of the ethical strategy of the *conatus*.

The logic formulated by our first point about a 'return' is not a look back to an *a priori* order or principle, since the norm is itself, in the relational existence of acts, susceptible to modification. We could even say that the *conatus* constructs its own norm of action in its relational activity. This is evidently the case in the transition from the state of childhood to that of adulthood or from the state of ignorance to that of wisdom. Philosophy's real moment is the Real and its autonomy. The Spinozistic imperative of ethics (and likewise in politics), is the 'return to the origin'. But it is not a conservative return toward an order postulated as 'natural', nor toward that of a life which before its modality had organized its materiality. Rather it is the return to the origin as the real moment of the Real, the moment of nature essentially equilibrated in its autonomy and its immanence. This equilibrium has neither excess nor lack, it is an auto-normative movement that is a self-organizing law of nature that one discovers both as the power of idea and that of bodies or of the multitude. This is to say that the logic of return—which, due to our condition of finitude and of "human weakness and inconstancy" (EIVp18s) supposes a conjectured state of imbalance—is a dynamic of active resistance. As in the case of *titillatio*, certain parts of our being resist the authority (of a true *imperium*) of other parts that tend, by subjecting the individual in its totality, to put its entire life in danger. The oppressed parts oppose this hegemony in solidarity with one another through their particular *conatus*. Thus an affect is bad inasmuch as it simultaneously hinders the soul from thinking (EIVp26, EIVp27), and all the parts of the body from fully fulfilling their function. In a phrase, a "bad pleasure . . . would prevent the body from being rendered more capable."[8] From this point of view, the pain of certain oppressed parts of our body that tend to resist the exclusive and excessive authority of a single one of these parts is good so far "as being able to check titillation [or pleasure] so that it does not become excessive, and to that extent. . . it would prevent the body from being rendered less capable" (EIVp43d). We could reason likewise concerning excessive pain that the other parts of the body also resist (as they do excessive pleasure).

But with melancholy, since this is itself a balanced depression—because all the parts of our body are equally affected with sadness—nothing allows us to resist it in an internal manner. The entire defense system is neutralized and made to serve the depression: this is the true dynamics of suicide. In the case of melancholy, unless an external cause happens to unsettle it to the advantage of a pleasurable affect, by which the *conatus* of one of the body's parts could be able again to resist the totality of the other parts in their depression, the individual, logically and unavoidably, is headed for destruction. For the love of self, which is an active center of resistance, is totally neutralized by melancholy. Therefore it is necessary in this case *melancholiam expellere*—to expel melancholy, to resist it with all one's forces. This is a major categorical imperative of Spinozistic ethics. EIIIp37d underlines the necessary active resistance of the individual *conatus* to pain:

> [T]he *conatus* of a man affected by pain is entirely directed to removing the pain. But . . . the greater the pain, the greater the extent to which it must be opposed to man's power of activity. Therefore the greater the pain, with that much greater power of activity will a man endeavor to remove the pain.

And in EIVp45c2s, in an all too rare, personal interruption of the geometric order of the *Ethics*—too rare to be ignored—Spinoza firmly says:

> Why is it less fitting to drive away melancholy than to dispel hunger and thirst? Th[is] principle . . . guides me and shapes my attitude in life. [9]

Melancholy is, then, a prime adversary. Through it the *conatus* can be totally vanquished by neutralization. It becomes paralyzed, and its forces of life invert to become forces of death. Death insinuates itself in us through the dynamics of associations (totally harmful in this case) and thus uses the same means by which life itself otherwise could be affirmed and unfolded.

The second aspect that characterizes the strategy of dynamic power of affirmation underlines the productivity of the *conatus* itself. This productivity is always favorable to the conservation of the individual if the latter does not encounter external obstacles to this affirmation. Thus, the idea of a perfect strategy, though abstract, is itself deducible causally and outside any teleological consideration of "man's essence, from the nature of which there necessarily follow those things that tend to his preservation" (EIIIp9s). If one posits the essence of a finite mode, one necessarily deduces from it all the useful acts for its conservation. And if the finite mode, through an exceptional destiny that may happen to befall it, were capable of actually thinking according to the norm of a given true idea (correlative to a real activity of the body whose affections would thus be actively ordered), it would directly develop a perfect strategy for the absolute affirmation of its existence. But "this rarely or never happens" (TIE 44). EIVp19, EIVp24,d, EIVp61d, and EIVapp6 underline the identification of a perfect strategy with autonomy. This is what was already posited in the opening of EIVpref, where *sui juris* (the man who depends on himself and thus preserves himself adequately) is opposed to the man who is tossed about by external causes and depends to the highest degree on 'fortune'. At EIVdef8 and EIVax, Spinoza successively posits: 1) the mode's intrinsic infinitude in the "power to bring about that which can be understood solely through the laws of his own nature" (or the power of autonomy), and; 2) its extrinsic finitude through its relationships of force among finite things. These two principles yield from the very beginning of *Ethics* IV the necessary link between the power of autonomy and the necessary active-resistance to which autonomous affirmation is led *vis-à-vis* obstacles from outside. It is in this sense that the *conatus* is indissoluble in its very productivity as both the power of affirmation and the power of resistance. For the *conatus* does not merely resist, rather, in its very resistance as affirmation, it constructs and constitutes. The entire ethical endeavor is in this process of the autonomous auto-arrangement of active resistance of the singular modality. It consists in the tendency to return to the essential equilibrium that we first experience in *hilaritas*. This equilibrium is at the same moment and on a certain level of perfection, the productivity of new desires and new pleasures with new true ideas: *acquiescentia in se ipso*, that is, the love of self adequately conceived.

This spiraling process through which equilibrium can be regained, although always at different levels of perfection, has for itself no model, finality, or limit. This is a dynamics of infinite perfection. This is, in some way, Epicureanism multiplied and put into endless movement. In Spinoza, as well as the Epicureans (applying a strategy of indefinite productivity of desire, or that of pleasure in a "natural and necessary" tranquility), it is a matter of regaining the equilibrium which allows the wise man's life, who is like a god to other men (EIVp35c2s), or, as Epicurus puts it in his Letter to Meneceus, "a god among men."[10] In fact, Spinoza will show in *Ethics* V that what the best men could ever aspire for is to substitute for a loved object which affects us in different and often contradictory manners, and throws us into constant flux[11] (making us enemies to ourselves and to others), a new object, one which would affect us "with a continuous and supreme pleasure to all eternity" (TIE 1), and "equally" for all men (EIVp36), as well as all the parts of our soul and our body. This object would offer a kind of delight in tranquility already found, if precariously, in *hilaritas*. Here, however, to follow the expression of EIVp47s, we "command fortune as far as we can."

This new object (if we can speak this way) is God or Nature, the knowledge and love of which we can aspire to as soon as our body possesses a great number of capacities to be affected and to affect. This is expressed at EVp39,d, which is founded on EIVp38 and EIVp30. Let us look at the demonstration:

> He whose body is capable of the greatest amount of activity
> is least assailed by the emotions that are evil (Pr.38, IV), that
> is, (Pr.30,IV), by emotions that are contrary to our nature.
> Thus (Pr.10,V) he has the capacity to arrange and associate
> the affections of the body according to intellectual order and
> consequently to bring it about (Pr.14,V) that all the affections

of the body [*omnes corporis affectiones*] are related to the idea
of God. This will result (Pr.15,V) in his being affected with
love towards God, a love (Pr.16,V) that must occupy or constitute the greatest part of the mind. Therefore (Pr.33,V) he
has a mind whose greatest part is eternal.

In the knowledge of God and our affects, *hilaritas* thus changes
to *beatitudo*. This is a blessedness of our whole being, or man in his
totality. It affects the "entire man" (*totius hominis*) in all the parts of
his body and mind (EIVp60,s), and not only in the contentment of
"that part of us which is defined by the understanding, that is, the
better part of us" (EIVapp32). If we held ourselves exclusively and
in a restrictive manner to this last affirmation, we would thus
believe that fortune—an occasional and yet necessary cause for
hilaritas—could better bring about the happiness of man than did
his reason or his virtue themselves. As was already announced in
the *Short Treatise on God, Man, and His Well-Being*, he who searches
and finally "rests in the good which is all good and in which is
found the plenitude of all joy and all satisfaction" (KVII 7:3),
achieves a "love" which is "unlimited, that is, that the more it
grows, the more it becomes excellent since it bears itself toward an
object which is infinite and which permits him to grow continually" (KVII 14:5). And the more we live in and by this integral
love, the less we will need "fortune's help" (EIVp46s).

Thus, the definition of *hilaritas* at the very heart of *Ethics* IV
indicates that a sense of blessedness is found in fleeting experience, and also marks, to a degree of completeness, the direct,
dynamic, and autonomous path to its achievement. Through this
pleasure, by which we gain "knowledge" of an integral good
(EIVp8), we can reach the knowledge of God and of ourselves. We
can regain the highest degrees of perfection and the tranquility
gained thereby, a tranquility that we have already known as children. As children we were (if very transiently) easily gratified by
fortune; this is the free gift of blessedness which suits us, and
which Parts IV and V of the *Ethics* have us both construct and
regain, in accordance with the dynamics of our own virtue, i.e., in
accordance with the very laws of our own nature (EIVdef8,
EIVp24). *Hilaritas* is at once both a force and precious indication of
this endeavor of and toward *acquiescentia in se ipso*.[12]

The question of the strategy is thus shifted from the domain of
representation (that of the practical and ethical subject under the
determination of reason, who works up means for an end) to the
domain of the production of an adequate idea following an order

of affections identical in body as in thought. This domain matches (in the sequence of active affections) the very order by which nature produces and affirms itself in its total plenitude. And this new logic—which in reality has been from all eternity—is the same as the essence in its actualization or the existence in its absolute and perfect affirmation. This is the perfect strategy for the mode, which, without the abstract mediation of a model of means and ends, applies its open autonomy so as to really master problems posed in its effort of total adequateness to the Real, hence also to itself. Through adequate ideas, man accesses the real moment of active affect; wisdom is the real moment wherein the actual state of bondage is abolished, but it is also the struggle of the strategic subject who, on the basis of a true knowledge, participates in the construction of the objective conditions of this moment.

Translated by Steven Barbone

NOTES

1. EIVp42d. All references to the *Ethics* and to the *Treatise on the Emendation of the Intellect* (TIE) are taken from *Ethics, Treatise on the Emendation of the Intellect, Selected Letters*, trans. Samuel Shirley (Indianapolis: Hackett, 1992). [All other translations are my own—Trans.].

2. This topic is taken up in Chapter 4 of my book, *La Stratégie du Conatus: Affirmation et Résistance chez Spinoza* (Paris: Vrin, 1996).

3. Spinoza also speaks of children's mimetic pleasure of laughing in EIIIp32s.

4. Martial Gueroult, *Spinoza: L'Âme* (Paris: Aubier, 1974), p. 336.

5. Paul Nizan, *Les matérialistes de l'antiquité* (Paris: Maspéro, 1965), pp. 17-8. Cf. Niccolò Machiavelli, *The Prince*, trans. and ed. Q. Skinner and R. Price (Cambridge: Cambridge University Press, 1988), ch. 19, p. 64.

6. EIVp46s and EIVapp11. See also TTP, particularly chaps. 11-4.

7. In his sixteenth lecture on the fine arts, Alain clearly relies on the Spinozist theme of the singular essence, its "formula of equilibrium," to use his phrase, and the logic of the love of ourselves: "For every man, Peter or James, says Spinoza, there is necessarily in God an idea or essence, formula of equilibrium, of movements, of linked functions, which are his soul and which is the same thing as his body . . . [And] it is completely necessary not to believe that this essential architecture could ever be sick through itself, end, wear itself out, die by its own hand. . . . The tide of existence does not cease to beat against our cliffs; but, Spinoza energetically expounds, man cannot possibly kill himself, nor even point a dagger against his own chest, unless another hand, stronger than his, twist his own. Here we find, in the austere philosophy, the center of hope and courage and the true foundation of love of self." Alain, "Vingt leçons sur les Beaux-Arts," in *Spinoza* (Paris: Gallimard, 1968), pp. 171-2. On the center of hope and of courage, or the center of resistance to everything which blocks our self affirmation or tends to destroy us, see EIIIp6d.

8. EIVp43d, EIVp44d, EIVp59d, EIVp65.

9. This personal interruption is nonetheless more vibrant as it borrows the words from Terence who is cited there without being named. Cf. *Adelphi*, v. 68: "Mea sic est ratio et sic animum induco meum." Spinoza writes, "Mea haec est ratio, et sic animum induxi meum" (EIVp45c2s).

10. Epicure, *Lettres et Maximes*, ed. Marcel Conche (Paris: PUF, 1992), p. 227. For a comparison of the two philosophers, see my article "Epicurisme et spinozisme: l'éthique," *Archives de philosophie* (juillet-septembre, 1994), pp. 471-84.

11. EIVp33d.

12. In a recent essay, Antonio Negri, after having emphasized "the true and proper ontological function of *ridere*," likewise points out the concept of *hilaritas* as one of the major developments in the Spinozistic phenomenology of passions. He writes that it is a development in which Spinoza "acknowledges in the process of subjectification (i.e., about the subject's identification of the origin of the innovation of being) a fundamental, ontological intensity for the process, i.e., in the 'experience' that leads man to freedom." Antonio Negri, "Necessité et liberté chez Spinoza: quelques alternatives," *Multitudes* 2 (May 2000), pp. 163-80.

Spinoza and Freud: An Old Myth Revisited

Cornelis de Deugd

The present paper is intended to question frankly the prevalent assessment that Benedictus de Spinoza and Sigmund Freud have, in many respects, much in common. The assessment of these thinkers as kindred spirits even goes so far as to present Spinoza as the predecessor of Freud. Because these notions have been around for such a long time (at least since the 1920s), and have become so widespread, while having been verified only to a limited extent, they have come to bear a strong resemblance to what is traditionally designated as myth.

Not all of the authors who have studied this relationship have spoken of Spinoza literally as a precursor to Freud. But even for these authors, this thesis is still implicitly present. To my knowledge, there is no study that is truly critical of this thesis while at the same time examining the fundamentals of Spinozistic and Freudian thinking. The unfortunate absence of this double-edged approach has resulted in an accumulation of untenable and sometimes wild ideas. Fortunately, during the last two decades a few articles have been published by authors who, critical of the hagiographically-inclined writings of the last eighty years or so, have tried to correct such writings within the margin of what has threatened to become canonical. The names of Nails, Fóti, and Yovel spring to mind; I shall return to them later on. Most of the authors, however, have apparently been satisfied with the status quo.

Admittedly, Spinoza and Freud are not just ships that pass in the night; there is one noteworthy similarity in their work, i.e., their psychic determinism. Spinoza, like Freud, unequivocally defends a determinism that is both unqualified and rigorous. This one characteristic links them together, and in so doing, links them to several others as well. And that is about all; the congruencies, similarities, and parallels that can be named in addition are, in relation to the vital issues of each thinker, of such insignificance as to be completely unimportant. Remarkably, other authors, writing on Spinoza or Freud have avoided the topic altogether, and I am inclined to think that this is not merely accidental. They may well have seen that, once one leaves the level of superficial similarity, it is a deceptively problematic matter. Furthermore, it is not unthinkable that they noticed substantial vested interests of an emotional nature that would make for strenuous discussion. To illustrate this feature (but also somewhat for the sake of curiosity) I need no more than name a few works of outstanding quality in which the topic is not discussed at all.

There is the perspicuous study by Errol Harris, *Salvation from Despair* (1973); Ruben Fine's *The Development of Freud's Thought* (1973); H.F. Hallett's *Creation, Emanation and Salvation* (1962) and, of course, Frank J. Sulloway's more recent *Freud, Biologist of the Mind* (1979), a 600-odd page study notable for its minute historical scholarship. In this work every philosopher, even in the remotest sense 'related' to Freud, is examined, but Spinoza is not even mentioned.

In the pages to follow, I propose to discuss four major areas in which Spinoza and Freud are alleged to be of one mind and on the basis of which Benedictus de Spinoza is said to be the predecessor of Freud. My contention is that the two are worlds apart, and that at least in these four areas this thesis is demonstrable.

Although I am inclined to see the Freud-Spinoza *discussion* during the twentieth century somewhat from the angle of light comedy, and treat it with a smile rather than a frown, I do not see the elucidation of their relationship to be a matter of secondary importance simply because both men have deeply influenced the Western view of man.

1. Reason—Unreason

The concept of reason appears to have two main facets. In view of the various comparisons and the ensuing claims as to similarities and congruencies between Freud and Spinoza, and, generally, the claims that Spinoza is a 'predecessor' of Freud, the question arises why Spinoza is a representative of an anthropology diametrically opposed to Freud's. Spinoza's view of man is that of Rationalism and the Enlightenment; man is conscious of being able to obtain knowledge by the power of reason which—whenever it manifests itself—excludes all things irrational.[1]

Freud's view of man shows an almost complete reversal of the rationalist legacy: consciousness as a relatively unimportant, if not 'superficial', dimension, dominated by forces stemming from the irrational unconscious, which Freud considers to be more prominent and influential than the rational part of man. Both the rationalist and the irrationalist (Freudian) view of man have, as said, deeply influenced present day anthropology. Even if it were only in these terms, a clarification of the Spinoza/Freud discussion can hardly be seen as a matter of minor importance.

As to the second facet, repeatedly it has been maintained that Spinoza's rationalistic way of thinking finds its equivalent in psychoanalytic practice. Both, it is said, attempt to understand human (mental) phenomena, that is, to bring them within reason's radius of action. When Freud receives various kinds of information from a patient (part of which he sees as related to the unconscious) he interprets and explains them, communicating his findings to the patient. In doing so he applies new, revolutionary methods that will always remind us of his pioneering and original spirit: the analysis of dreams, transference, free association, etc. That these methods have been called "woefully inadequate from a scientific point of view" (Eysenck) is at present none of our concern.[2] For Freud's psychotherapeutic activity is, of course, a *rational* procedure. It is an attempt to grapple with the emotional vicissitudes, that is, the problems of his troubled patients and, finally, to arrive at an *understanding* of them.

The application of the term 'rational' seems an obvious move; it is inconceivable that it could be formulated otherwise. All medical activity, including both the accompanying and ensuing communication, is based on the same principles, whether we observe methodological innovation or not. However, it remains rather unclear what this has to do with Spinoza's rationalism, in which the paramount emphasis is on the criterion of truth, and in which the logical attributes of true knowledge—universality and necessity—are not derived from experience and its generalizations, but are intellectual and deductive. One could say that Freud does what, according to Spinoza, most people do. In his *Theological Political Treatise*, Spinoza remarks that "people prefer to be taught by experience rather than deduce their conclusions from a few axioms" (Chapter 5, GIII 77:9-11), thereby indicating in a strikingly simple way the difference—that was to arise three centuries later—between Freud's method (case studies) and his own (deductions/generalizations). In this respect, Spinoza's rationalism is the opposite of empiricism. If we categorize Spinoza's labor in the vineyard of philosophy as rationalism *tout court*, Freud's arduous, novel approach in the field of psychiatry may well be called empiricism. In a somewhat different vein, we may apply the terminology of Paul Tillich and speak of Spinoza's ontological reason versus Freud's technical reason. What looms here is one of the many cases in which the ideas of Spinoza and Freud oppose each other in the sense that Spinoza's rationalism is the equivalent of universalist thought, whereas Freud cannot but proceed on the basis of particularistic thinking.

These distinctions are not merely significant in a theoretical sense; they spell out the fundamental difference between Spinoza and Freud. The confusion in this respect is manifold. For now I shall give only one example out of many and shall return later on in different contexts to other consequences of these distinctions. Kaplan quotes Spinoza as having said: "We must know both the strength and weakness of our nature, so that we may determine what reason can do and what it cannot do in governing our passions."[3] Indiscriminately using the term 'reason', the author proceeds with an attempt at elucidating what, according to Spinoza and Freud, reason can do, all the while implying that in both cases 'reason' functions the same way, and that Freud does the same thing Spinoza did three centuries earlier. That he does not notice the discrepancy between Spinoza and Freud becomes apparent from the fact that no mention is made of Spinoza's concept of the *adequate idea* that, in the *Ethics,* should drive out the confused idea and take its place. In a comparative analysis of Spinoza's and Freud's thinking, the 'adequate idea' cannot be excluded without resulting in embarrassing confusion. Freud's observation and subsequent intellectualization of phenomena in the patient's emotional history, that is, his subsequent rationally formulated insight, has next to nothing to do with Spinoza's rationalism. In other words, it is essentially different from Spinoza's pursuit of the adequate idea. I shall have occasion to discuss further consequences of the distinctions made here.

That these doctrines are opposed to each other is to a great extent connected with two equally opposing anthropological views. Spinoza's philosophical undertaking is in every respect dominated by one goal: the *summum bonum,* the highest good, "of which the discovery and attainment" would enable one "to enjoy continuous, supreme, and unending happiness" (TIE 1). Spinoza is unswervingly certain that only *reason* can carry one to the blessed life, the consummation of the highest good. Never wavering in his certitude as to the exclusiveness and all-encompassing power of reason, he devotes his life to this goal and attains—primarily, one is inclined to think, in writing the *Ethics*—the coveted happiness. Although Spinoza does not say that every human being has to travel precisely the same road, the result of his journey reflects a very positive view of man: man *can* attain supreme happiness. Spinoza is as much the rationalist in a methodological sense as he is in a doctrinal sense. His rationalism is inextricably linked with his positive anthropological view of man, which was to become dominant in the period of the Enlightenment, an age for which Spinoza himself was to a certain degree responsible.

Freud, whose *œuvre* is wholly permeated with irrationalism—as will be seen in greater detail in the next section—could, naturally, not take the road Spinoza took. But though we can say that Spinoza's rationalism is the backbone of his positive view of man, it does not follow that Freud's irrationalism is the cause of his pessimistic anthropology. However, this is not to the point. What is evident here is the glaring contrast between Freud and Spinoza as concerning the value they place upon reason and the use they make of it. Having seen these contrasts we may consider the cause of Freud's pessimism as irrelevant at present, and demand at least one example of Freud's negativity about man. As far as that is concerned, it would be difficult to find a clearer picture than the one in his *Civilization and its Discontents* (1930): the whole of 'creation'—as we may succinctly paraphrase his position—harbors no happy human beings.[4]

2. Conscious—Unconscious

As a logical follow-up to the preceding section there now looms, predictably, the problem of Freud's theory of the unconscious, which deals with a set of questions most closely related to irrationalist thinking. The hypothesis of the unconscious is the cornerstone of the theoretical edifice Freud has created and is, at the same time, the very point of departure for his analytic-therapeutic practice.

Surprising though it may seem, there is not one thorough analysis of any length of the Freudian conception of the unconscious[5] in the literature on the Spinoza/Freud relation. Even Bidney, extensively and masterfully examining Spinoza's psychology—and, in a most levelheaded way, relating it to the position of Freud—does not delve into the obscure realm of Freud's Id. Neither does he confront it with Spinoza's epistemology or the doctrine of the affections. He merely refers to the unconscious in a few rather non-committal, fringe remarks.[6]

This neglect on the part of scholars interested in the history of ideas and specifically in Spinoza's impact on the modern world is so unusual and unexpected that a conjecture as to the reason for it can only be a hazardous one. However, it could also be extremely simple: have we perhaps become all too familiar with the unconscious and the accompanying terminology as something that simply *is* there and is, as it were, taken for granted? I am paying attention to these omissions because they have influenced the discussion on the Freud–Spinoza issue for decades. It seems to me that if Freud's concept of the unconscious had been analyzed, described, and put to work in the Spinoza–Freud comparison, there would in all likelihood not have been the myth that in this day and age still remains to be dissipated. Whyte, having studied the development and history of the unconscious, has given rise to the erroneous idea that Freud's conception has been around for many centuries;[7] Eysenck, Freud's most vocal adversary for decades, has conveniently stretched this point out to two thousand years.[8]

However this may be, not having room for a detailed handling of (erroneous) pronouncements of a genetic and historical nature, I do wish to stress that Freud, taking the road back into Europe's cultural history, merely went back to the Romantics. I stress this point as it is critical for the understanding of the *character* of Freud's theory of the unconscious. It is what I would call 'modern', which in this context means that it is active, vital, dynamic. What Freud utilized and elaborated for his own purposes was, *mutatis mutandis*, the picture that the Romantics had presented to the world. There was no trace of it in the static picture to be found as late as Descartes and Spinoza: here we should think of the Germans who, from the earliest representatives (Jena School) up to 'full' Romanticism, were almost exclusively responsible for exposing and developing the 'modern' idea of the unconscious. One thinks of philosophers and theorists of literature and the arts like Schelling, both the Schlegels (A.W. and Friedrich), Fichte, Novalis, and Willem Bilderdijk in The Netherlands.

Among these men a distinction was made between two kinds of imagination: on the one hand, the general, 'philosophical' imagination, which is the property of all men and which is instrumental in 'calling forth' (calling into being) the world of extra-mental reality ("without imagination there is no outside world"—an exclamation of Friedrich Schlegel)[9] and, on the other hand, the artistically-creative imagination of the poets and artists. I fancy I need but refer to three passages to clarify the theory of the two kinds of imagination and point to the explicit romantic conviction that the 'general' imagination (that is 'world-creating'; Fichte's term: *weltschaffende Einbildungskraft*) works *unconsciously*, whereas the 'artistic' imagination is of a definite *conscious* character.[10]

At this point it might be clear why understanding the new and trail-blazing romantic position on the unconscious is indispensable for understanding Freud's new metapsychological conception. The power, which in this idealistic view brings forth ('creates') the entire world of outside reality, is relegated by the Romantics (echoing Kant) to the realm of the unconscious—a truly revolutionary step having far-reaching consequences. For now it makes superfluous any further elucidation of the new characteristics I have indicated before: active, vital, dynamic, which characterize both the romantic and the Freudian unconscious. Whether Freud went directly to Romantics like Fichte or Schelling or whether he reached them through, e.g., Schopenhauer, Nietzsche, von Hartmann, etc., is immaterial at present.[11]

The question of decisive import here seems to be: what did Freud do with it? How and why did his labor result in *his* version of a dynamic unconscious and ultimately in what has been called a dynamic psychology? I take this to be an important question, first, because the unconscious is, as I said, Freud's point of departure in theory and practice; second, because an epistemological status unparalleled in the history of Western thought has been ascribed to it; and, third, it would prove to be impossible to speak in comparative terms about Spinoza's doctrines of *conatus*, the affections, ignorance, causation, etc., without having recourse to its genesis, its dynamic character and at least to its basic tenets.[12]

In Freud's division of the individual's mental apparatus both the regions of the Ego and the Superego are in part unconscious, but for present purposes I shall concentrate on the Id. According to Freud, the Id is the dark, inaccessible part of our personality (*Studienausgabe*, vol. 1, p. 511); all there is in the Id is instinctual cathexis wanting to be discharged (p. 512). The Id knows no value judgments, no good and evil, no morality (ibid.). The logical laws of thinking are not applicable to whatever happens in the Id (p. 511). Freud calls it a chaos (ibid.) and describes it later on as primitive and irrational (p. 512).

Apart from Freud's therapeutic intentions, which have also been accredited to Spinoza, we might well wonder how this picture of a dungeon of hidden forces—inaccessible, chaotic, illogical, primitive, and irrational—could be linked up with the *rationalist* Spinoza, and drawn with the help of genuine Spinozistic notions: *conatus*, freedom, ignorance, affections and the like. And yet, this has been done repeatedly; some authors even have gone so far as to apply unalloyed Freudian terms to Spinoza's thinking (*libido*, drive, unconscious, dark libidinal forces, etc.). Yet in Spinoza's rigorous rationalist system we nowhere find a trace of anything even remotely resembling a conception of the unconscious or any other Freud-like conception. Spinoza leaves no doubt that to him the human mind, being the idea of its body, is of necessity conscious of whatever happens in it: "nothing can take place in that body without being perceived by the mind" (EIIp12). Elsewhere he argues: "Now as the mind . . . is necessarily conscious of itself through the ideas of the modifications of the body, the mind is therefore. . . conscious of its own endeavour" (EIIIp9d; see also EIIp21s). Once more the protagonists of our story prove to be worlds apart.

However, in the case of the unconscious as well as in other cases one can come across authors endeavouring to bring these worlds together. This sometimes results in contradictions, the minimizing or explaining away of differences; comparisons are occasionally made that fall short, and ways of reasoning are advanced that do not hold water. Also, now and then certain deviations are tactfully avoided. We need not expand these matters, having already laid out the enormous discrepancy between Freud and Spinoza. To further exemplify my point I shall discuss one case of a somewhat broader scope, adding a few illustrations abundant in the literature on the two men.

As was seen in the preceding paragraphs, the difference between Spinoza, who holds that everything occurring in the mental world occurs at the conscious level, and Freud is fundamental. What then is the basis of the numerous allegations to the contrary found in the secondary literature? The answer is that there is no such basis. All there is behind those contrarily formulated opinions is a series of misunderstandings and a considerable eagerness to find in Spinoza whatever was brought into Western culture by Freud. This phenomenon seems to me rather inexplicable, but at present an explanation of it is not needed. Without having explained it, we notice that it has been said repeatedly that certain ideas, constructions, and phenomena of discernible Freudian lineage can be found in Spinoza. One of the recurring themes is the idea that the unconscious 'hidden forces', with which Freud and other psychoanalysts have busied themselves for almost a century, are part and parcel of Spinozistic thought. Thus Bernard claims that Spinoza evidently "had understood what Freud calls the 'adhesiveness' of the *libido* and the resultant 'fixations', 'obsessions' and 'repressions' . . .";[13] Bickel considers the unconscious 'implied' in Spinoza's thinking[14] while Feuer praises Spinoza highly (the *Ethics* as a "landmark in man's achievement of self-understanding") for his "discovery of the distinction between conscious and unconscious forces in man's psychological life."[15]

These are but three examples out of many that fly in the face of the evidence gathered thus far, showing that Spinoza would not have had the faintest idea of what is being imposed on him.

An interpretative move, putting the hidden ('libidinal') forces on a par with Spinoza's confused ideas, could here properly be contextualized. I shall discuss this (I am tempted to say) custom rather extensively in the next section, which will be devoted in part to confused (inadequate) ideas.

Unconscious forces have also frequently been invoked in cases where Spinoza confesses ignorance about things "hidden from the understanding." I refrain at present from referring to the secondary literature, with which everyone who knows something about Spinoza is familiar. But it seems imaginable (though not so understandable) that Spinoza admirers arrive at such conclusions. After all, did not Spinoza occasionally speak of phenomena, events, causes with which he was not acquainted, which he could not explain and about which he did not know anything even though he knew them to exist or to happen?

Naturally, in a situation like this and especially in case of formulations as used here, it is understandable that at least fragments of the psychoanalytic discourse come to mind. For that reason the question should be asked, what exactly is Spinoza speaking about and—most importantly—how does it function in the totality of his philosophical thought. Endeavouring to answer this question I will advance a few fragments from Spinoza's works about man's ignorance that might solve the problem at one go. It is connected to, and forms a unity with, his defense of his determinism, and is at the center of his argument about man not having a free will, both forming cardinal elements in his thinking.

In EIIIp2s Spinoza says: "Experience teaches us no less clearly than reason, that men believe themselves to be free, simply because they are conscious of their actions, and unconscious of the causes whereby those actions are determined." That he could not have used the word "unconscious" in the twentieth-century sense has not only been discussed in this section but is also clear from the general trend of the argument elsewhere. What is really on Spinoza's mind is that people *do not know*. They are in some respects simply *ignorant*. They do not know a great many things and in this particular case they do not know these causes. He similarly points to our ignorance in other cases, for instance, when discussing our attempts to understand the will of human beings. As for the causes discussed at present, Spinoza is eager to make transparent that it is a matter of man not knowing what is going on. In one of his letters he follows the same reasoning in slightly different words, saying that "human freedom . . . consists solely in the fact that men are conscious of their own desire, but are ignorant of the causes whereby that desire has been determined."[16]

If these deliberations do not suffice to make Spinoza's standpoint with regard to knowledge versus ignorance completely clear, I should like to put a little less emphasis on the aspect of the 'not knowing' and a little more on Spinoza's determinism, which is, as almost everywhere, involved here. Thus, in EIIp48 Spinoza lays bare the underlying determinist nexus in admirably simple words:

> In the mind there is no absolute or free will; but the mind is determined to wish this or that by a cause, which has also been determined by another cause, and this last by another cause and so on to infinity.[17]

Once more, it should be emphasized that Spinoza treats only of knowing and not-knowing. His rigorous psychic determinism makes him point to his own and all people's ignorance in certain cases: things that are 'hidden' from the human mind and its fathoming. Obviously there is no Freudian unconscious 'hidden-ness' here. In other words, there is no trace of anything behind the curtain of consciousness, in an unconscious 'world' of its own. Whatever Spinoza argues and demonstrates comes under the heading of normal epistemological considerations. By 'normal' I mean that everything is approached on the level of consciousness, the only place where philosophical thinking thrives, be it rationalist thinking or not.

That there could be a world of hidden forces stemming from an illogical, immoral, and chaotic realm of the human mind could not have occurred to Spinoza, first, because his rationalist, optimistic, and positive anthropology would have prevented it; second, because it is wholly at variance with his rationalist epistemology; and third, because the concept of a dynamic unconscious which Freud accepted, and which he elaborated, had to wait until the Romantic period (even then, it was still almost another century until Freud's *die Traumdeutung.*)

3. Affects and Adequacy — Affects and Pseudo-science

> Our mind is in certain cases active, and in certain cases passive. In so far as it has adequate ideas it is necessarily active, and in so far as it has inadequate ideas, it is necessarily passive. (EIIIp1)

These memorable words carry us to the heart of Spinoza's predilection for seeing the problems at hand in the light of the dichotomy activity/passivity, and for doing so in relation to another distinction: the one between the adequate and the inadequate idea. When it is evident that the adequacy of an idea is related to activity and the inadequacy to passivity, the question could be asked: what, to Spinoza, is the inadequacy of an idea? For this question I propose to go to Part II of the *Ethics*, getting deep into the metaphysics. This is necessary in order to uncover the basis of Spinoza's thinking on this point, and to refrain from taking at face value terms like adequate and inadequate—so frequently used in everyday parlance—as must have happened in the Spinoza/Freud discussions. Only by avoiding this pitfall shall we be able to discern, again, the essential difference between Spinoza and Freud.

In EIIp11c Spinoza posits his far-reaching conviction that "the human mind is part of the infinite intellect of God." His elaboration is of such interest to the present topic, and has such directness and clarity, that there seems to be no need to apologize for a lengthy quotation:

> thus when we say, that the human mind perceives this or that, we make the assertion, that God has this or that idea, not in so far as he is infinite, but in so far as he is displayed through the nature of the human mind, or in so far as he constitutes the essence of the human mind; and when we say that God has this or that idea, not only in so far as he constitutes the essence of the human mind, but also in so far as he, simultaneously with the human mind, has the further idea

of another thing, we assert that the human mind perceives a
thing in part or inadequately. (EIIp11c)

The inference may be formulated rather succinctly: this is the
metaphysical basis of Spinoza's conception of adequacy versus
inadequacy. Now, combining this with the passive–active
dichotomy, I would like to refer to the quotation which opened
this section (EIIIp1), pointing to Spinoza's conviction that in so far
as it is a matter of the working of man's *conatus*, man is active,
and in so far as it is a matter of external causes, man is passive.
Man fails to adequately understand these external causes, and this
results in confused ideas. Now Spinoza wants us to replace the
confused, inadequate ideas, and thus move towards adequacy. At
this juncture I should mention that it has been repeatedly alleged
that Spinoza, the 'predecessor', resembles Freud, the latter being
concerned with bringing unconscious materials to the level of consciousness, making them subject to rational consideration.

Asserting that this is a possibility would be to grossly under-
state the case: it is simply untenable. I shall come to this presently.
For now, one should refer to EIVp17s, where Spinoza is eager to
mention the power of reason over the affects, anticipating (and
referring to) his extensive discussion on the use of this power in
Part V. This is a well-known matter, and I shall but briefly point to
a few pronouncements taken from this Part.

In Proposition 3, its Demonstration and Corollary we read that
a confused idea ceases to be confused as soon as we form a clear
and distinct idea of it. This is done by means of the power of reason, and in the Corollary Spinoza emphasizes that when this
occurs, an emotion becomes "more under our control and the
mind is less passive in respect to it, in proportion as it is more
known to us."

From EVp4 one can deduce, in addition to the approach to
clearness and distinctiveness, a relation to Spinoza's anthropology. In this Proposition Spinoza states: "There is no modification
of the body, whereof we cannot form some clear and distinct conception." It appears that Spinoza has thought of giving a total
(overall) validity to the foregoing three propositions. However, I
take it that the consequence he draws in the Scholium is at least as
important. He states there that "it follows that everyone has the
power of clearly and distinctly understanding himself and his
emotions . . . ." This is a far-going pronouncement. One notices,
first, that adequacy is attainable by the power of reason only, and
in a state of activity (see also the above discussion on

passive/active and adequacy/inadequacy). This is another affirmation of Spinoza's optimistic, positive anthropology, which has been described in the section on reason above. Both standpoints are opposed to Freud's, and both amount to a Spinozistic principle that stands in contrast with Freud's theory and practice: with Spinoza everything that happens, happens on the level of consciousness.

This basic tenet can be approached by still another road. The first Proposition of *Ethics* V refers (and literally so in its Demonstration) to EIIp7: "The order and connection of ideas is the same as the order and connection of things." This means, implicitly, that knowing something is necessarily connected with the consciousness of it. In the Scholium to EIIp21 ("The idea of the mind is united to the mind in the same way as the mind is united to the body") Spinoza says that "if a man knows anything, he, by that very fact knows that he knows it."

To sum up: having quoted in full the metaphysical exercise as to God, man, and inadequacy, having discussed a number of related aspects, and having ended with Spinoza's emendation by means of the power of reason, by which everything remains on the level of consciousness, I need not discuss any further the central issues of the 'replacement move'. It would make sense, however, to call it what it is: a rationalist procedure rooted in a rationalist metaphysics.

All this proves to be wholly opposed to anything Freud believes in this respect. Evidently, he cannot but stop short of the adequate idea, not to mention the underlying and at the same time all-encompassing metaphysics. But this opposition between the two still has far broader implications when seen specifically in the light of the previous discussion of Freud's unconscious. This is not just because Spinoza is in a general sense the inheritor of the Cartesian view of mind as awareness—implicitly but constantly present in the preceding discussion—but because Spinoza himself explicitly states his certainty about the mind's awareness. In the foregoing section I have referred to three pertinent places in the *Ethics*[18] and I shall return to them in the last section. For now it is relevant, too, that the partial quotation from EIIIp9 in the preceding section does not make it clear that Spinoza speaks with reference *both* to the adequate and the inadequate ideas. In other words, the mind is not only aware (conscious) in the case of clear and distinct ideas, but also in the case of confused ideas.

For the sake of a minimum of completeness I would like, finally, to pay a little more attention to those inadequate, confused ideas—first, as they are compared or equated (in the secondary literature) with the occurrences (*Vorgänge*) in the unconscious as sketched by Freud, and, second, as they are treated by Spinoza himself.

Rather than unnecessarily piling up a series of quotations from secondary sources, I give only one example, which is representative in the sense that, written by different authors and in various modifications, it has been around for at least half a century:

> The super-ego being formed largely by the early prohibitions of parents and by the imposition of environmental standards is in part unconscious and so for Spinoza would be a complex of confused ideas.[19]

From statements like these, the conclusion is usually drawn that whereas Spinoza's 'problem' would be to replace the inadequate ideas with adequate ones, Freud's would be to bring the unconscious materials to consciousness. This would indicate one of those basic similarities between the two,[20] bringing something of intrinsic value but of inferior quality to a higher level, e.g., the level of usefulness. However, we have seen thus far that Spinoza entertains no relation whatever with occurrences in the unconscious—'in part' or totally. This is confirmed also, as was seen, by the place of the confused ideas—by themselves or 'as complex'— and this provided a refutation of particularly the last sentence of the quotation: even a complex of confused ideas would have been dealt with by Spinoza wholly on the conscious level and by purely rationalist means.

But, rather than restricting myself to the particulars of this section or the others, I shall expound how Spinoza acts when encountering confused, inadequate ideas. In the *Treatise on the Emendation of the Intellect*, §78, Spinoza describes 'doubt' as follows:

> The idea which causes us to doubt is not clear and distinct. To take an example. Supposing that a man has never reflected, taught by experience, or by any other means, that our senses sometimes deceive us, he will never doubt whether the sun be greater or less than it appears. Thus rustics are generally astonished when they hear that the sun is much larger than the earth. But from reflection on the deceitfulness of the senses doubt arises, and if, after doubting, we acquire a true knowledge of the senses, and how things at a

distance are represented through their instrumentality, doubt is again removed.

This brief account, including the simple example, explains, rather abstractly and without minutiae, what Spinoza means by what I have called, somewhat loosely, the replacement move. But there is more to it. In this way of ratiocination there is still, somewhere in between, a) an act called 'suspension of judgement' (of the 'spirit'), and b) a detailed enumeration of conditions to be demanded, if one searches the doubtful idea and wants to attain what Spinoza calls the 'due order in investigation.' Both activities are indispensable for understanding the way in which the doubtful idea (being nothing but the inadequate one) is brought to adequacy.

In TIE 80, Spinoza speaks of the 'suspension of the spirit'.[21] Later on, in the *Ethics*, he uses the more common expression 'suspension of judgement', but there is no indication that he conceives of any difference in meaning; and therefore the explanation in the *Ethics* must hold good for both contexts. What, then, is explained? In other words, what does this act of suspending mean in relation to the topic of the inadequate ideas? "When it is said that someone suspends his judgement," Spinoza explains, "we mean that he sees, that he does not perceive the matter in question adequately." (EIIp2s; GII 134:11-14) Apparently, from that moment on, the demands for the sake of successfully investigating the matter, on which I quoted Spinoza, must go into full force, pointing out to the 'investigator' the road to adequacy.

I will now quote TIE 80 in its entirety. One finds there, on the one hand, Spinoza's 'demands', and, on the other, the suspension, in what are almost two formulations: the brief one (". . . for doubt is . . . ") and the explicatory extension of it. This may still remove a few obscurities and bring to a close the discussion about the difference between Spinoza's confused ideas and Freud's libidinal materials.

> Thus, if a man proceeded with our investigations in due order, inquiring first into those things which should first be inquired into, never passing over a link in the chain of association, and with knowledge how to define his questions before seeking to answer them, he will never have any ideas save such as are very certain, or, in other words, clear and distinct; for doubt is only a suspension of the spirit concerning some affirmation or negation which it would pronounce upon unhesitatingly if it were not in ignorance of something, without which the knowledge of the matter in hand must

needs be imperfect. We may therefore, conclude that doubt
always proceeds from want of due order in investigation.

Looking back on the sections now completed one grapples with
the impression that there are not just differences of a technical,
philosophical and anthropological nature, but that nothing less
than a chasm exists between the two thinkers: Spinoza is a representative of a consistent rationalism, consistent in every respect,
moving in the clear sunshine of human awareness, clear as the
ideas are in God; whereas Freud is a representative of a well-
meaning pseudo-science, pursuing irrational materials by means
of unavoidable guesswork, often even guesswork in a roundabout
way: through dreams, mental slips, associations, etc.

4. Conatus—Libido

At first glance there may be considerable resemblance and paral-
lelism between Spinoza's idea of the *conatus* and Freud's conception of the *libido*. This may lead to the assumption that here we
find the exception to the rule, observed thus far, that Spinoza and
Freud are worlds apart. This conclusion, however, can only be
reached and maintained on an unsatisfactory basis; the actual situation is different. We shall now have a look at it, starting with
three instances from secondary literature.

A well-known British philosopher was the first to point to what
he called "an evident parallel" between Freud's conception of
libido and Spinoza's *conatus*, and goes on to boldly explain that
both Spinoza and Freud "conceive of emotional life as based on a
universal unconscious drive or tendency to self-preservation
...."[22]

Feuer, while diligently studying the philosopher to whom
knowledge is freedom, makes actual headway in turning Spinoza
into a Freudian psychoanalyst; thus ensues the Freudian vocabulary that goes with Spinoza's new vocation: "What, then, is the
technique of therapy which Spinoza proposes to those who are
slaves to forces of which they are unconscious?"[23]

Also, it is difficult to decide whether or not we are witnessing
still another step further away from both Spinoza and Freud when
reading about what looks like some kind of exchange between the
two: "Psychoanalysis has substituted for Spinoza's *conatus* the
term *libido*, the creative outgoing life force of the individual . . . ."[24]

We may be slightly surprised to see what has become of
Alexander's interpretation, which he advanced in the 1920s, and

which was modest, common-sensical, and not uncritical. Here we are confronted with three examples of the topic at hand being pushed *ad absurdum*.

Had I adhered to a more historical approach it would have been possible, surveying this extended period, to show how various authors (usually great admirers of Spinoza and Freud), little by little, bring the two closer together (e.g., Alexander had not yet mentioned anything about *conatus–libido*), resulting in inferences and pronouncements like the three quoted here. But this seems at present less significant than examining the anthropological and methodological aspects in themselves in order also to look for—possibly veritable—substitutes for the opinions quoted above.

In a case like this where there is admittedly an apparent undeniable resemblance between two ideas or phenomena, there is nothing so much needed as accurate definitions. Whereas Freud's own conception of the *libido* has been portrayed in a previous section, in the present context Spinoza's *conatus* makes its appearance. For that we turn to *Ethics* III, from which I pick but two propositions, the seventh (for the second time) and the ninth:

> The endeavour, wherewith everything endeavours to persist in its own being, is nothing else but the actual essence of the thing in question. (EIIIp7)

> The mind both in so far as it has clear and distinct ideas, and also in so far as it has confused ideas, endeavours to persist in its being for an indefinite period, and of this endeavour it is conscious. (EIIIp9)

These words about the *conatus* as power of self-preservation could be juxtaposed with Freud's testimonies and the three commentaries cited in illustration. What can be elicited by a comparative scrutiny of these divergent materials?

For one thing, the thesis concerning *conatus* and *libido* being by and large the same phenomena results in Hampshire transferring the unconscious character of the *libido in toto* to the *conatus*: the "universal unconscious drive" is attributed to "both." But, *nota bene*, the conception of a conscious and rational *conatus* is vital to the entire warp and woof of Spinoza's philosophical fabric, and therefore any change in its character would be incomprehensible. The imagination boggles: if this position—the *conatus* is of an unconscious nature—were pursued to its last consequences, Spinoza's philosophy would be afflicted (to apply Kierkegaard's terminology) by a sickness unto death. However, Spinoza himself provides an effective remedy in advance. Comparing Hampshire's words with EIIIp9 (itself reminiscent of claims raised earlier, in a different context): ". . . the mind . . . endeavours to persist in its being . . . and of this endeavour it is conscious" (see also EIIp12).

As for the character of the *conatus,* Spinoza's words exclude not just any far-fetched libidinal characterization of it, they exclude even the faintest hint of anything remotely related to a realm of the unconscious. The reference to the conscious realm is too explicit to assume otherwise.

Feuer's words have something in common with Hampshire's— the belief that something like an unconscious could ever have been integrated and have functioned in Spinoza's philosophy— but an additional aspect has now been introduced. Setting aside his question about Spinoza's "technique of therapy"—it demonstrates even in the choice of words how great the emphasis is on what Freud and Spinoza are supposed to have in common, but it does not touch the present issue.[25] The author further speaks of people being slaves to unconscious 'forces'. This again is an instance of how Spinoza is pushed into a straightjacket of Freudian ideas and doctrines. Nowhere in his *Ethics* (or in any of his works, for that matter) does Spinoza use this psychoanalytic language. He simply does not know of forces that are unconscious. Admittedly, the fourth book of the *Ethics* is entitled *Of Human Bondage;* but one need only read the Preface to learn that the bondage is bound up with the affects; as early as the first sentence we read: "Human infirmity in moderating and checking the emotions I name bondage." As was unraveled in the foregoing section, the unconscious does not enter the discussion at all except for having to be dismissed as being inapplicable.

Seeing that the Freudian grip on Spinoza has been strengthened more and more through the years, we see at the same time what one might call the ultimate step (though made rather early in time) with respect to the 'relationship' between *conatus* and *libido*—the claim, in the third example given above, that psychoanalysis has *substituted* for Spinoza's *conatus* the term *libido*. It is one of the most conspicuous results of the approach, repeatedly practiced, of wanting to see as many Freudian traits in the Spinozistic *œuvre* as possible. Conspicuous but invariably consistent; reducing this matter of consistency to the simplest possible summary: what is found in Freud must be found in Spinoza also.

I should like to add a few notes both to this section and to the paper as a whole; they are primarily of a corroborative nature but may also serve to enlarge somewhat the picture, seen thus far, of the handling in the secondary literature of a great philosopher.

Apart from whatever further differences between *conatus* and *libido* still might be found, and for now also leaving aside that one cannot do anything with an unconscious *conatus* (a misconception, I think, and a contradiction in terms at that), there is still another palpable difference between the two when viewed as phenomena *per se.* Freud's concept of *libido*—the (repressed) psychic energy of primarily sexual instincts—may not be of an entirely satisfying exactitude, but is sufficiently exact for a comparison in general terms with Spinoza's conception: the *conatus* applies to every existing thing, animate and inanimate; without it, *natura naturans* would in all likelihood be an incomprehensible state of affairs. In comparison, the limitations of Freud's psychic energy are obvious, even when *libido* is defined in terms of self-preservation and the like. This note still entails another and ominous cleavage between our two men in that we know since Bidney that "Spinoza . . . has no conception of repressed psychic energy."[26]

And there is yet another angle from which one can approach these matters. Speaking of sexual love, implicit in the preceding lines, one could recall Spinoza's definition of it: "Lust is desire and love in the matter of sexual intercourse" (EIII deff.aff.48). In other words, it is a mode of desire. This theoretically is the farthest one could enter the *libido*—being in the company of Spinoza, that is. However, this love would still not take another place in human existence than that of one of the modes of desire, of which there are a great number. This, evidently, is a far cry from Freud's *libido*. All this is closely related to a twofold point in Spinoza, i.e., that a mode of desire does not express the essence of man as does the *conatus* and, consequently, that Spinoza refuses to identify the *conatus* with even a major part of what Freud would classify as libidinal—the mode of desire which is lust. There is not a word of it in any of his works.

There appears to be no way of bridging the gulf between *libido* and *conatus*, irrespective of the road taken. Yet a number of authors never arrived at this conclusion, and went on bringing the two as close to each other as possible. The degree of closeness differs widely from one author to another. It ranges from complete identification to mere participation. All this holds good especially for what I think should be called the antithesis *conatus/libido*, the most tenacious (if not obstinate) element of the myth. I'll make but a very limited, random choice.

Having previously observed Rathbun substituting one of the two terms for the other (which means identification of the two), it may be surprising that Kaplan, more than four decades later, still says basically the same thing, even though his article is written with many nuances and differentiations. Kaplan claims that when the two concepts "are applied to man" Spinoza's position is virtually indistinguishable from Freud's.[27] With respect to the 'contents' of Freud's *libido*, both Spinoza and Freud, according to Bernard, "have pointed out the existence of dark primitive libidinal forces in man, the origin and nature of powerful asocial drives . . .."[28] The wording seems to be more moderate, but the element of identification is present just the same. And again in Hampshire we find the kind of identification that we have found previously when the word 'substituted' was used; Hampshire speaks about ". . . their common central conception of *libido* or *conatus*."[29]

There are also authors who, clinging by and large to rather similar interpretations, seem to take a step back, in that they express themselves in a rather restrained and affable manner, speaking of Spinoza 'anticipating' Freud. Anticipation (or synonyms such as 'foreshadowing') is almost always hard to prove or to disprove, the word being one of the vaguest in the history of ideas and the humanities generally. In the main it flourishes in the twilight zone where similar terms (all about as vague) like 'influence', 'affinity', 'likeness', 'congeniality', are rampant. Thus anticipations are often multi-interpretable. This is also discernible with respect to the matter now under discussion: certain ideas are said to be anticipated whereas other writers (they have been quoted) have used far stronger expressions, occasionally reaching the point of identification.

How far one can proceed in this atmosphere of vagueness and intangibility becomes apparent when it is said that, though the Freudian death instinct "is not found in Spinoza's concept of the *conatus*," the *conatus* nonetheless "might be said to foreshadow the theory of the death instinct."[30] Freud's *thanatos*—the idea of the death instinct! Apart from Spinoza's famous words about the "free man . . . whose wisdom is not reflection upon death, but upon life" (EIVp67), to my knowledge there is no idea in Freud's extensive writings that is so utterly incommensurable with Spinoza's *conatus*. It is a late development in Freud (1920), and because of it the fundamental idea of self-preservation had to be abandoned. True, no other writer on Freud and Spinoza has written anything in this vein; if they mention it at all, they are invariably critical about its merits for the Freudian system and defend no worthwhile relation of it to Spinoza.

As was implied in the foregoing, 'anticipation' is a much-used expression among those interested in the Freud/Spinoza relationship. Hamblin Smith's article, from as early as 1925, is worth noticing if only for its title, "Spinoza's Anticipation of Recent Psychological Developments,"[31] in which one finds the contention that the concept of the unconscious is anticipated throughout the *Ethics*; and in the sixties, Sours still says by and large the same, adding this specification: Spinoza anticipated it "by his general interpretation of the affective life of man."[32] Just to keep the record straight: Bernard had used literally the same words in 1946.[33] Elsewhere he links Spinoza's anticipation of Freud with the distinction between adequate and inadequate ideas, which seems even more susceptible to question.[34]

This choice of a few examples of Spinoza's alleged anticipatory labor should suffice, because they are so numerous as to appear, in whatever terms, everywhere in the secondary literature. This, after all, should not surprise anyone knowing that Spinoza has been named "the ethically minded psychiatrist."[35]

In the introductory section I have said that the Spinoza/Freud story is still largely intact, but that in the last two decades a few studies have been published bearing a more critical character, although they have not done away with it. To be a little more precise: they do not accept the totality of what can hardly be called anything but the current folklore about Spinoza and Freud—the whole gamut from the merely questionable features to those essentially alien to Spinoza's thought. But neither do they, *expressis verbis*, reject it totally (as I am inclined to do). However, questioning certain features and suggesting certain changes, the authors did administer some amendments. The harvest is not as plentiful as could be expected considering the prolonged life span of the myth, but it is promising: at least there's a light at the end of the tunnel.

Bound up with this part of the discussion is the name of David Bidney, a scholar of a much older generation; he ought to be mentioned first. In addition to what I wrote about *The Psychology and Ethics of Spinoza*, I should like to point out that it was Bidney's contention that, contrary to a number of other voices, the distinction between adequate and inadequate ideas "does not by any means correspond to that between the conscious and the unconscious";[36] it was he who rejected the idea of a relationship between the *conatus* and Freud's *Thanatos*[37] and who without hesitation stated that Spinoza "has no conception of repressed psychic energy."[38] These are a few examples but they convey valuable insights. As can be deduced from this paper, they have been neglected for more than half a century since their publication in 1940. His influence thus appears to have been regrettably meager.

Much closer to the twenty-first century is Nails' comparative article about *conatus* as opposed to *Eros / Thanatos*,[39] in which she concludes that "it is possible to provide descriptions of human psychology, organic behavior, and physical activity without recourse to a second principle. Spinoza's doctrine of *conatus* is able, alone, to account for all these phenomena."[40]

Along with Nails, Fóti should be named as the one who meritoriously contributed to exposing a few dubious features of the old myth. Her article "Thought, Affect, Drive and Pathogenesis in Spinoza and Freud"[41] goes right to the heart of the matter, displaying some of the myth's weaknesses. It is difficult to highlight merely one or two passages because it is a stringing together, as it were, of questions and analyses entailing conclusions on almost every page. The general upshot is that there is, on the points discussed, less agreement between Spinoza and Freud than has hitherto been maintained. The article is outstanding on the *conatus*, especially on its interpretation, in teleological terms, of the role of the imagination and Freud's and Spinoza's understanding of necessity.

Among those whom I here mention in conclusion, Yovel ought to be included.[42] Apparently captivated by his interest in the emancipation of Spinoza and Freud—an approach of thematic originality affording ample opportunities for comparison—he hardly touches upon any of the topics which I have discussed as 'the main four'.[43] Thus he practically remains outside the subject matter of my paper. But there is more than one reason for including him. Like the few others referred to in this context, he is clearly not impressed by what can well be called the tradition of the twentieth century; rather, he ignores it, which is also a form of extricating oneself from it. There is, further, a complete absence of the urge, repeatedly spotted in the foregoing, to observe, unwarrantably, more and more Freudian thought and practice in Spinoza's works. It looks like he sees more differences between the two men than similarities and congruencies. This, too, may be a sign that he belongs to the generation that commenced in the latter part of the twentieth century. These reasons may suffice to explain why I enjoy being able to bring this paper to a close with a conclusion of his, not directly related to that paper, but which opens up yet another perspective: "Human liberation in Spinoza leads man to the infinite; in Freud, liberation leaves man in his impotent finitude in the universe."[44]

NOTES

1. "No man can better display the power of his skill and disposition, than in so training men, that they come at last to live under the dominion of their own reason" (EIVappIX).

2. H.J. Eysenck, *The Decline and Fall of the Freudian Empire* (Harmondsworth: Penguin, 1986), p. 213.

3. Abraham Kaplan, "Spinoza and Freud," *The Journal of the American Academy of Psychoanalysis* 5 (1977), p. 317.

4. "man möchte sagen, die Absicht, dass der Mensch 'glücklich' sei, ist im Plan der 'Schöpfung' nicht enthalten." Sigmund Freud, *Das Unbehagen in der Kultur* (II), in *Studienausgabe*, eds. A. Mitscherlich, A. Richards, and J. Strachey (Frankfurt am Main: Fischer Verlag, 1976), vol. 9, p. 208.

5. The discussion commenced in the 1920s; one of the first articles was that of Bernhard Alexander, "Spinoza und die Psychoanalyse," *Chronicon Spinozanum* 5 (1927), pp. 96-103.

6. David Bidney, *The Psychology and Ethics of Spinoza, A Study in the History and Logic of Ideas*, 2nd ed. (New York: Russell and Russell, 1962).

7. Lancelot Law Whyte, *The Unconscious Before Freud* (London: Julian Friedman, 1979).

8. Eysenck, *The Decline and Fall of the Freudian Empire*, p. 213.

9. "Ohne Fantasie keine Aussenwelt." Friedrich Schlegel, *Prosaische Jugendschriften*, ed. J. Minor (Vienna: n.p., 1906), p. 264.

10. A.W. Schlegel, *Vorlesungen über schöne Literatur und Kunst* (Heilbronn: n.p., 1884), vol. 2, p. 84; F.W.J. von Schelling, *System des transzendentalen Idealism, S.W.* (Stuttgart/Ausburg: n.p., 1858), vol. 3, p. 626; A.W. Schelegel, *Vorlesungen über schöne Literatur und Kunst*, vol. 1, p. 329. In an enumeration of romantic names, Whyte lists S.T. Coleridge, but without any explication. However, Coleridge did not contribute anything to the discussion, nor did any other British Romantic. The only passage in his *oeuvre* that formulates the above distinction has been proved to be an unacknowledged paraphrase of the German position, particularly Schelling's. See S.T. Coleridge, *Biographia Literaria*, ed. J. Shawcross (London: n.p., 1958), vol. 1, p. 202.

11. The road between the German Romantics and Freud is to a certain extent delineated in my article "Filosofische antropologie en literatuur, Freud als bemiddelaar," *Wijsgerig perspectief op maatschappij en wetenschap* 19 (1978-9), pp. 56-65.

12. I take these tenets from the *New Introductory Lectures* in the first volume of the *Studienausgabe*, paraphrasing or translating as needed (see note 4).

13. Walter Bernard, "Freud and Spinoza," *Psychiatry: Journal of the Biology and Pathology of Interpersonal Relations* 9 (1946), p. 108.

14. Lothar Bickel, "Über Beziehungen zwischen Spinoza und der Psychoanalyse," in *Probleme und Ziele des Denkens* (Zürich: n.p., 1939), passim.

15. Lewis Samuel Feuer, *Spinoza and the Rise of Liberalism* (Boston: Beacon Press, 1958), p. 210.

16. Letter 62 to Schuller.

17. See the famous Appendix to *Ethics* I, where Spinoza expresses himself in slightly stronger words, saying that "men never even dream, in their ignorance, of the causes which have disposed them so to wish and desire."

18. EIIp12; EIIp21; EIIIp9.

19. Constance Rathbun, "On Certain Similarities Between Spinoza and Pychoanalysis," *The Psychoanalytic Review* 21 (1934), p. 8.

20. The author conveys the gist of the quotation again on pp. 13-14, and in a remark like the one about the two 'problems' on p. 3.

21. He avoids the expression 'suspension of judgement' (*suspensio indici*), using instead the very unusual 'suspension of the mind' (*suspensio animi*). This goes back to a quarrel with Descartes and the latter's analysis of the judgement. It need not detain us here.

22. Stuart Hampshire, *Spinoza* (Harmondsworth: Penguin, 1951), p. 141.

23. Feuer, *Spinoza and the Rise of Liberalism*, p. 211.

24. Rathbun, "On Certain Similarities," p. 7.

25. Bernard had used the same terms more than a decade earlier, employing a very similar reasoning ("Freud and Spinoza," p. 107). Transferring this term to Spinoza has since been rather frequent.

26. D. Bidney, *The Psychology and Ethics of Spinoza*, p. 405; see also p. 391.

27. A. Kaplan, "Spinoza and Freud," p. 311.

28. W. Bernard, "Freud and Spinoza," p. 108.

29. S. Hampshire, *Spinoza.*, p. 143.

30. C. Rathbun, "On Certain Similarities," p. 3. See also Bidney, *The Psychology and Ethics of Spinoza*, p. 404.

31. W. Hamblin Smith, "Spinoza's Anticipation of Recent Psychological Developments," *The British Journal of Medical Psychology* 5 (1925) pp. 257-78. Also, this author identifies the two conceptions *libido* and *conatus*, proposing that psychoanalysts should use "conatus, in place of the somewhat unfortunate term libido" (p. 265).

32. John A. Sours, "Freud and the Philosophers," *Bulletin of the History of Medicine* 35 (1961), p. 337.

33. W. Bernard, "Freud and Spinoza," p. 108.

34. Ibid., p. 106; as to the questioning, see also Bidney on consciousness and adequacy (*The Psychology and Ethics of Spinoza*, p. 405.)

35. L.S. Feuer, *Spinoza and the Rise of Liberalism*, p. 215.

36. D. Bidney, *The Psychology and Ethics of Spinoza*, p. 405.

37. Ibid., p. 404.

38. Ibid., pp. 391 and 405.

39. Debra Nails, "*Conatus* vs. *Eros/Thanatos*: on the Principles of Spinoza and Freud," *Dialogue* 21 (1979) pp. 33-40.

40. Ibid., p. 40.

41. Véronique M. Fóti, "Thought, Affect, Drive and Pathogenesis in Spinoza and Freud," *History of European Ideas* 3 (1982), pp. 221-36.

42. Yirmiyahu Yovel, "Spinoza and Freud: Self-knowledge as Emancipation," *Spinoza and Other Heretics*, vol. 2, *The Adventures of Immanence* (Princeton: Princeton University Press, 1984), pp. 130-66.

43. The exception is the section on *libido* versus *conatus* (pp. 145-7). He speaks there, on the one hand, of a "fundamental kinship", and on the other hand of "important differences." The first refers to both Spinoza and Freud seeing man "consituted by some principle of desire." There can of course be no objection against the thesis thus formulated, provided one does not—and Yovel definitely does not—locate the *conatus* in an unconscious realm.

44. Y. Yovel, *Spinoza and Other Heretics*, vol. 2, p. 165.

List of Contributors

Laurent Bove is Professor of Philosophy at the Université de Picardie Jules Verne, France.

Menachem Brinker is Professor Emeritus of Philosophy at the Hebrew University of Jerusalem and Crown Professor of Modern Hebrew Studies at the University of Chicago.

J. Thomas Cook is Professor of Philosophy at Rollins College in Winter Park, Florida.

Cornelis de Deugd is Professor Emeritus of Philosophy at the Free University of Amsterdam and of Comparative Literature at the University of Utrecht.

Herman De Dijn is Professor of Modern Philosophy at the Catholic University of Leuven (Louvain).

Michael Della Rocca is Professor of Philosophy at Yale University, New Haven.

Daniel Garber is Professor of Philosophy at Princeton University.

Ursula Goldenbaum is Professor of Philosophy at the Technische Universität Berlin – Institut für Philosophie, Wissenschaftstheorie, Wissenschaft- und Techniksgeschichte.

The late **Bernard Rousset** was Professor of Philosophy at the Université de Picardie Jules Verne, France.

Dr. Gideon Segal is Lecturer at the Hebrew University of Jerusalem and Holon Academic Institute of Technology.

Timothy L.S. Sprigge is Professor Emeritus of Logic and Metaphysics at the University of Edinburgh.

Elhanan Yakira is Assistant Professor at the Philosophy Department, The Hebrew University of Jeerusalem.

Yirmiyahu Yovel is Hans Jonas Professor of Philosophy at the New School University and Professor Emeritus at the Hebrew University of Jerusalem.

Name Index